A Distant Shore

A Distant Shore

Irish Migration & New Zealand Settlement

❧

EDITED BY
Lyndon Fraser

University of Otago Press

Published by University of Otago Press
56 Union Street/PO Box 56, Dunedin, New Zealand
Fax: 64 3 479 8385
email: university.press@stonebow.otago.ac.nz

First published 2000
Volume and Introduction © Lyndon Fraser 2000
Individual essays © Individual authors as listed in the Contents 2000
ISBN 1 877133 97 3

Printed by PrintLink Ltd, Wellington, New Zealand

Contents

	Acknowledgements	6
	Contributors	7
	Introduction	9
1	No Petty People: Pakeha History and the Historiography of the Irish Diaspora **Donald Harman Akenson**	13
2	Varieties of New Zealand Irishness: A Meditation **Patrick O'Farrell**	25
3	The Invisible Irish? Re-Discovering the Irish Protestant Tradition in Colonial New Zealand **Alasdair Galbraith**	36
4	Irish Migration to New Zealand to 1915 **Terry Hearn**	55
5	The Irish on the Otago Goldfields, 1861–71 **Terry Hearn**	75
6	Irish Migration to the West Coast, 1864–1900 **Lyndon Fraser**	86
7	'In Prospect of a Happier Future': Private Letters and Irish Women's Migration to New Zealand, 1840–1925 **Angela McCarthy**	105
8	'Shaming the Shoneens': The *Green Ray* and the Maoriland Irish Society in Dunedin, 1916–22 **Seán Brosnahan**	117
9	'The Importance of Being Irish': Hibernianism in New Zealand, 1869–1969 **Rory Sweetman**	135
	Notes	155
	Index	189

Acknowledgements

This book would not have been completed without the advice, support and encouragement of many people. First, I want to thank all the contributors to this volume for their generosity, patience and willing co-operation. My task as editor was made easier by the work of several individuals who commented on draft chapters or assisted directly during the editing process. I would like to extend my sincere gratitude to Malcolm Campbell, Angela McCarthy, Anna Rogers, Katharine Sillars and Angela Wanhalla. Many thanks, also, to Wendy Harrex and the University of Otago Press for accepting and processing the manuscript.

This project began while I was working as a Postdoctoral Fellow in the School of History, Philosophy and Politics at Massey University, Palmerston North. I received generous financial assistance from the Massey University Research Fund and Historical Branch of the Ministry for Culture and Heritage. I am also deeply indebted to a number of archivists and family historians throughout the country. In this regard, I want to acknowledge the work of Barrie Lynn Callinan, Father Kevin Clark, Brother Gerard Hogg, Brian Nolan, Ron Patterson, Peter Read, John Tourelle and the staff at National Archives, Christchurch. Finally, I offer a very special thanks to Keith Beattie, Trevor Burnard, John Cookson, Bob Hall and my students in the Department of Sociology at the University of Canterbury.

LYNDON FRASER
University of Canterbury

Contributors

Donald Harman Akenson is Professor of History at Queen's University, Kingston, Ontario, and concurrently is Beamish Research Professor of Migration Studies, in the Institute of Irish Studies, at the University of Liverpool. He has published several books on the Irish at home and abroad, including *The Irish Diaspora: A Primer* (Toronto: P.D. Meany and Belfast: Institute of Irish studies, the Queen's University of Belfast, 1993) and *Half the World from Home: Perspectives on the Irish in New Zealand, 1860-1950* (Wellington: Victoria University Press, 1990).

Seán Brosnahan is a Dunedin curator who graduated with an Honours degree in history from the University of Canterbury in 1986. He is descended from early Irish settlers in Otago, Southland and South Canterbury. 'Wherever I delve into the Irish past of the southern region, I inevitably find myself tripping over relations and connections. I have delighted in bringing some of their neglected stories to a wider audience, particularly the far-flung descendants of the Irish diaspora's southernmost contingent.'

Lyndon Fraser teaches in the Department of Sociology at the University of Canterbury. He was the Concept Developer and Oral Historian for the *Passports* exhibition at Te Papa. His first book, *To Tara via Holyhead: Irish Catholic Immigrants in Nineteenth-Century Christchurch* (Auckland: Auckland University Press, 1997), won the Keith Sinclair History Prize.

Alasdair Galbraith recently graduated with a Masters degree in history from the University of Auckland, where his thesis examined Irish Protestant migration to nineteenth-century New Zealand. He currently works at the Auckland University Library and as a part-time researcher for the Crown Forestry Rental Trust.

Terry Hearn graduated with an MA (Hons) degree from the University of Otago in 1971. He completed his PhD thesis in 1982 and currently works as the Historian of British Immigration in the Ministry of Culture and Heritage.

Angela McCarthy recently completed a PhD in the Department of Modern History at Trinity College, Dublin. Her study utilised personal letters to explore individual accounts of Irish migration to New Zealand. Angela also runs a website

devoted to Irish migrants in New Zealand at http://homepage.eircom.net/
~McCarthy.

Patrick O'Farrell is Emeritus Scientia Professor of History at the University of New South Wales. He is the author of books on Irish history, Anglo-Irish relations, Catholics and the Irish in Australia, and the history of his own university. His first book was a biography of the New Zealand labour leader Henry Holland, and in *Vanished Kingdoms* (Kensington: University of New South Wales Press, 1990) he has written about his New Zealand Irish family background.

Rory Sweetman is a freelance historian who has written extensively on the history of Catholicism in New Zealand. His latest book, *Bishop in the Dock: The Sedition Trial of James Liston* (Auckland: Auckland University Press, 1997), won the Keith Sinclair History Prize. He is currently working on a popular history of the passage of the Private Schools Conditional Integration Act (1975).

Introduction

Lyndon Fraser

From the end of the Great Famine to the beginning of the First World War, thousands of Irish men and women made their way to New Zealand from Great Britain, the Australian colonies and other places. As manual workers, domestic servants, farmers and housewives, these newcomers and their descendants played an important role in shaping the economy and society of the new nation. Even today our physical landscape is heavily invested with memories of an earlier Irish presence: one thinks of place names such as Killinchy, Lismore or Dargaville; the imperial ruins of abandoned Orange Lodges; grand monuments to an Irish spiritual empire like St Joseph's in Dunedin; and the graves of John and Ann Quinlan from County Clare in the cemetery at Gillespies Beach. Yet we still know very little about the great chains of mobility that tied New Zealand to various points of origin in Ireland and to other Irish diasporic communities scattered around the world. This book is an attempt to remedy this state of affairs. It is a collaborative venture that pulls together exciting new work by a small band of writers with an interest in the Irish diaspora. We hope that our interpretations will stimulate further research in a neglected area of historical scholarship and – in keeping with the historian's calling – provide glimpses 'into the lives of those otherwise silenced by death'.[1]

Donald Akenson's essay surveys recent developments in Irish diaspora studies and assesses their significance for New Zealand historiography. He challenges local historians and social scientists to abandon restrictive bicultural approaches to the past that mask the complex nature of colonial society in the nineteenth and early twentieth centuries. Irish migrants, he argues, need to be woven into our own historical narratives 'not as ethnic stereotypes or 'filiopietistic burlesques of reality', but as 'real, complex peoples'. Such a task requires the selective use of tools borrowed from the field of ethnic studies. At the same time, Akenson urges us to relinquish the term 'emigration' and re-conceptualise Irish mobility as a global phenomenon with invisible threads 'that stretch out infinitely and in all directions'. One of the great virtues of this move is that it makes the entire Irish diaspora 'a big deal in world history' and calls attention to the globe-circling impact of its commercial, educational and religious institutions. We need to expand the context of our work to embrace the intimate connections between huge structural changes, geographic locations and people's everyday lives.

The main themes of Akenson's chapter are further extended by Patrick O'Farrell and Alasdair Galbraith. Professor O'Farrell's contribution is 'a meditation' on the various shades and textures of New Zealand 'Irishness'. He alerts us to the 'intricacies and convolutions' of the interaction between Old World cultural forms and local social settings. Readers will find a wonderful illustration of these complexities in his parents' reaction to a young Irish curate who visited their Greymouth home unexpectedly 'for tea and talk'. O'Farrell contrasts their 'embarrassed unhappiness' at these intrusions with 'fond recollections' of French Marist priests and their high standard of spiritual care and personal conduct. The diversity that he describes here made New Zealand Catholicism into a 'curious amalgam' of Irish, French, English and Australian influences. But we know much less about the transplantation of distinctive Irish Protestant cultural traditions in this country. Alasdair Galbraith's ambitious essay explores the multiple dimensions of Irish Protestantism and seeks to account for the 'cultural amnesia' that has erased it from our historical memory. He argues persuasively that the Protestant Irish were active participants in the construction of a pan-British identity which replaced Old World affinities and represented a crucial first step in the process of becoming 'New Zealanders'. The imperial enthusiasms and 'low-church, Old-Testament-driven Protestantism' shared by these newcomers blended easily with the dominant values of colonial society and facilitated their disappearance 'into the crowd'.

The next three chapters examine the main features of Irish migration to New Zealand before the First World War. Terry Hearn's detailed statistical overview answers the most basic questions about these transoceanic population movements. He insists that the depiction of New Zealand's Irish intake as a dualistic phenomenon – one part '"Celtic", southern and Roman Catholic and the other English or Scottish, northern and "Protestant"' – is erroneous. The surviving documentation shows that the Irish migrant stream comprised a number of strands differentiated by social class, religious affiliation, occupational background and geographical origin. Although the colony's inflow shared many of the features of the wider Irish diaspora, there were important variations over time and from region to region. The two chapters that follow provide solid empirical support for Terry's conclusions. Both case studies highlight the crucial role played by the eastern Australian colonies in shaping the volume and composition of New Zealand's Irish intake. Along with Angela McCarthy's chapter on the private correspondence of Irish women, these essays demonstrate the importance of Old World social ties in structuring the migration process and raise important questions about the assumption – made by some historians – that mobility leads inevitably to weak kinship networks.

Seán Brosnahan and Rory Sweetman direct attention to the role of radical nationalists and Hibernianism within local expatriate communities. Seán's meticulously researched essay documents the activities of 'genuine' Sinn Féiners in Dunedin between the years 1916 and 1922. Few readers will be able to resist his intriguing portrait of 'a hidden Ireland' peopled by shadowy figures like James Bradley and the underground networks of friends and relations that sheltered defiant Irish fugitives from the authorities during the First World War. He provides fresh insights into the impact of Irish issues on New Zealand society and forces us to re-think the relationship between Irish radicalism, working class Catholics and the rise of the Labour Party. In the final chapter, Rory Sweetman lucidly portrays the organisation and development of the Hibernian Australasian Catholic Benefit Society in New Zealand. This institution contained some of the colony's most prominent Irish Catholic men and provided its financial members and their families with important benefits such as mutual-aid and fraternalism. Rory offers a comprehensive account of Hibernian responses to political events in Ireland and insists that the Society's 'remarkable longevity' owed more to its religious dimensions than to any particular notion of 'Irishness'.

Detail from 'Emigrants Embarking', 1880, Australian Sketcher, *18 December 1880.*

1

No Petty People
Pakeha History and The Historiography of The Irish Diaspora

Donald Harman Akenson

I

A good form of occasional discipline for scholars in the humanities and social sciences is to re-read at intervals once-fashionable items of the scholarly literature. That is a valuable bit of self-mortification, for one learns two things: first, that one's own work will eventually be out of style and thus out of the conventional academic mind and, secondly, that even in items no longer fashionable there frequently are *aperçus* that are long lasting because they are wise. A case in point is found in Emile Durkheim's observation, in his classic, *The Elementary Forms of the Religious Life* (1912), that 'there are societies in Australia and North America where space is conceived in the form of an immense circle, because the camp has a circular form, and this spatial circle is divided up exactly like the tribal circle, and is in its image'.[1]

That is a metonym for most human cosmologies. Most societies' – and most individuals' – view of the way the universe is organised is a product less of objective data collection than of the assumptions with which such data collection begins. That is: we think the world is organised the way we are. And this holds especially true for our social cosmologies. We are an inherently immodest and self-venerating species.

To an outsider (a sympathetic outside observer, but still definitely an outsider), one of the most intriguing aspects of New Zealand's collective behaviour is the degree to which it illustrates Emile Durkheim's observation. More than most countries that I study, its historical and sociological literatures and, especially, its social policy formation, operate along bi-modal lines. This is not in any sense a condemnation, for in fact digital thinking can produce very precise results, as anyone familiar with basic computer language knows. It is just one way of thinking. On its primary axis, the world is seen to be organised bi-culturally, because that is the way the world around the New Zealand campfire is organised. There is lip-service to multiculturalism, but it is only that. There are just two teams playing on the big field and everyone else is relegated to the reserves.

Now, in terms of the present-day polity the opting of New Zealand for biculturalism rather than multiculturalism is sensible and bids fair to be a successful social analgesic. However, the degree (perhaps unconscious) to which New Zealand scholarship in the humanities and social sciences has followed the tramlines of recent political necessity is just a trifle unsettling. Dichotomous thinking makes it difficult for New Zealand scholars in the human sciences to deal with the rest of the world: there are a lot of places – most of North America and Europe for example – towards which a bi-modal approach just will not work. Nor does it work concerning New Zealand society in the nineteenth and early twentieth centuries. Without consciously intending to do so, it appears to me that many (perhaps most) historians have systematically denied the complexity of the individuals and the congeries of the Pakeha culture.

That last observation might be the basis for pessimism, but in fact I am an optimist about the future direction of 'Pakeha history'. This is because I see younger scholars moving into the field who understand that the history of New Zealand does not begin on these islands. Only recently has the shackle of anti-colonialism been shaken off. Younger historians have the self-confidence that an earlier generation did not possess: they are sufficiently sure of their own cultural identity that they can operate under the realisation that New Zealand became a 'neo-Europe' and that an understanding of the individuals and groups who forced this transformation can only be achieved by an in-depth knowledge of the cultures from which these peoples came – and especially knowledge of the four nations of the British Isles. (That present-day governmental *apparatchiks* are still trying to torch the evidence for New Zealand's European historical background is hardly grounds for cheer: but I believe the Philistines will be unsuccessful in the long term.)

My optimism is also based on the fact that a new generation of historians is more socially secure and less unconsciously racist when chronicling developments within 'Pakeha history' than was a recent generation. Specifically, it is increasingly understood that some (not all, certainly, just some) of the conceptual tools of ethnic history and ethnic studies as done in other cultures may be applicable to nineteenth and early twentieth century New Zealand. Specifically, the recognition that 'charter groups' can usefully be conceived of as ethnic collectivities is now being granted. Not so long ago, the idea that, say, the early Scots or the English, could in some ways be understood as 'ethnics' in New Zealand was contemptuously rejected, with the assertion (all too often clearly and racially articulated) that ethnics were various Polynesians, or East Europeans, or, well, just not people like our grandparents.

Of course there are exceptions to any generalisation one could make: and these should be celebrated, because frequently they point the way to richer forms of understanding our past. Most importantly they remind us of a central epistemological fact. That as scholars of human societies, we are not limited to any single way of conceptualising and observing our subjects. Nor is there usually a single 'correct' mode of perceiving patterns of historical reality. There are usually several 'correct' solutions to most historical puzzles. Some are more elegant than others, but as long as the narrative and the deductions fit the verifiable evidence, each is valid. The best historians play with several conceptual schema simultaneously.

This leads us back to Durkheim's campfire, and tells us that we can both honour New Zealand's present-day goals of social amity and respect the complexities of the past. The wiring of the human mind is sufficiently robust to permit our carrying simultaneously within it not just one, or even two, but several cosmologies, or models of how the world operates. To apply that richness to 'Pakeha history' one simply needs to jump past the conundrum laid down by the great American humorist Robert Benchley, who declared that the world was divided into two sorts of people: those who divided the world into two and those who did not.

II

My optimism concerning future developments in New Zealand historical writing is consonant with developments I am absolutely sure are occurring in the field of Irish history. We are at a bend in the long road of Irish historiography, considered worldwide. I am firmly convinced that the next generation will see a remarkable change in the way that the experience of the Irish people and of their ethnic derivatives throughout the world will be understood. And at the heart of this change will be a radically different conceptualisation of where 'emigration' fits into the picture.[2]

Concepts are not to be confused with real things. They are ways of talking about real things. Concepts are neither true nor untrue. They are therefore to be judged on whether or not they are useful and, if useful, to what degree. Concepts inevitably merge with attitudes and attitudes meld into action. So, useful concepts not only help us to see our world more clearly, but also help us to act more sensibly. Thus does clear thought lead to humane action.

There are three major tests of the usefulness of any concept: accuracy, robustness, and fecundity. That is, does any given concept cover the known empirical phenomena without cheating; does it embrace them in such a way as not to be a mere restatement of the empirical phenomena, but to point out underlying systematic relationships; and does it lead to further concepts? Does it keep the pot boiling? Now, the key thing to be understood about any concept is that it is a disposable item. An historical or social scientific concept that has accuracy, robustness, and fecundity at one moment can, a few decades later, possess none of these qualities. Facts change as new research progresses: concepts that robustly relate empirical phenomena and produce testable hypotheses gradually become less robust as the data-world changes; and concepts that once inspired new advances in research now produce only tired old repetitions.

I am convinced that emigration as a concept in the analysis of Irish history is virtually mined-out. Let me be clear here. I do not mean that the term 'emigration' as a descriptive reference to out-migration from Ireland has lost its validity. To the extent that we can ever hold in common the meaning of words, 'emigration' is one that we can share to describe a real historical process, a common life-tactic employed by many members of Irish society. In the historical literature, however (and, indeed, in present-day policy statements), 'emigration' as a higher-level concept has become almost useless because it is used both to denominate a set of events (a set of effects, in other words) and the cause of those events. It has become an omnibus construct because many observers use 'emigration' both to mean the leaving of Ireland and the effects upon Irish society of those departures. And 'emigration' has become a term so emotion-laden as to preclude clear historical and political thought, for it wraps the behaviour of individual human beings in a smothering blanket of implied judgement. Och, emigration, the forever tragedy.[3]

Too often, the application of 'emigration' as a concept involves a tiny, constant bullying, and at the heart of that bullying is the tyranny of the Irish homeland. (I'm speaking here, obviously, of the home country as a cultural icon, not as a physical force.) You see, in its present usage, 'emigration' is usually understood as a vector that starts in a primary place and slides towards a second one. Emigration is always from Ireland. Well and good: that's a matter of linguistic definition. But, if we are trying to understand the larger world, this privileging of the Irish homeland may have less value than if we were to reverse the valence, for explanatory purposes. That is, instead of thinking of movement being from Ireland, let's conceive of it as being towards someplace else. The gradations on the metre stick by which one assesses the activities of the migrants (and of their children and their grandchildren) alter radically and thereupon the meaning of the act of migration is transformed.

The iconic tyranny of the homeland also must be exorcised in a second way. It is generally, albeit unconsciously, assumed that whatever social, cultural, and intellectual practices occurring 'abroad' (that is, outside of Ireland) most approximate those that occur in Ireland, are most 'Irish'. That is a standard which often results in a lead sector – an area of very rapid social adaptation by migrants – being assayed in some way as pernicious or iniquitous. And cities, provinces, neighbourhoods wherein people of Irish background adapt new economic and social mores are seen as less historically important than those that resemble the old home country.

Instead of seeing the homeland as the equivalent of ancient Rome – the capital by which all other locales are judged, it might be more productive if we conceive (if only for brief moments) of the sum total of Irish migration patterns

– the entire Irish diaspora – as being a phenomenon that has no single metropole. Instead of seeing it as a flat-earth exercise, judged from 'Rome', we might well conceive of the Irish diaspora as a massive reticulation of invisible webbing, stencilling itself all over the face of the globe. That webbing has no centre, but instead, if one stands at any point, it possesses lines that stretch out infinitely and in all directions. Viewing this diaspora from Wellington, Sydney, Cape Town, Boston, Toronto, Liverpool, is just as revealing and just as legitimate an exercise as is the adoption of the Customs House, Dublin, as our vantage point.

Obviously, I am implying that Irish migration forms a text that is polysemous and that it should be multiply conceptualised. I am particularly evangelical on this matter, because one of my missions over the years has been to convince historians of countries that previously avoided doing so, to build Irish migrants into their own national histories as fully articulated entities.[4] But the Irish will be given their appropriate place in the various national histories as real, complex peoples – not as ethnic stereotypes and not as filiopietistic burlesques of reality – only if the data on Irish migrants can be appropriated by each national history.[5] This requires that the vantage point not be limited to Dublin, nor the meaning of migration determined solely by Old World criteria.

Both as part of my small crusade to convince historians of other nations that the Irish migrants really are much more important than those national historians realised, and as a general improvement of Irish historiography as well, I hope to coax as many scholars as possible to consider the availability of a doctrine that runs through Irish historiography. This is the 'Doctrine of Irish Exceptionalism', and the belief – more an unconscious attitude than a specific articulation – that Irish history has worked by different rules than those which apply to the rest of the western world.[6] Of course Ireland has been unique – every culture is – but much of what we view as Irish history is a local subset of a much larger, general pattern, and this is as true in migration history as in any other area. In particular, Irish migration patterns from roughly 1600 onwards were part of the larger phenomenon which, for want of a better term, is often called 'the expansion of Europe'. The promise of the next generation is that it will meld the Irish research base with the databases of other European countries. There is especial promise in working with scholars of migration from other, relatively small nations on the periphery of Europe. The Scandinavian material, for example, is particularly rich. But non-European comparisons are also possible. For example, some of the post-Famine labour flows seem to bear comparison to data being produced by the Southern African Migration Project at Queen's University, Ontario. And there are other examples.[7]

Now, in melding the research base of Irish migration studies with those of other countries, the work will in the first instance be historical and social scientific. One recognises that within the community of Irish scholars social scientists have not had the influence that they deserve to have had. (Still, one has to stretch far to find in Ireland the dour sense of vengeance served found in a Toronto *Globe and Mail* back-page headline [25 July 1997] 'Social Scientist elected president in Albania'.) To my mind, the great virtue of social scientists as they approach the global matter of the Irish diaspora is that they are not afraid to draw generalisations: tight, rigorous, limited in scope – testable generalisations. This is in contrast to the practice in my own line, history, in which the cheap trick that we teach all honours students and post-graduates is that everything is unique, and thus outliers in any data-set are taken to mean that central propensities and common properties can be ignored. And the social scientists, in framing their generalisations, operate in contrast to most of those scholars engaged in what is vaguely called 'cultural studies', wherein no generalisation is uttered unless it is incapable of being either proved or disproved, but merely illustrated. Or so it seems.

Actually, if there is a danger in social scientists having a major, perhaps dominant, position in Irish diaspora studies, it is only the general one that affects that broad band of disciplines worldwide: a curious propensity for reversing cause and effect. In that regard, I instance only an American example, from the *Journal of Fallacious Research*. Therein it was reported that a physical geographer who had collected hundreds of video tapes of violent meteorological phenomena had demonstrated, at a high level of statistical significance, that mobile trailer parks cause tornadoes.

One of the sets of inhibitions that we are in the process of slipping off could be called 'the spancel of the migrant generation'. Because of the way that information on Irish migration was collected (and this holds virtually worldwide), we tend to know quite a lot about the migrating generation in each historical moment and relatively little about the people who are the majority of the Irish diaspora: a group that then-President Mary Robinson estimated in 1990 as being over 70 million persons worldwide.[8] In most cultures, the sense of Irishness (however defined) both changed and diminished over generations, but I would argue that for at least two or three generations it was a significant determinant of the behaviour of most people of Irish descent. Further, I think that even after that, it remained (and indeed remains) as a enduring stream, subterranean, but still partially determining personal behaviour, and this long after the individuals in question ceased to think of themselves as Irish. Any concept of Irish migration, then, must not be merely physical and must not deal only with the first generation, but must be cultural and institutional and must deal with the entire multi-generational ethnic group. Operating with such a rich concept of migration is much more challenging than working with simple 'emigrant' history, but it has the potential to be infinitely more productive.

I emphasise the potential here, because I think that the Irish diaspora is being sold short by its historians (I include myself here). For, even when building the Irish into our own separate national histories, we have been excessively

modest in the following respect: put bluntly, we have not emphasised sufficiently strongly that the Irish diaspora is a very big deal in world history. It deserves to be presented as part of a multi-generational cultural and institutional web that interacts with other diaspora. Those that are especially important are:
1 the Spanish diaspora. One of the great virtues of present-day scholarship is that attention finally is being paid to the Irish and the Hispanic world, for the Hispanic diaspora has interacted with the Irish one from the earliest days of European expansion;
2 the African diaspora, the intersections with the Irish diaspora being frequently tragic; and
3 that of the English (more of that later).[9]

Notice that I included 'cultural and institutional' reference in the preceding paragraph. From that you can infer that I believe it is self-defeating to limit migration studies simply to the geographic transfer of human beings from one spot to another. The really interesting part is the migration of cultural patterns – physical culture, technology, institutions, and 'soft' culture – into and out of Ireland as part of a great globe-circling matrix. Let me mention only three examples as instances of the sort of phenomenon that deserves further investigation.

The first is in the field of Irish commercial relationships with other countries. A case that easily comes to mind is that of Beamish and Crawford. Founded in 1792, the firm had assimilated a technological history that ran back to the outbreak of the Irish civil war of 1641, being built on one of the oldest brewing sites in Ireland. How does an enterprise that has a mercantile genealogy that goes back before Cromwell come to be part of one of the massive commercial empires of our own day (the Scottish-Courage Group, which now has one-quarter of the beer market in Ireland and England)? And what does it say about the iconographic enthusiasms of the Irish as an ethnic group that Beamish remains a cult drink among Hibernophiles from Mombasa to Montreal?[10]

Second, I think a really important book lies in tracing the globe-circling impact of the Irish national schools and, simultaneously, of the Irish Catholic church's attitudes towards primary education. Whoever takes on this task will discover that in several important places in the English-speaking world the 'official culture' of the masses – that is, the state-approved and government-funded culture taught to children – had as its direct genealogical antecedent the national system of education in Ireland. The school systems of Ontario, British Columbia and parts of the Canadian prairies were modelled directly on those of Ireland, and in their early days professors of education were imported directly to the Canadas to show the locals how things should be done.[11] Related to this is the seemingly globe-circling fact that the Roman Catholic church fought, first, to bend the Irish national system of education into a form that it could approve, and then held this up as a model to be emulated. It achieved these ends – involving a segregation of Catholic from Protestant children and a clerical control over state-provided tax monies – in most of Canada, in New Zealand and (partially) in some Australian states. And, mostly, these patterns of 'official culture' were won by Irish-educated priests and bishops, or by clergy trained in Irish-founded seminaries in their respective countries.[12] Irish ideas migrated; Ireland ruled.

This brings me to the third example of cultural migration. Curiously, the migration of Christianity to Ireland and its migration from Ireland is relatively little studied. More than any other ideational matrix, Christianity influenced (some would say determined) the pivotal aspects of Irish cultural and social life. And, more importantly to historians of other nations, nineteenth- and early twentieth-century Ireland was the source of the numerically greatest diaspora in the history of the Christian religion. For the better part of a century, the heart of the Catholic church in the United States of America, in English Canada, in Australia and in New Zealand was Irish. Only within living memory has this changed. So, Christianity and its flow in and out of Ireland should be one of the central themes of Irish historical writing. Yet, when one looks at the literature, one encounters very little that embodies the appropriate sense of wonder, or attempts to see the wholeness of the process. Instead, one has (with one or two notable exceptions) narrow institutional studies and isolated chapters plucked from the M.Litt. theses of antiquarian parish priests.[13] Christianity deserves better. I suggest this with both disappointment and strong conviction, because I have spent a portion of my own research time over the last two decades writing a book which has recently appeared entitled *Surpassing Wonder. The Invention of the Bible and the Talmuds*. It has as its dominant tone my own awe at just how magnificent an achievement the invention of our Judaeo-Christian heritage actually was and how fundamentally determinative of most of our later social and intellectual concepts were the texts, the poetry, the hymns, and the historical narratives of the Ancient Near East.[14] Something akin to that same awe should seize Irish historians as they see those same concepts interact with a proud and unbroken Celtic world and thereby produce a culture that, in its religious components, was enduring, adaptable, and thus, ultimately, transportable the world around.

III

I am optimistic about the future of Irish diaspora studies, in part because it appears that the parochial concept of Irish emigration is being replaced by the more robust, more international, more ecumenical one of 'migration'. And the accompanying concept of Irish exile, gurning and vaguely paranoid as it is, is being replaced by the idea of Irish diaspora so that scholars of Irish migration are empowered to approach with confidence topics of genuine international significance, and to discuss matters within their ken from which the historians of other countries can learn a good deal.[15] But perhaps I am being blithe and Pollyannaish. (Though my being descended from several generations of stern and unbending Swedish Baptists – the sort of people who conducted winter baptisms by the expedient of sawing large holes in frozen lakes – makes this unlikely.) So, let me conclude my conspectus of Irish migration studies by citing some of the sub-fields in which scholars have turned the corner and are producing a good deal of work distinguished simultaneously by imagination and integrity. (I do not detail specific scholars here, because it is the contours of the field as a collective enterprise that are important in this context.)

The most significant of these developments, in my view, is the creation virtually *ex nihilo* of a substantial literature on female migration. Such a literature would be necessary in virtually any culture, but for the Irish it is particularly salient, for Ireland was unusual among European countries in having nearly as many women who chose to out-migrate as men. There are still scores of unsettled basic questions concerning women in the Irish diaspora – the most difficult to ponder being whether or not migration out of Ireland was an emancipating experience – but the grounds of debate are now becoming clearly established.[16] (As an aside, thus far Irish work has for the most part avoided the lugubrious solemnity of, say, some of my Canadian colleagues. Recently, a friend of mine returned from a seminar on Marian Engels's novel *Bear* in which the bear has physical relations with a woman. This offended one of the participants who said, 'I don't know ... I mean, about the morality ... She'd only known the bear a week.')

Indeed, the work on women's migration has had an impact on Irish diaspora studies in general: it has helped to spur a recognition of Irish migrants as active participants in their own life stories, not mere flotsam on the running tide of social history. Just as a recognition of the personal independence and personal agency of females has been a central item in the field of women's history in general, so the demonstration that Irish women were capable of a remarkable degree of self-direction in the migration process has led to a recognition that the entire group of migrants – men included – had a greater degree of agency than previously was granted. The notion of the Irish emigrant as passive victim served for several generations as an analgesic within the Irish homeland, and to a lesser degree throughout the diaspora, but it was patronising to the emigrants and culturally debilitating to those who promulgated it. If one reads the classic documents on Irish emigration – for example, the Commission on Emigration and Other Problems of 1948-54 – one finds a pervasive sense of the failed male.[17] The tone is the same as that of the first generation of men in our own time whose wives went to work. They had a sense of failure, that they were not real men because they could not 'keep' their wives. The same sense of failed maleness holds for most Irish discussion of out-migration conducted before, roughly, the early 1980s: we have failed because we cannot keep our young people. No, it's all right if your wife works in Dunne's stores, and it's okay if your kids work in California. That's just the way the world is: no fault implied.

Now, further, I am optimistic because we have learned within the last decade or so to live with the fact that ethnicity – which is a construct central to understanding the behaviour of the Irish diaspora – is a hollow concept: hollow not in the sense of being meretricious, but as being susceptible to situational modification. The best work that I read now assumes that ethnic identity is both a matter of self-identification and of taxonomies developed by the host society, and thus the nature of Irish ethnic identity evolves both over time and according to locale.[18] So, really good ethnic history is simultaneously a rigorous documentation of the behaviour of a specific group of individuals and equally a chronicle of their evolving consciousness. Thus, what begins as migration history becomes part of what is sometimes called 'the history of consciousness'.

Moreover, I am delighted to encounter, year-by-year, an ever-diminishing amount of 'ballgown and tiara history'. That is a term from the museum trade. It refers to a phenomenon universal in both material and cultural history: the most ubiquitous and widespread items disappear and the unusual ones – the tiaras and ballgowns of a previous culture – are those that are most often preserved. So it is relatively easy, but very misleading, to set up a museum exhibit which gives pride of place to the unusual and the atypical, while ignoring what was general, and perhaps universal. Similarly, in the New Worlds to which the Irish migrants ventured, it is important to document and honour the cultural treasures that were brought from the homeland and were preserved – the Irish language in some places, ascetic Presbyterian psalmody in others – but only if they are placed in societal context. To judge the historical importance of any given practice according to the degree to which it either preserved or replicated usages from the Old Country is to confuse migrants with curators. Fortunately, most historians of the Irish diaspora now do not privilege, say, early twentieth-century male migrants who played Gaelic games, but rather, follow the bulk of the migrants to the places they really played: baseball parks, rugby fields and football pitches, depending where in the wide world they turned up. That is a metonym of a larger and promising historiographic development, attending to the migrants on their own historical terms, not ours.

Further, I am heartened that, finally, historians of Irish migration and historians of the Irish diaspora have begun to face directly what has until recently been the single most avoided matter in the field, namely the relationship of the Irish and empires (note the plural: empires). In particular, we are beginning to analyse the way the successive ranks of Irish migrants to New Worlds were, however unconsciously in most instances, the foot soldiers of empire.[19] This requires a breaking of the perceptual set, the idea that Irish migrants were not like other Europeans (the 'Doctrine of Irish Exceptionalism' again); that because they had been imperialised, and at home had frequently fought against imperialism, they could not be imperialist. To break this misleading perceptual set, several focal recalibrations are in train. First, focus is being shifted from formal activities that relate to empire to informal ones. Crucially, the actions of individual migrants (whether in rural or urban areas) made them participants in imperial systems, and this despite most of them having no involvement with any official imperial apparatus.[20] Second, a confusion of cause and effect is being erased. It is true that the motives of most Irish migrants leaving their homeland had nothing to do with enthusiasm for imperialism – many were virtually forced to migrate – but the effects upon native cultures in the various New Worlds occurred nonetheless. Behaviour, rather than motivation, is becoming our chief focus. Empires are very complex social systems, and whether an Irish migrant joined a regiment in the New Zealand Wars or was a tally man in the Winchester arms factory in Connecticut made little difference: participation in the system inevitably implied an effect. Crucially, the American Empire is becoming recognised as the place where Irish migrants and their descendants made their most underestimated contribution to imperialism, not least in the displacement and destruction of indigenous cultures.[21] The post-1850 expansion of the United States to embrace most of the habitable portions of North America was nothing less than the creation of a kingdom; and, in our own century, the American Republic has become, first, the world's leading imperial power and, in our own time, the only one of any consequence. And, at last, scholars are facing the possibility that the educational and religious institutions that issued forth from Ireland – both Catholic and Protestant – were more effective in breaking down indigenous cultures than were entire regiments of the armies of the British Empire or of the various American governments.[22] Tough issues, certainly, but the discipline is sufficiently mature to engage them.

Finally, I am most optimistic about the direction and energy of Irish migration studies because each year I see just a little less of the unconscious, but pervasive, sectarianism that has bespeckled so much of the historiography of Irish migration. Sectarianism is a very easy disease to catch, not least because one of the chief causal determinants of Irish history has been (and still is) the existence of hostile, mutually hate-ridden sects. The chief way that the historiography of the global Irish diaspora exhibited the effects of this toxin was either to segregate the history of the Protestant migrants or, more commonly, to ignore that history completely.[23] Those practices are fading, but building the Protestants (I am here using the term in its modern sense, to include all the Protestant denominations, not just the Church of Ireland) into the worldwide story is notoriously difficult: they left fewer markers than did their Catholic counterparts and they held more complex and protean multiple identities, so they disappeared more quickly into host populations than did the Catholics. In this context, I should recommend a book published recently by Liverpool University Press, Donald MacRaild's *Culture, Conflict and Migration. The Irish in Victorian Cumbria*.[24] It is a nice example of how to develop a balanced and inclusive non-sectarian ethnic history of a local Irish community.

IV

If I think that we can look forward to a very productive, paradigm-shifting decade or two in Irish migration studies, I am also aware that this work eventually will be found factually insufficient and its conceptual base inadequate by some subsequent generation. Good: that is one version of how the Great Chain of Being operates and it should not bother us a bit. We should be mildly concerned, however, with a side-effect of the way that we use, wear out, and discard concepts. Although that is the way professional scholars do their work, it can be very unsettling to the general public, who confuse the verities with the unvarying. And, often, the general public wants historians not to uncover the facts, but to obscure them.

I recently received a letter from my old Harvard mentor John Kelleher, the founding-figure of Irish Studies in North America. He was talking about a set of pictures in the *New York Times* which showed various sets of paramilitaries posing without their balaclavas on. 'Makes one sense the real reason for the ski-masks', he noted.

Within Ireland at the present time, a strong minority within the scholarly community and (probably) a minority of the general public are in search of heritage rather than history, belief rather than evidence, sectarian and political exclusivity rather than cultural diversity. They want the old songs, the old methods, the old hatreds. They want the ski-masks back on.

It is much too early to guess how the *Methodonenstreit* within the scholarly profession in Ireland will be resolved. I am confident, however, that the scholars who study the Irish migrants worldwide, their culture, their institutions, their ethnic consciousness, will not do an abrupt about-face and march back to the false security of the tiny walled towns constructed by the frightened and the resentful. We have already come too far for that.

2
Varieties of New Zealand Irishness
A Meditation

Patrick O'Farrell

I

One of the things an historian learns (hopefully) is the limited utility of labels, and of convenient generalisations, even those that carry obvious and agreed meanings. Thus 'Irish' means inhabitants of Ireland or – and here is the first area of debate or at least discussion – their descendants in other countries. Are, in fact, such diaspora 'Irish' really 'Irish'? The whole matter of their interaction with the host country is essentially what diaspora history is about and it will come to complex conclusions on the kind and degree of that interaction. And it is beset by major problems in regard to the nature of its basic central material. What *is* an Irishman (or woman – to ignore the gender complications for verbal convenience)? An Anglo-Irish aristocrat, a Dublin jackeen, Corkmen, Kerrymen, spalpeens, mountainy men, Ulstermen of various kinds, men of the west, and of the Western Isles, and so on ... Answer: all of these and more. And with very different answers over time: the 'Irishman' of the eighteenth century is not the same person as today's emigrant.

But what's new? Historians from the beginning of time have faced these kinds of problems. Encountered them, but sometimes not noticed. Obviously historians of diasporas are confronted by the interaction between the influences of two (or more!) different environments and cultures. They must deal with those as best they can: recognise them, not evade or ignore. And that goes for not only 'Irish' but 'New Zealand': that too is a complex and multi-faceted entity.

We all fall short of illuminating or comprehending the intricacies and convolutions of such interactions, but that does not mean we should not try. The contrary: we should try harder, the challenge being such as to extend the capacities of even the angels.

Down on earth, we learn. Something new every day. In my case, and in relation to the New Zealand Irish (Catholics only in this case), I was first compelled to think about this in relation to a book I was reviewing in 1976. As against what I thought was the author's monolithic concept, I remarked:

there has been no single Irish Catholic experience in New Zealand history. To refer to some of the personal published testimonies, Dan Davin's Southland is different from Pat Lawlor's Wellington, which is different from Ian Cross's Wanganui, which is different from the present reviewer's Greymouth and South Canterbury. Any treatment of Irish Catholic experience or activity in New Zealand ought to explain why such differences existed'.[1]

Which was true enough as far as it went, which was not all that far. It did not avert to the very different temperaments, gifts, abilities attitudes and life experiences reflected in the writers named – to say nothing of others, such as H.M. Wilson or Eileen Duggan or Maurice Duggan, who also depicted the New Zealand Irish scene. From brief personal acquaintance I can contrast the personae of Dan Davin and Pat Lawlor, in ways that would be generally accepted. How do their contrasting perceptions and sensitivities, to say nothing of differing literary capacities, affect the character and accuracy of their depictions of their 'Irish' worlds?

And my comment did not include reference – and this is basic – to the curious and unique variegated amalgam New Zealand Catholicism was, formed not only by direct Irish influences, but also, and that strongly, by French and English (to say nothing of Australian, given the large numbers of Irish who came via there). Nobody with any knowledge of New Zealand Catholic history can miss that. In Michael King's *God's Farthest Outpost*,[2] Chapter Two is entitled 'A French Church?' The question mark is removed in Chapter Three, 'An Irish Church', but nevertheless the Irish were in the position of Johnny (or Seán) come-lately. Mother Aubert, immortalised in Jessie Munro's *The Story of Suzanne Aubert*, did not die until 1926.[3] And I did not need Neil Vaney's massive and excellent thesis 'The Dual Tradition. Irish Catholics and French Priests in New Zealand: the West Coast Experience, 1865-1910', with its mastery of detail, to persuade me of the reality of that duality.[4] I already had experienced it personally, through my Irish parents' fond recollections of a French clerical presence extending much later.[5] And from the reaction of my parents to the young Irish priests – seculars from All Hallows rather than the French-influenced Marist Order – assigned as curates to Greymouth in the 1950s. They did not measure up to the standards, religious, personal, and social, set by the French. I recall the case of a certain such priest who often visited our house for tea and talk – unexpectedly. He always opened the back door without knocking and then announced his presence by shouting, in the broadest possible caricature brogue, 'How'r ye living'! This constantly enraged my father, given the intrusion, and the stage Irishman act, but he never revealed a sign of this – until after the priest had gone. My mother went along with the performance and always laughed politely and made him welcome. But even she was unhappy with his bursting in.

This parental reaction might be explained away as the usual abrasion between generations – the priest was the same age as my older brother – but there was much more to it than that. It was an example of the frequent distaste, the feeling of embarrassed unhappiness, that came over the emigrant Irish, and their children, when they visited Ireland. They were affronted by the poverty, the begging, the shortcomings of personal hygiene and sanitation, the drunkenness, the indolence and inefficiency, by the dominance of priests, eccentricity to the degree of being weird or destructive, even the weather. (This list is historical, not applicable to the economy of the Celtic tiger.) These things had to be balanced off against the extraordinary human warmth, the natural piety, the fascinating subtleties, and the open charming welcomes and enchanting hospitality.[6] Visiting Irish and their children had diverse reactions and came to different appraisals of this mix, but the general conclusion is obvious: Ireland was The Old Country, the diasporas the New. And 'old' meant a good deal more than 'former'. Some of that meaning is suggested in Paula Meehan's 1991 poem, 'The Man Who Was Marked by Winter':

> We are old: a species gone to seed
> Run wild under the stars
> And our talk is old talk.

Old in the sense of smelly, incontinent, tired, careless of appearance, boring, backward-looking: people looked on by the young sometimes with affection, but also with impatience, even contempt.

This is the structuring into which the New Zealand, and other diaspora Irish fitted. They saw themselves as pioneers in new dynamic situations, crammed with hitherto undreamed possibilities, challenged by the offer of big rewards for hard work, in contrast with Ireland, clean and efficient. Superior environments.

The tension between the elements of this situation is real and obvious. Given that it existed not only between New Zealand and Ireland, but within New Zealand itself, then that multitudinous set of variables offers both a valuable source of potential explanatory insights and a bewildering set of possibilities. Unless she has incontrovertible evidence, the historian who has sufficient perception to explore below the surface will often be reduced to doing no more than offering fruitful suggestions. But is not that always the way in which the best history, particularly in such a subtle field as immigration history, is conducted? Make no mistake, this field, once one has gone past the area of simple statistics – and that in itself can be very elusive and problematic – is subtle indeed.

Imponderables abound. And in 1976, my own information on Irish regionalism was limited to matters of general knowledge. It was not until the 1990s that I became conscious of the need to add to and refine my regional diversification – Rangiora, Loburn, Kerrytown, and Timaru in Canterbury, the Lace Curtain Irish of Dunedin, to mention merely some. And the Lace Curtain phenomenon raised the whole matter of status and occupation, wealth and attitude.

This regionalism factor is all the more important because of the particular nature of New Zealand Irish settlement. It tended to be dispersed, scattered, and rural, lacking the concentration of America, even Australia. Thus my Irish farming uncle in South Canterbury had two switches of land-owning location, Makikihi and Waimate, in the sense of these settlements being the focus of shopping and religious services, offering merely occasional, accidental, casual and brief social encounters with fellow Irish. Even family visits within the districts involved significant travel, and such were the demands of a farming life, that, before the day of the telephone, the rural mail service was the way in which even virtual neighbours kept in touch. Common residual Irishness might survive in such conditions, but it was bound to be in a mild form.

At least in the early 1970s I was very much aware of the Ulster Protestant Irish and their presence in concentrated form in the settlement of Katikati in the Bay of Plenty. That awareness did not spring from any experienced New Zealand consciousness. In the 1976 review I quote above I wrote 'the present reviewer has never regarded himself as Irish ... It might be wondered, in relation to the period spanned by this book (1868–1922), how many New Zealanders with similar origins saw their identity in the same way.' I still consider this to be a good question, particularly in the case, of which I am an example, of first generation Irish New Zealanders. It has been often suggested in diaspora studies that it is the second generation that embraces a sense of Irishness. I see no sign whatever of this amongst my own children, who have all lived in Ireland, with my wife and me, for two years of past time. They value and enjoyed their Irish experience, and particularly some aspects of their schooling there, and still have affection for the country. This situation of my never feeling Irish or judging it consciously as relevant to my own identity, I put down to my father's almost complete identification with New Zealand, as a place and as a social and political system which he participated in actively: he never inflicted Ireland on me, and very seldom referred to it. It was not relevant. His Ireland – all of his five brothers and sisters – came to New Zealand.

I see very recently, in the Australian novelist Gerard Windsor's memoir *I Asked Cathleen to Dance* (1999) that he had a somewhat similar experience with his Cork-born father, though his grandfather (I never met mine) whetted his curiosity. But his Irish seduction he attributes to seeing David Lean's spectacular *Ryan's Daughter*. He was later to find that the film's apotheosis, the storm scene, was in fact filmed in South Africa. Which prompts a relevant aside: how much was New Zealand Irishness, or any other kind of Irishness, derived from reality or from visions? Misremembered, or worse still, from created images – Ireland as fraud?

Not intentionally, but one wonders about the concepts and motivation driving some of the genealogical interest in Ireland. Questions obtrude that do not, of course, apply only to New Zealand Irish. Some few descendants are holy pilgrims, genuine explorers of their links with the land of their forefathers, some are simple tourists seeking a place to go which has some point of personal reference, others are sentimental nostalgia buffs. And this situation and these attitudes have been radically changed by the relatively recent travel revolution – air travel plus prosperity. The whole concept of emigration has changed, from permanent relocation, exile, to the prospect of temporary, even very brief, sojourning.

II

Which raises the general question of Irish dream-worlds, and more interestingly, did the Irish ever really leave home?

I have pursued this general question before, at some length,[7] but not in relation to New Zealand. It requires proper investigation: it is merely raised here. For instance, what is to be made of the mentalities of the founders of Canterbury, that most 'English' of New Zealand's colonies – John Robert Godley, James Edward Fitzgerald and Charles Bowen; Fitzgerald went on to be New Zealand's first premier. They all spelt out variations on standard Anglo-Irish themes. Edward Gibbon Wakefield opined that Godley was the only Irishman he ever knew who was not at all Irish. Yet Godley exhibited that salient characteristic of the Burkeian Anglo-Irish colonial visionary – the determination to create in the colonial world a society the reverse of Ireland, a society which reflected the lessons learnt from Britain's Irish mistakes, a dream capsule. In farewelling his colony in 1852, Godley said:

> I often smile when I think of the ideal Canterbury of which our imagination dreamt, yet I see nothing in that dream to regret or be ashamed of, and I am quite sure that without the enthusiasm, the poetry, the unreality if you will, with which our scheme was overlaid, it would never have been accomplished.

As to Fitzgerald, Wakefield judged him super-Irish, wild enough to hunt his own sheep, volatile, charming, an accomplished watercolourist. Bowen, romantic conservative rather than a liberal like the others, saw education (he was central to the 1877 Act) as a social salvific. All these Anglo-Irish were in postures of reaction from Famine Ireland, of which they had direct personal experience. Surprisingly, none of them are even mentioned in Miles Fairburn's *The Ideal Society and its Enemies*.[8] As far as these pivotal men are concerned, there is a case for seeing the New Zealand colony as ideally unlike Famine Ireland.

Elsewhere I have raised, rather than pursued, the apparent fact that the framework the British government set out for the New Zealand colony was Irish – New Ulster and New Munster in 1846 – and there were many other links evident in administrative, police and military structures.[9] That raises the question of the extent to which New Zealand was a British, a United Kingdom, colony rather than the English one its socially dominant élites wished and pretended. Which is all to say that the Anglo-Irish influence on, and in, New Zealand remains to be investigated.

To move from the narrowly historical to broader humane and literary concerns: what is to be made of the particular and individual operations of chance, preference, whim, accident and the like? Life, in any experience, is full of such factors. And people on the move are more children of Providence than most. Friends, opportunities, schemes, impulses, the interplay between this and that, the complex and individual interaction that makes the whole migrant story such a fascinating one. Sure, there are patterns, groupings, trends, but also the idiosyncratic, the unexpected, the maverick, the mysterious arise, as in any human affairs.

Why did these particular Irish come to New Zealand rather than elsewhere? For any number of reasons: land schemes, chain migration, adventure, the attractions of a similar climate and landscape, membership of the British Army in the New Zealand Land Wars, and so on. But did any come because it was as far away from Ireland as it was possible to be? The greater the distance, the more intense the feeling of independence? To take the point of Allen Curnow's 'Landfall in Unknown Seas': [10]

> Simply by sailing in a new direction
> You could enlarge the world

Or, striking a different note in 'Spring 1942':

> We do not choose our islands
> But mountains are magnets where
> Our Fathers sailed in under
> Heroes or hang-dog exiles
> Or (it doesn't matter) marooned.

And to take up Curnow again with his insight into the New Zealander:

> Wholeheartedly he cannot move
> From where he is, nor love
> Wholeheartedly that place.

It could be that Curnow's perceptions are relevant to all immigrant experience, but they bring squarely to mind my own father – or at least the emanations I took from his attitudes – and mine. Yet is this simply to pose the awkward and basic question: were the Irish in New Zealand much the same essentially as all other immigrants? Is this whole separate historical treatment a falsity, a contrivance? Obviously not, but where are its legitimate borders? How are the New Zealand Irish distinguished from other immigrants, or from Irish immigrants in other countries, in America, Australia, Britain, elsewhere. What makes the New Zealand Irish themselves?

On the face of it, these seem vital questions, and so they are. They may not be the only questions to which we would like answers.

One question might be the general effects of distance on immigrant reactions and attitudes. What significance has the implications of the very title of Donald

Akenson's excellent and vastly stimulating *Half the World from Home. Perspectives on the Irish in New Zealand 1850-1950.* Or for that matter, of this book – *A Distant Shore*? Where (and when) is Home? What Shore is distant? Depends on your location, which way you are facing. And is it facing both ways at once? Of course it is: that is what both books are about.

It might be worth enquiring of our Irish in New Zealand if their view of Ireland was coloured, even determined, by status, class and personal experience, personal tastes and values. Put that way, the answer is inescapable. Take Eileen Duggan, New Zealand-born of Irish parents, never to visit Ireland. George Russell (A.E.) reviewing her 1921 *Poems in Ireland*, wrote that 'we might almost suppose she lived in Ireland.'[11] But what is to be made of a poem such as 'The Famine Wind'? A feminised Famine Ireland is seen thus:

> And she knew that the King of Sorrows
> With his sceptre of pain and loss
> Had touched her brow as an equal,
> And said, 'Thou must bear the Cross.'[12]

It is a fact, discovered by the Irish Folk Lore Commission in the 1930s, that the Famine of 1845-50 carried an element of peasant tradition that saw the disaster as a punishment from God; but from the 1860s, and John Mitchel's propagandist journalism, the virtually exclusive view was that England was to blame. Is Duggan's interpretation a reversion to Irish historical folkways? No, in keeping with her whole poetic treatment of Irish subjects, it is rather one expressive of her personal religious value structures and of her disposition to adopt the 'Celtic mood' – 'a nameless melancholy, a consciousness of grievance, a sense of foreboding, or at other times a romantic vision of a land of faery'.[13] A combination of J.M. Barry and 'The Sorrows of Werther'. The brothers Grimm perhaps. This facetiousness masks the serious question: how much is being 'Irish' of this kind merely a version, a particular application, of a universal romantic agony? A widespread and non-specific human tendency to what might be harshly described as maundering sentimentality?

But Eileen Duggan's 'Irishness' was very much subordinate to her New Zealand nationalism. It is this very characteristic, or at least the poetic mode in which it was expressed – the use of words like kowhai, rata, and tui – that drew the disapprobation of New Zealand's literary avant-garde in the 1940s and thereafter. This raises the matter of the location of Ireland, and Irish New Zealandishness, in cultural and intellectual spectrum.

A modern effort to conflate the two historically can be found at its eccentric extreme in Michael O'Leary's *The Irish Annals of New Zealand* (Seacliff, 1991). Written in a style parodying both the James Joyce of *Ullysses* and *Finnegan's Wake*, with a dash of Flann O' Brien, this mixes Irish and New Zealand history in what seems to me a crude and unreadable fashion, but it is none the less methodologically interesting as a literary possibility. However the fact is, however unfairly, any kind of Irishness was seen as a mark of cultural inferiority, a dimension of the terrain of the working class, or the lower bourgeoisie. There has been some excellent study of aspects of religious sectarianism, but little of the cultural sectarianism directed towards what was Irish.

Against this it could be argued that popular Irish influences were major factors in rescuing New Zealand from its dominant tendency towards an English cultural cringe. They exercised, on a smaller scale and in collaboration with others, a liberating social role, similar to that wielded by the Irish in Australia. Contrast R.A.K. Mason's self-pitying plaint:[14]

> Garrisons pent up in a little fort ...
> here in this far-pitched perilous hostile place
> this solitary hard-assaulted spot,
> fixed at the friendly outer edge of space

with the sentiments of Thomas Bracken, of Clones, Co. Monaghan:

> We greet you, stranger, to this land
> Where slaves have never trod –
> The breeze which sweeps our mountains
> Is the breath of freedom's god. [15]

Or Bracken's more famous second stanza in the National Anthem 'God Defend New Zealand'!

> Men of every creed and race
> Gather here before Thy face
> Asking Thee to bless this place
> God defend our Free Land.

Certainly Mason has a valid point, but it is in sharp negative contrast to Bracken's confident and expansive optimism. And it is Bracken who proclaims the value and sentiments of the National Anthem. The only Irish-born (and tempered) celebrity to comment on New Zealand was G.B. Shaw, on a visit in 1934. He said: 'Probably all the people of New Zealand should be exterminated to make place for a more advanced people', an observation which was accepted without question by an adoring crowd of dazzled reporters.[16] It was of a piece with all the other outrageous Shavianisms of which Shaw delivered himself – that Britain knew nothing about and was totally uninterested in New Zealand, that New Zealand should stop venerating, kowtowing to, and allowing itself to be exploited by Britain, and stop pretending it was the dairy of the universe, and start producing people with brains. However these opinions sinned against orthodoxy there was, on personal recollected experience, widespread Irish New Zealand sentiment which supported critical attitudes of that general kind. However, as with so much that might be located among the Irish, these were broadly popular views, the common property of the 'ordinary bloke', and thus beneath the notice of élite society's formative and recognising elements.

III

A meditation? To ponder, reflect on, muse over. That includes a present orientation, the linking of past and present – and the present is both instructive and problematic.

Today, New Zealand has two sets of Irish links. The Ulster New Zealand Trust based in Northern Ireland, and formed in 1988, exists to promote historical, cultural and economic links between Ireland and New Zealand – and to care for the (beautifully) restored birthplace of the New Zealand premier, John Ballance (1839-93). Ballance House is at Glenavy, near Lisburn, County Antrim, a substantial middling farmhouse, open to visitors, with amenities, and a full-time curator and assistant who promote not only the House, but New Zealand cultural affairs generally. The New Zealand visitors – a constant flow among the 33,000 since 1990 – tend to be those of Ulster heritage, people interested in gardens, old houses, respectable elegance, scones, with raspberry jam, cream, and tea – a sharp contrast in interest, age groups, and choice of liquid refreshment to some of the visitors to Dublin. Ballance House is the base for Mrs Jill McIvor, Honorary Consul for New Zealand in Northern Ireland. On her frequent visits to New Zealand Mrs McIvor's particular interest is historic houses, whose names indicate the importance of Ulster influence woven into New Zealand commercial and political life – Lisburn House in Dunedin, Donegal House in Kaikoura, Stafford House in Wellington – and, of course, Antrim House, home to the New Zealand Historic Places Trust. Antrim House was built by Robert Hannah, that 'shrewd' and 'hard' Antrim bootmaker, who, from 1874, built a business empire to become one of New Zealand's wealthiest citizens at his death in 1930.

In contrast are New Zealand's links with the Irish Republic. The formal connection is with the Irish Embassy in Australia, which has contacts with twelve Irish Societies in New Zealand centres, from Auckland to Dunedin. Their character tends to be social, sporting, and commercial. And here, as distinct from the Ulster situation, the reflex exists – a New Zealand Ireland Association in Dublin, formed in 1986, 'To promote the social, cultural and sporting interests of New Zealanders living in Ireland and to keep Kiwis in touch with events back home'.

Home? What is home? These societies, in Ireland and New Zealand, depend very substantially on particular individuals, but their disparate and distinctive existence throw up questions which reverberate back into the complexities of past Irishness – too complicated to pursue here in brief compass.

In 1994 I published an article entitled 'How Irish was New Zealand?' Perhaps I should have asked 'How New Zealand were its Irish?' They are, of course, different questions and it is the latter I wish to pose here.

I have used the term 'colonial' elsewhere to denote the response to the new environment and the change, transformation, to something different and new.[17] To repeat:

> 'Colonial' is used precisely when it denotes the settlers and culture of new territories connected with parent states: It is a term of convenience when it is used to take the descriptive emphasis away from terms whose structural balance is misleading – Irish-Australian, Irish-New Zealander. My quarrel with these terms is that they point back to the old culture, whereas the direction of this enquiry is forward. It is towards the formation of a new culture which is 'colonial' to the extent that it is derivative, but distinctive and unique to the extent that the derivation itself has a life and character of its own. The use of 'colonial' also obviates making inappropriate distinctions between Australia and New Zealand: earlier in this century Irish immigrants made no great distinction between the two countries, hardly more than was made between Australian States. Interchange was frequent and casual, particularly at the level of labouring men. It would be absurd not to recognise the different histories and characters of the two countries, particularly the greater English and Scots flavour of some parts of New Zealand, but equally silly not to be aware of their close similarity and relationship.

In a way, like Ireland and its enormous diaspora, New Zealand is a residual country, that is the entity that is left, remains, after the elements which cannot be, or do not wish to be, absorbed, have left. It has the peculiar psyche of such a residue. It is closed. Clement Freud's ancient joke – 'I went to New Zealand once, but it was closed' – had a wider application than to former trading hours. The positive side of this was loyalty, pride in place, independence, the negative – so far as this commentary is concerned – the mythology of homogeneity: there was no sense of being multicultural, though that, while muted, was the case.

In regard to the Irish, why muted? Here was a distinctive minority group, 14 per cent of the population in 1871; why was it not more vigorous, more noticeable, more self-promoting?

Because not only was it small, but it was scattered. It is tempting to suggest that there is a critical size and concentration applicable to the efficacy of minority groups and their role in social interaction. The Irish proportion in Australia was large enough to compel majority attention, and to generate the confrontations and stand-offs which distinguish their role in Australian history.

Again, one might answer that it had no concerted national leadership of the kind the Irish Catholic clergy provided in Australia. The confrontationalism of Bishop Moran in Dunedin went against the grain of a Catholicism deeply influenced by French and English origins.

And finally, the response might be that such was the timing and nature of New Zealand's settlement – no convicts, post-1798, post-1848, post-Famine – that it was spared those big Irish issues which had conditioned and agitated the aggressive Irish in Australia. It was not until 1916 that Irish issues attracted national attention in New Zealand.

Then there was the matter of Irish immigration, such a controversial and bitter issue in Australia. The Irish percolated into New Zealand in a quiet manner and in such small numbers as provoked relatively little hostility, and then dispersed. Their arrival generated no such massive anti-Irish reaction of the kind so important in conditioning Irish immigrant communities elsewhere. They were not perceived as a threat to the character of the new colony.

Nor were they. Gold-diggers, construction workers, coal miners, were, largely, merely passing through, following the forces of international demand for their pioneering labour. Those who came to stay, for commerce or farming, identified almost immediately with their location. After all, that is what they had deliberately chosen. They adopted the general tone and purposes of the colony: they did not wish to be apart; there is in early New Zealand Irishry no celebration of itself, and even its later manifestations – such as Dan Davin's – are apologia rather than affirmations.

Aggressive culture is invented, built as builders make a house, from available materials, according to the plans of architects and the skill and motivation of the builders. The structure is for necessary protection, habitation, the pursuit of one's own life-style. But what if the prevailing climate does not demand such protection, is balmy and open? An aggressive culture is also created in response to those who hate it: its enemies seek to foster and give reality to whatever it is that they fear, so that they may denounce and oppose a reality and not a phantom.

New Zealand did not lend itself to the internal creation of garrisoned fortresses: perhaps R.A.K. Mason's implied assertion of beleaguered commonality applied ' at the friendless outer edge of space'.

The Irish are renowned for their friendship, but is it even more that place was irrelevant to them? that is, place outside, other than, Ireland. New Zealand was a satisfactory material environment: their house. But their home was in their head and their hearts, Irish people and places, Irish gods and God.

3
The Invisible Irish?
Re-Discovering the Irish Protestant Tradition in Colonial New Zealand

Alasdair Galbraith

On 10 May 1875 a lavish public reception was held in Auckland's Choral Hall for a group of Irish migrants. Several hundred people attended the affair, including a large number of Irish-born settlers who gathered to welcome their compatriots to New Zealand. The chairman of the public reception committee, Joseph MacMullen Dargaville, a prominent local Irish politician, rose to address the audience. His speech celebrated the arrival of the settlers and the strength of their identification with the British empire:

> It was his pleasing duty that night [Dargaville announced] on behalf of the many thousands, not only in Auckland but of the country, to bid them a hearty welcome to the shores of New Zealand. They welcomed them with full hearts, for their arrival brought back vivid memories of that dear old land which they all loved so well, the land in which their forefathers lived, and struggled, and died; the land in which the happy years of childhood had been spent. He welcomed them the more heartily because he could assure them they had come to a land in which industry, perseverance and frugality were the chief requisites, virtues which he knew [them] to excel in, and which would be sure to lead to success under any circumstances. He welcomed them further, because he and they had a deep seated love for their Queen and mother country, and because he knew that they would hand down those feelings of loyalty to Britain, which would help to maintain that halo which surrounded their native land.[1]

Dargaville's rhetoric struck a deep chord with those present because it appealed to their beliefs about the values and characteristics that lay at the heart of their community: industry, perseverance, frugality, a 'deep-seated love for Queen and country', and loyalty to Britain. His words also conveyed something about their shared sense of identity. Clearly, the 'dear old land' so beloved to Dargaville and his 'fellow countrymen' was Ireland. Yet 'loyalty' to Britain and the British monarchy were crucial too. The community's ethno-religious identity was double-sided: Irish, but at the same time defiantly British.

Readers familiar with the history of the Irish in New Zealand will recognise this group as the 'Protestant Irish' settlers who founded the well-known settlement at Katikati, near Tauranga.[2] Its members are still the best known historical representatives of Irish Protestant immigration to New Zealand in the nineteenth century. Yet they are so isolated in the historical record that one could be forgiven for thinking that it was the whole story. There is, however, a great deal more to tell. The Protestant Irish comprised between one-quarter and two-fifths of Irish migration to New Zealand in the nineteenth century. Of the estimated 450,000 New Zealanders who can today claim Irish descent, somewhere between 120,000 and 180,000 can claim Irish Protestant descent.[3] In addition, Irish Protestants contributed an immeasurable amount to the process by which the diverse peoples who settled the colony eventually became 'New Zealanders'. By leading the way in embracing a pan-British identity that replaced Old World regional and national identities, these newcomers helped to 'define the emerging Pakeha consensus'.[4]

Irish Protestants who emigrated to nineteenth-century New Zealand were representatives of a distinct minority tradition within the Irish population. Mostly they were descendants of Scottish and English settlers who were 'planted' in confiscated territories in Ireland, particularly in the northern province of Ulster, during the seventeenth and early eighteenth centuries. In the ensuing two centuries, Protestants were as affected as Catholics by the profound structural changes in Ireland that sent millions of Irish emigrants to the United States, Canada, Australia and New Zealand. None the less, most studies of the Irish in New World societies have tended to overlook the Protestant dimension and emphasise Catholic and nationalist themes.[5] My chapter attempts to remedy this neglect. In the sections that follow, I want to address a series of key research questions about New Zealand's Protestant Irish. Who were they? What distinguished them from the Catholic Irish? What patterns characterised their settlement? How did they contribute to the development of New Zealand society and culture? Why are they so hard to detect in either popular or academic visions of New Zealand's history?

I

Irish Protestantism had deep colonial roots. The plantation of British colonists in Ireland from the time of James I was intended to subjugate unruly regions of the country and create a loyal population of Protestant settlers who would secure English rule. Land confiscated from rebellious Irish chiefs and lords was granted by the Crown to English and Scottish entrepreneurs on the condition that they undertook to populate them with Protestant English or Scots tenants. The plantations met with mixed success. Those in the south of Ireland failed to take root and largely withered away. The Ulster plantations, however, were reinforced by waves of new migrants from Britain and flourished. By the nineteenth century Protestants comprised about half the population of Ulster. Throughout the rest of the country, they comprised less than one-tenth of the population. Over the three centuries that followed the plantations, the Catholic Irish population and the descendants of the planters failed to assimilate and remained distinct and mutually exclusive groupings with fundamentally different religious and national loyalties. On a number of occasions this antagonism flared into widespread armed conflict.[6]

The nature of the plantations and the subsequent centuries of uneasy co-existence shaped the character of the Protestant Irish who later emigrated to New Zealand. By the mid-nineteenth century, this group was composed of two main elements: Anglicans, mostly English-descended, who were found throughout Ireland, but most strongly concentrated in Dublin and south Ulster; and Presbyterians, mostly Scots-descended, who were concentrated almost exclusively in Ulster, particularly the coastal counties of Antrim, Down and Londonderry. Anglicans were numerically stronger and comprised around 12 per cent of Ireland's total population, while Presbyterians made up about 10 per cent. In Ulster, where the great bulk of Protestants were found, Presbyterians were the larger group.[7] Prior to the late nineteenth century, Presbyterians and Anglicans retained differences of identity and interest which were only marginally less divisive than those between Catholics and Protestants generally. In Ulster, as late as the 1840s, local terminology reflected these differences: Presbyterians were commonly referred to as the 'Scotch' and Catholics as 'Irish', while Anglicans were usually termed 'Protestants'.[8] Hostility between Presbyterians and Anglicans, partly provoked by the legacy of the penal laws that discriminated against all non-Anglicans, was evident well into the nineteenth century.

The most useful way to analyse the Old World background of New Zealand's Protestant Irish population is to distinguish between Ulster and non-Ulster origins. The Protestants of Ulster came from quite different cultural backgrounds to their counterparts in the southern provinces. Anglicans and Presbyterians living in the north covered a complete social spectrum: they comprised about one-half of Ulster's population throughout the nineteenth century and were represented in every strata of local society. The Protestants of the South, on the other hand, are best viewed as a small and privileged minority or 'ruling caste', whose cultural heritage came to be known as the 'Anglo-Irish' tradition. It is important to make a distinction between the cultural mores captured by the historian's term 'Anglo-Irish' and the culture of the Anglican Irish more generally.[9] There are obvious connections between the Anglicans of the north and south, but it is essential to understand the degree of difference between the Trinity College educated landowners and Dublin civil servants of the south, for instance, and low-church Anglican tenant farmers of the Ulster border counties. In short, Ulster Anglicans had more in common with northern Presbyterians and Methodists than with their southern co-religionists. Overall, the cultural distinction between Ulster Protestants of all denominations and the southern Anglo-Irish remains the more useful division for consideration.

In the next chapter Terry Hearn shows that Ulster provided a disproportionate share of Irish migrants to New Zealand. To understand the distinctive Old World background of these settlers, we need to examine closely the region from which they came. Ulster was unique in nineteenth-century Ireland. The province contained a large Protestant population and a relatively advanced and diversified economy. Although there were no political cleavages between Ulster and the rest of Ireland, cultural differences were particularly obvious. Paschal Grousset, an exiled French journalist, ex-Communard and liberal social commentator who travelled through Ireland in 1887, noted that

> If you did not know beforehand that you are entering a new Ireland through Enniskillen, an Ireland, Scotch, Protestant, manufacturing, a glance through the carriage-window would suffice to reveal the fact ... No more uncultivated fields, no more endless bogs and fens. Instead of those long, red, or black streaks of peat, alternating with consumptive oat and potato-fields, green, fat meadows, mown by steam, studded with cows, in the most prosperous condition, spread themselves before your eyes. Some trees are to be seen now. The hedges are in good repair, the horses well harnessed to solid carts; the hay stacks have a symmetrical outline, and vast fields of flax nod under the breeze; the farm houses are well built, flanked by neat kitchen gardens; in short, all gives the general impression of a properly cultivated land.[10]

Grousset attempted to explain the visible changes in his surroundings by pointing to the role of the landowners in ensuring more efficient agricultural practices:

> [The] tenant is three times out of five of Scotch origin; three times out of five he belongs to the Protestant persuasion (Episcopal, Presbyterian, Methodist); there is not between him and his landlord the antagonism of race and worship which is to be found in the other provinces. The landlord himself fulfills his duty better, and does not effect to spend abroad the money he draws from his estate.[11]

Many commentators identified Ulster's cultural landscape as the main reason for the stark economic contrast with the south. Contemporary explanations for the differences between Ulster and the rest of Ireland revolved around the perceived qualities of the Protestant inhabitants, who were all too frequently stereotyped as Scots-Irish Presbyterians, even though almost half of them were Anglican.[12] William Makepeace Thackeray, who toured Ireland in 1841, claimed that

> A sort of weight seems all at once to be taken from the Englishman's mind on entering the province, when he finds himself once more looking upon comfort and activity, and resolution. What is the cause of this improvement? Protestantism is, more than one Church-of-England man said to me; but for Protestantism, would it not be as well to read Scotchism? – meaning thrift, prudence, perseverance, boldness, and common sense, with which qualities any body of men, of any Christian denomination, would no doubt prosper.[13]

The strength of cultural differences between the Catholic and Protestant populations of Ulster is clear from contemporary accounts. *The Ordnance Survey Memoirs of Ireland*, compiled in the 1830s and 1840s, provide a rich source of ethnographic information on everyday social life in the north during the period immediately before the settlement of New Zealand. The memoirs contain a systematic set of parish-by-parish accounts about Ulster's economy and society undertaken by engineering officers of the British army and designed to accompany the first accurately surveyed scale maps of Ireland. Although the memoirs construct cultural stereotypes that reflect the biases of the British surveyors, they tell us a great deal about the cultural differences that existed in the north. Moreover, the vivid descriptions of Ulster religious communities in the extant listings are particularly useful because they suggest that we need to distinguish between these groups in a New Zealand context.

The English surveyor J.R. Ward, for example, described the local population of Longfield West, in County Tyrone, in stereotypical terms:

> The people in this parish are very civil and obliging, whereas if you proceed 4 miles northwards you will meet with a very uncouth race. The former are mostly Catholics, the latter Presbyterians. The former race are, however, very often dishonest and insincere, the latter on the contrary are mostly upright men. Both parties are very superstitious.[14]

The supposed laziness and lack of industry of Catholics was also alluded to in an unsigned memoir for Donacavey, County Tyrone, in 1835: 'The numerous saint's days are regularly kept by the Roman Catholics and the idle and dissipated are never in want of an excuse for quitting their work'.[15] Surveyors linked the supposed lack of industry of Catholics to their lower socio-economic position, which they regularly invoked as a cause and effect of their idle habits. In west Tyrone, where Catholics were recorded as 'generally compris[ing] the poorer classes', these lower orders were said to have little interest in self-improvement.[16] One surveyor claimed that 'they have no inclination to turn their thoughts to improvement or cultivation, they are reckless of all appearance of neatness either in their houses or persons, and indigence is, with them, an all-sufficent [sic] excuse for dirt'.[17] Catholics were often portrayed as priest-ridden. In Kilskeery, J.R. Ward commented that 'early marriages ... are common among the Roman Catholics. It is said their Priests encourage them'.[18]

Surveyor James Boyle recorded many colourful descriptions of the Presbyterian population of Antrim. Boyle made much of the Scottish descent of the Presbyterian locals, whom, he claimed, 'retain almost all the characteristics of their forefathers, their manners and customs having been as yet little altered by intercourse with strangers'.[19] Their 'dialect, idioms, customs and manners', he continued, 'are purely Scottish and by no means pleasing'.[20] Boyle also averred to the supposed lack of civility of the Antrim Presbyterians, whose manners he described as 'uncourteous and anything but agreeable or civil'.[21] They were 'rather rough and blunt', he reported, 'though honest in their manners ... a stranger would term them rude, but politeness they look on as servility'.[22] Boyle even went so far as to claim that they were 'by no means bright', unlike the inhabitants of the mountainous regions of the county, who 'partake more of the character of the aboriginal inhabitants'.[23] Narrow-mindedness and bigotry were traits often alluded to in descriptions of Presbyterians. Boyle claimed that this group displayed 'bigotry towards any other persuasion', including their fellow-Protestant Anglicans. Indeed, he asserted, their prejudice against Anglicanism was almost on a par with that towards 'Popery', 'which creeds', he pointed out, 'they look on as being closely allied'.[24]

Portrayals of Anglicans tended to reflect positive qualities such as 'honesty', 'civility' and 'efficiency'. In the predominantly Church of Ireland parish of Glenavy in south Antrim, Boyle reported that the locals were 'free from either the Scotch accent or the Irish brogue, and speak with a pure and agreeable accent'.[25] In appearance and manners, too, Boyle found evidence of a people more to his taste. He described the inhabitants as having 'very fine, high and broad foreheads, and generally light hair'.[26] In manners, he asserted, they were 'more agreeable than those of the people of the County Antrim generally, being much more gracious, communicative and civil without being at all servile … They are a manly race both in their persons and in their manners.'[27]

It is not difficult to detect in these accounts evidence of the surveyors' value system that emphasised 'Englishness' and Protestantism as the most desirable qualities. Anglicanism constituted an ideal, whereas depictions of Presbyterians and Catholics reflected their failure to embrace one (in the former case), or both (in the latter) of the two key qualities. Presbyterians, therefore, were criticised for their 'Scotch' character and blamed for sectarian animosities. Catholics were deemed unfit to administer their own affairs, an unflattering portrayal that served the interests of the British authorities. Beyond these stereotypes, the memoirs point to the existence of strong cultural differences between Catholics and Protestants in Ulster and shows that studies of the Irish in New Zealand need to take them into consideration.

II

It is very difficult to assess the relative numbers of Protestants and Catholics among the Irish who emigrated to New Zealand. Yet the question remains a crucial one if we are to understand the identity of the New Zealand Irish as a group. As noted, Ulster provided a disproportionately large share of Irish immigrants to New Zealand in the colonial era. One of the reasons for this was simply that the region was a consistently high provider of emigrants to the New World, and had been since the eighteenth century. Traditions of large-scale emigration had deeper roots in the nine northern counties than in the remainder of Ireland. Despite the greater numbers sailing from other provinces in the latter half of the nineteenth century, particularly during the Famine years, emigration from Ulster to various destinations (including New Zealand) remained important.[28]

Ulster's prominence in Irish migration to New Zealand is best explained by two closely related factors. The first is the prevalence of widespread contemporary stereotypes and prejudices regarding the Irish and, in particular, the Catholic Irish. The second is that, as a result of these prejudices, New Zealand's immigration networks in Ireland discriminated heavily in favour of mainly Protestant Ulster.

The existence of negative stereotypes of the Irish in Victorian New Zealand is well documented. Briefly put, the Irish in New Zealand were 'widely stigmatised for their Catholicism, poverty, violent and drunken tendencies and willingness to work for low wages'.[29] Regardless of the accuracy of this stereotype, it was widely applied. Although Catholicism held a prominent place in the list of negative traits, Donald Akenson has argued that anti-Irish prejudice was directed 'at all the Irish, Protestant and Catholic alike'.[30] In the popular mind, he suggests, 'Irishness' equated with Catholicism and 'Irish Protestants were mistakenly understood to be Catholics'. One illustration of this broad sentiment is found in colonial objections to George Vesey Stewart's Ulster Protestant settlements in the Bay of Plenty on the grounds that they 'brought too many Irish into the country'.[31] Clearly, on some occasions, anti-Irish feeling outweighed religious differences.

There is little evidence to support the view that anti-Irish prejudice was directed at Irish Protestants quite as viciously as it was at Catholics. On the contrary, Irish Protestants deliberately distanced and distinguished themselves from their Catholic compatriots in ways that deflected criticism. There also seems to have been some recognition of an Irish Protestant identity in New Zealand and a set of less widely held stereotypes relating to it. On the whole, these stereotypes were positive, and served mainly to offset the supposed inadequacies of their Catholic compatriots. Irish Protestants were ascribed qualities such as thrift, prudence, the ability to progress economically, loyalty to Britain, and, of course, Protestantism; by contrast, Irish Catholics were held to be religiously suspect, economically stagnant, and disloyal to Britain and the empire. It is significant that the *Cyclopaedia of New Zealand*, a biographical compendium that celebrated turn-of-the-century colonial values, described Ulster as 'a country which has given New Zealand men who, through ability and perseverance, have taken the front ranks in politics and enterprise'.[32]

Positive attitudes towards the Protestant Irish are also found in the political arena, particularly in reference to the immigration issue. In 1870, the cabinet minister representing Otago Province, the Hon. Mr Holmes, argued that among the most desirable emigrants from Britain would be 'small farmers from the lowlands of Scotland, the north of Ireland, and the best agricultural counties of

England'.[33] Holmes's reference to the 'north of Ireland' must be noted for its specificity: it was, in the context of its time, a deliberate allusion to the distinctively Protestant character of Ulster. William Grahame, a prominent member of Auckland's early Presbyterian Church, and John Morrison, New Zealand's emigration agents in Ireland in the mid-1860s, used similar language, explaining that the need for a superior class of emigrants justified 'the selection we have made from the northern counties'.[34] Premier Edward Stafford argued that 'amongst other places, the north of Ireland would be eminently a useful field for the selection of emigrants'. The people of this area, he maintained, had a 'special aptitude', since 'there [were] not better skilled husbandmen in the world than they are'.[35] Alexander Bradley, who in 1874 lobbied Premier Daniel Pollen on the subject of Irish immigration, complained that 'the North of Ireland' had been overlooked, and asserted that the inhabitants of this area were frugal, hardworking, superior in character to English immigrants, and of 'a class equal to any in the British Dominions for making prosperous colonists'.[36]

An illustration of the extent to which anti-Irish prejudice was directed more strongly at immigrants from the predominantly Catholic south is provided by the different responses to three ships that arrived in New Zealand in the mid-1870s. The first of these vessels, the *Asia*, sailed from Queenstown (now Cobh) in the south of Ireland on 8 February 1874, and arrived in Otago on 27 April. The passengers were mainly recruited in the southern counties of Ireland, and included a substantial number of single young women from a Catholic servants' home attached to a workhouse in Cork. Within three days of the *Asia*'s arrival in Dunedin, the *Otago Daily Times* published a stinging editorial attack on the character of the ship's immigrants. The editorial made much of the presence of thirty-three girls from the servants' home, which it misrepresented as a 'reformatory', and argued that 'while immigration was desirable, the importation of "certified scum" was indefensible'. 'As a rule', the editorial maintained, 'immorality and crime breed quite fast enough in a town, without granting free passages to import the double-distilled article'.[37]

Local response to the arrival of the *Conflict* in Lyttelton less than two years later was dramatically different. This vessel had sailed from Belfast and the city's New Zealand agent, Samuel Cochrane, had recruited its complement of immigrants throughout the northern counties of Ireland. The ship's arrival was greeted with approval in Canterbury. The commissioners' report on the ship noted that the immigrants 'appear to be of a very suitable class for the colony, being for the most part considerably above the average in physique, and exceedingly well conducted and respectable in appearance'.[38]

A third ship, the *Queen of Nations*, sailed to the North Island, arriving in Auckland in July 1874. Like the *Conflict*, the *Queen of Nations* sailed from Belfast, and carried a cargo of immigrants recruited throughout the north of Ireland. The *New Zealand Herald* of 10 July 1874 commented on the 'exceptionally high character of the *Queen of Nations'* passengers', but overlooked the charges of assault laid against some migrants that featured in the same edition's court pages. It lamented the lack of more direct emigrant voyages from Belfast.[39]

The lobbying and political machinations of Irish Protestant politicians and residents in New Zealand were instrumental in promoting the recruitment of immigrants from Ulster. During the 1860s and 1870s, Protestant Irishmen were a numerous and influential group in the higher echelons of provincial and central government. Among the most prominent of these figures were premiers Daniel Pollen and Edward Stafford, provincial superintendents John Williamson and James Edward Fitzgerald, and leading politicians such as Joseph Dargaville, George Maurice O'Rorke, Charles Bowen, Crosbie Ward, Hugh Carleton and William Travers. Perhaps the clearest illustration of the influence of Protestant Irish politicians in the field of immigration is provided by the wrangling surrounding the Katikati Special Settlement. There was strong opposition to the government's grant of land to an Orange group in the midst of a furore over Irish immigration.[40] This criticism came from quite influential figures like Isaac Featherston, the government's Agent-General in London, and Julius Vogel, the Premier. None the less, these opponents were confronted at every turn by a powerful Irish Protestant clique that was successfully led by the scheme's promoter, George Vesey Stewart.

Donald Akenson and Richard Davis have already provided detailed accounts of the intricate negotiations that preceded the establishment of the first and second Katikati settlements.[41] While the details will not be revisited here, it is worth noting the role played by Irish Protestant politicians. When Stewart's initial advances to the New Zealand government were spurned in 1873, John Williamson, the newly re-elected Provincial Superintendent of Auckland, and local politician Joseph Dargaville, were instrumental in ensuring that his proposals were accepted by the Auckland Provincial Council. The council committee that investigated the matter was chaired by Dargaville, a fellow-Orangeman of Vesey Stewart, who was elected Grand Master of the New Zealand Orange Lodge in 1874.[42] The other members included an Anglo-Irishman, Hugh Carleton, and William Kelly, whom Stewart described as 'a true Irish patriot', by which he meant a loyalist and a Protestant.[43] Not surprisingly, the committee voted its approval for Stewart's proposal, and the New Zealand government, in light of Auckland's commitment, and the pressure of two of its own members, was obliged to provide its support. The two ministers who helped ensure the scheme's success were Daniel Pollen, the Anglo-Irish colonial secretary, and the Galway-born son of an Anglican landowner, George Maurice O'Rorke, who was the Minister of Crown Lands and Immigration. Pollen insisted that the original terms offered to Stewart by the Belfast agent, Harry Farnall (including assisted passages *and* free land), should be honoured.[44] O'Rorke was instrumental in finalising the details of the scheme and the allocation of the much-coveted Katikati block to Stewart's party.[45]

Persistent calls to discourage Irish immigration from places outside Ulster placed considerable pressure on colonial authorities. It gave rise to recruitment practices which were strongly biased against the south of Ireland, while maintaining a thin public veneer of impartiality. These biases found expression in three main areas: the location of emigration agents, the placement of advertising, and the provision of shipping. With the notable exception of Ulster, New Zealand's mobilisation drives in Ireland during the 1860s and 1870s were gravely deficient in each of these areas.

The location and conduct of New Zealand's emigration agents in Ireland provides strong evidence of the bias towards Ulster. The Waikato Immigration Scheme of the mid-1860s, for example, was conducted jointly by the Auckland Provincial Council and the New Zealand government and constituted the first large-scale campaign that the colony implemented in Ireland. The efforts of the Auckland Provincial Council were co-ordinated by William Crush Daldy, a prominent English pioneer settler of Auckland. Daldy arrived in Ireland in September 1864 and made Belfast his first port of call. Although he briefly visited Dublin in June of the following year, he appears to have confined the remainder of his Irish sojourn to lecturing and touring throughout Ulster. He concentrated on attempts to establish two special settlement schemes. The first of these was sponsored by a group of Presbyterian businessmen from Londonderry and Belfast, and fell through in the early stages of negotiation. The second was promoted by an Anglican clergyman from Tyrone, and was slightly more successful, eventually becoming the small Bay of Island Special Settlement in Kawakawa in 1865. Daldy was instructed to appoint assistant agents to aid him in his recruitment campaign. Of the two Irish agents he appointed, both were in Ulster: one in Newry, County Down, and the other in Armagh.[46] The representatives of the New Zealand government in Ireland in the same period, John Morrison and William Grahame, also concentrated their efforts in Ulster. Again, these agents made their first Irish visits to the north, and by their own admission confined their selection to 'the northern counties'.[47]

New Zealand's recruitment drives in Ireland during the 1870s followed similar patterns to the mid-1860s. The first colonial agent appointed there in this period was Harry Warner Farnall, who set up at Belfast in June 1872. Farnall was a leading figure in the Anglo-Israel movement in the colony, an international movement that combined unusual Old Testament interpretations with a supremacist racial focus. Its adherents believed that Anglo-Saxons were God's chosen people, the lost tribe of the Israelites. It was also popular among some fundamentalist Protestants in Ulster, where its ideas were used to 'provide a generalised justification for British rule in Ireland'.[48] This view was based on the assumption that Irish Protestants were Anglo-Saxon in racial origins (in contrast to the supposedly Celtic racial origins of Irish Catholics). The Anglo-Israelite Farnall was the sole New Zealand agent in the country at the time of his arrival. Although he claimed that he intended to lecture throughout the country, Farnell confined all his activities to Ulster. Farnall was instrumental in ensuring the success of the Katikati affair, an episode that left him bankrupt. Indeed, there is some evidence to suggest that he may have helped Stewart formulate the scheme from the start.[49]

The distribution of New Zealand's network of emigration sub-agents and newspaper advertising throughout Ireland in the 1870s clearly shows the Ulster preferences of the recruitment campaign. The two lists of agents submitted during the early 1870s to the Colonial Secretary, Daniel Pollen, listed a total of fifty-four Irish agents, of whom forty-one were located in Ulster.[50] The distribution of newspaper advertising to promote New Zealand's immigration policies and assisted passages showed a similar pattern. During the early 1870s, Isaac Featherston submitted two lists of British newspapers in which he placed advertisements. These lists show the regions most heavily canvassed in Ireland. Of the thirty-two newspapers mentioned, twenty-nine were Ulster-based publications.[51] Given that at this time Ulster's population comprised around one-third of the entire population of Ireland, the bias inherent in the recruitment campaign is obvious.

The provision of shipping to New Zealand-bound emigrants also clearly discriminated against Ireland, and the southern counties in particular. The vast bulk of Irish emigrants to New Zealand in the 1860s and 1870s sailed from Scottish and English ports. This was mainly because so few ships were laid on directly from Ireland. During the 1860s and 1870s only ten government-sponsored emigrant vessels made their way directly from Ireland to New Zealand, and no direct voyages took place in the 1880s.

In this 'sample' of ten ships we can detect the same patterns of bias which characterised the other areas of New Zealand's recruitment practices in Ireland at the time. Although the two Waikato Immigration Scheme vessels sailed from ports in the south of Ireland, both carried migrants recruited overwhelmingly in the 'northern counties'.[52] Of the eight ships dispatched from Ireland in the Vogel era, three sailed from Queenstown, in the far south, and five from Belfast. Five of the seven ships were recruited under specific auspices. The three ships that sailed from Queenstown, in the far south – the *Asia, Caroline*, and *Carrick Castle* – were chartered partly to carry emigrants recruited by Dunedin socialite Caroline Howard. They included a large number of female servants destined for the wealthier homes of Otago and Southland.[53] Two of the Belfast ships, the *Carisbrooke Castle* and the *Lady Jocelyn*, were also special charters to carry the parties of emigrants recruited by George Vesey Stewart. Only three ships dispatched from Ireland in the 1870s, therefore, were standard emigrant ships not attached to any particular scheme, and recruited by regular agents: these were the *Dover Castle, Queen of*

Nations and *Conflict*, all of which sailed from Belfast.[54]

The Ulster-focus of New Zealand's immigration recruitment in Ireland had a profound effect upon the composition of the local Irish population. It directly influenced the provincial and county origins of the colony's intake. And, it shaped the complex ethno-religious mix of Irish migration to New Zealand, while ensuring that the inflow featured a high proportion of Protestant settlers.

III

If Protestants played such a significant role in Irish migration to New Zealand, how did they handle aspects of their inherited Old World culture in the colony? In a detailed study of the Katikati settlement, Donald Akenson suggests that by the early twentieth century the residual traces of a distinctive Ulster character had largely disappeared. Instead, he identifies a 'blurring of cultural identity' that produced an indistinct set of British colonial identifications and values in the community.[55] A major reason for this configuration is that older affiliations were being challenged in Ireland as well as in the colony. As the nineteenth century progressed, Protestants began to qualify their Irish identity with British or Ulster emphases. The main reason for this change was the influence of dogmatic Irish nationalists, who tended to 'negate the Irishness of their Protestant countrymen'.[56] Other factors included the exacerbation of sectarian tensions in Ireland by events such as the Emancipation crisis and the Land War of 1879-83. The shift in Protestant identities wrought by these changes meant that later migrants to New Zealand possessed values that were quite different from those of earlier settlers. A similar situation existed in Australia where, in the early nineteenth century, Irish Protestant migrants 'could and did consider themselves Irish'. One historian has noted that among these newcomers 'bigotry was a luxury in which only later generations could afford to indulge'.[57]

There is considerable evidence to show that New Zealand's Protestants adhered to Irish and Ulster identities, rather than the undifferentiated 'British' outlook that Akenson found in turn-of-the-century Katikati. Typical in this regard was an Ulster-born Anglican, James Dilworth, who arrived in Auckland in 1841 and retained a strong Irish identity throughout his life. His biographer, Russell Stone, claims that he 'always considered himself Irish; identifying passionately with the land which his family had occupied for over two centuries'. In addition, Dilworth never lost his 'sense of kinship with Protestant Ulstermen'. It was these inseparable elements that provided his 'deep sense of Irish nationhood'.[58] Many other examples of the 'Irishness' of early Protestant settlers in New Zealand can be found. On the gravestones of the numerous Ulster migrants in the Pukekohe area, for example, inscriptions proudly proclaim Irish roots; among them were John Dynes, 'native of County Down, Ireland', and James Graham, 'of Co. Armagh, Ireland'.[59]

Like their compatriots at home, Irish Protestants in New Zealand qualified their identity as the nineteenth century wore on. They were Irish, but with a difference. When Hugh Maguire of Strabane, County Tyrone, wrote home to his sister in 1866 to instruct her to 'sell the Irish their property for what it will fetch', he revealed his Protestant credentials by invoking Ulster terminology whereby Catholics were termed 'Irish'.[60] William Gray, a staunch Orangeman from Belfast who emigrated to New Zealand in 1875, used similar language in his shipboard journal, though with a more disparaging tone. Whenever there was any petty thieving on the voyage, Gray claimed disdainfully, it was always traced to 'that unfortunate class of people known as Irish'.[61]

Later expressions of Protestant Irish identity strongly emphasised British and imperialist themes. Londonderry-born John Martin, who designed the New Zealand town that bears his name, Martinborough, in the shape of a Union Jack, is one case in point.[62] Alan Mulgan, the Katikati-born author and the son of Ulster Protestant settlers, is another. Mulgan's references to the community in which he grew up clearly illustrate the 'process of cultural blurring' which shaped Irish Protestant identities in New Zealand.[63] Despite the fact that 'Home', in Mulgan's Katikati, was Ireland ('or as some of these pioneers would probably prefer me to say, Ulster'), Mulgan grew up identifying more with England.[64] Mulgan thought that the settlers belonged to 'the ascendancy party' in Ireland and noted that 'they brought their politics with them'.[65] In Katikati, he wrote, 'our Imperial politics were very simple ... England was always right and Salisbury the man'. The great villain was Home Ruler Gladstone. 'In some quarters', according to Mulgan, 'the worst thing you could say of a man was that he was a Home Ruler'.[66] His summary of the Irish influences he inherited from a Katikati childhood was as follows:

> There was no one to tell us of 'Kathleen Ni Houlihan' and 'Dark Rosaleen' and their wrongs. To a boy who had been born in New Zealand and had never been out of it, Ulster was a shadowy place. England and English things were always before my eyes – the English army, the English navy, English statesmen, English power throughout the world. I had no English blood in me that I had ever heard of. Had I been brought up in a different atmosphere, I might have grown to manhood filled with the hatred of England which used to grow with such bitter luxuriance in the land that of all her territories, England had most deeply wronged. As it was, I had some affection for the country of my parents, but infinitely more for England.[67]

Akenson suggests that this kind of adherence to aspects of a British identity lay at the root of Irish Protestants' 'disappear[ance] as a separate group in New Zealand'.[68] The emergence of these patterns in mid-to-late nineteenth-century Ireland anticipated a similar process in the colony.[69] Although some local historians have depicted the development of settler society as an interplay between an inherited 'British' culture and the New Zealand environment, more recent studies acknowledge that there was no coherent British culture at the time of colonisation. Rather, the various national groups which comprised the United Kingdom were 'still distinct peoples, with different economies and societies as well as cultures'.[70] Even within those nations, regional variations were very strong. Among the English, for example, who are often presented as homogeneous, local identities like those of the Cornish 'Cousin Jacks' survived the journey to New Zealand.[71] Akenson's list of the main constituent elements of settler society — 'Welsh, English, lowland Scots, Highlanders, Irish Catholics, and Irish Protestants' — only hints at the diversity of ethno-religious influences and traditions involved.[72] The emergence of a shared 'British' identity among the settlers was the first step towards becoming New Zealanders.

Irish Protestants in the colony exhibited the desired tone of 'Britishness' so well that they merged imperceptibly into the host society. In a very real sense, they were 'perfect colonists': 'Protestant in religion, imperial enthusiasts by conviction ... their culture was almost perfectly designed to disappear into the rest of the New Zealand British population'.[73] The use of the word 'disappear' in this case is entirely appropriate. In other New World societies, Irish Protestants have been grouped with the English, and occasionally the Scots, as 'invisible immigrants'.[74] In demographic terms, the characteristics of the Protestant Irish certainly rendered them culturally invisible to those around them in New Zealand. They were Protestant, English-speaking, and possessed both regional and 'British' identities. All of these factors combined to locate them in the middle-ground of colonial culture. Irish Protestants conformed so well to the core values of the host society that they were over-represented among those who best articulated and manipulated such values.[75] New Zealand had four Irish Protestant Premiers or Prime Ministers before the end of the First World War: Daniel Pollen, Edward Stafford, John Ballance and William Ferguson Massey.

The relative absence of the Protestant Irish in New Zealand's historical literature is easier to understand when one considers their 'invisible' immigrant status. But how do we explain the lack of awareness of Irish Protestant roots among their descendants? Perhaps, as Donald Akenson suggests, these newcomers and their descendants 'merged with the general Protestant majority in their ... new land so successfully, that they have in large part forgotten who they are'.[76]

The 'collective memory loss' that Akenson identifies is not just abstract academic conjecture. Available evidence shows that, for whatever reason, many Irish Protestant migrants either discarded or subverted aspects of their Irish identity in New Zealand. Among descendants of the Anglican Irish evidence of this type of amnesia is hard to detect, because this group has so few markers to distinguish them from the majority culture in New Zealand. The Scots-Irish, on the other hand, are sometimes easier to trace because they often emphasised their distinctive Scottish heritage. There are numerous family histories written by genealogists with Scottish and Presbyterian backgrounds that allude to familial connections with Ireland. K.A. Hamilton, for example, writes about 'Grandfather James Hamilton ... a Scotsman who left Northern Ireland, Tully Wiggin, Tully Hogue, County Tyrone, in 1865'.[77] In another genealogical study, Kathryn Mooney examines the life of a west Auckland Presbyterian ancestor, William Kilgour, who once settled in the small Scottish community at Cornwallis to have 'the comradeship of other Scottish settlers'. 'It is interesting', Mooney suggests, 'that William Kilgour was born in Ireland'. In fact Kilgour's place of origin was Raphoe in County Donegal.[78]

Although it is possible that colonists like Kilgour and Hamilton were Scots who lived in Ireland prior to their departure for New Zealand, it is more likely that they were Scots-Irish. The work of genealogist Moira Neal underlines the prevalence of this type of cultural blurring. Neal, who is the convenor of the Scottish Interest Group of the New Zealand Society of Genealogists, was surprised to discover Irish roots on the side of her family she had always thought were Scottish. She knew that her father had been born in Ireland, but believed him when he 'vehemently declared that he was born in Ireland simply because his father had gone there to look for work'. In fact, she later found that her grandfather and great-grandparents had Irish birth-places.[79]

Presbyterianism and certain other characteristics that the Scots-Irish shared with the Scottish-born may have also confused contemporaries in colonial New Zealand. In both New Zealand and Australia, Ulster accents were frequently mistaken for Scots ones. Charlotte Godley, for example, noted that although she was 'not yet a connoisseur on the subject ... brogue [was] brogue, excepting that in the North of Ireland the people seem to speak almost pure Scotch'.[80] Clearly there was considerable scope for the kind of cultural amnesia that stands between New Zealand descendants of Irish Protestants and their Old World roots.

IV

The influence of Irish Protestants on the development of New Zealand culture extended from cultural mores and political attitudes to the colony's religious character. Indeed, historian Peter Lineham argues that Protestantism had as profound an impact on the colony as it did on English culture.[81] If we accept Lineham's view that Protestantism imparted an essentially conservative, 'respectable' and 'anti-Catholic' tone to New Zealand society, then what part did Irish migrants play in that process?[82]

The Irish contribution to the Anglican Church in New Zealand was extremely significant. An Auckland study shows that Irish-born adherents comprised around one-tenth of the Anglican congregation in the city.[83] More importantly, large numbers of Anglican missionaries and clergymen owed their training and background to Trinity College Dublin and the Church of Ireland. Among the most famous of these men were the missionaries John Morgan and Robert Maunsell, and clergymen such as Lorenzo Moore (who founded his own breakaway ultra-low 'Free Church of England') and Thomas Henry Sprott.[84] Akenson's hypothesis that the distinctively '"low church" tone ... evangelically oriented, liturgically somber' stance of the New Zealand Anglican Church owed much to the determinedly 'Protestant' position of the Church of Ireland may well prove to be correct.[85] As archdeacon of St Mary's in Parnell, Auckland, Maunsell was frequently involved in the celebrations and rituals of the Orange Order, and shared their concerns about the influence of 'Romanism' in spiritual and temporal life. In 1875, for instance, Maunsell warned Auckland Orangemen that 'they ought strenuously to guard against the Roman Catholics getting more than their share of influence in the community'.[86] The diary of clergyman Vicesimus Lush, the vicar of Thames, reveals that were tensions between the Irish and English factions over the direction of the ministry. After a clerical meeting at the Bishop's residence in Auckland in 1878, Lush recorded the following entry:

> At 7 the 'meeting' or korero began; to show how extremely low the Irish clergy are, amongst other things it was proposed that in every Church Gazette circulated in the diocese, one number of the Dawn of Day should be slipped in, so that the country settlers might find something attractive for the junior members of their families. This was violently opposed by Archdeacon Maunsell – Mulgan – Kidd and Hall – on the ground that the Dawn of Day was a High Church publication and would lead young people astray – i.e. towards Rome! And they would not allow such an erroneous publication to go forth under the implied sanction of the Clergy, as would be the case if enclosed in the Gazette. I not a little disgusted them by stating that I circulated 200 copies every month.[87]

Irish members of the congregation also played their part in shaping the low church tone of Anglicanism in New Zealand. At St Mark's church in Remuera in the late 1880s, for example, the church's principal benefactor and prominent parishioner, Ulsterman James Dilworth, joined others in denouncing the 'popish practice' of allowing the choir to wear surplices.[88] At Thames, Vicesimus Lush faced severe pressure from Irish parishioners who wanted services to be conducted in a manner acceptable to their tastes. Lush and many of his English flock preferred a certain level of ceremony and ritual enacted in church. Irish Anglicans, on the other hand, sought to reduce what they perceived as ritualistic idolatry. The Thames clergyman hinted at these tensions when he sympathetically reported the concerns of an English parishioner, who complained that 'the services of St. George's were not attractive enough ... he wanted to see the choir in surplices, to have candles at the altar, and to have the prayers intoned'. Lush agreed, but thought that these suggestions were largely impracticable, since 'we should have a schism at once – for I feel sure all the Irish Protestants would leave in a body at the very sight of candles and the very sound of intoning'.[89] Whether real or fanciful, Orangemen within the congregation were blamed for mounting pressure to modify his style of service. In 1876, Lush worried about the possible interpretations of an embroidered altar cloth: 'what the Orangemen will say to such a gorgeous piece of workmanship remains to be seen ... they will have to get accustomed to it, though they should never like it'.[90] On another occasion, the vicar was confronted by angry Irish parishioners over the style of a new stained glass window.[91] Lush's diary shows that Irish Anglicans were a significant and influential group who pursued their own agenda vigorously, even when this led to conflict with the English majority.

Evidence from Auckland reveals that the Irish-born comprised more than one-fifth of the city's Presbyterian population in the late 1880s.[92] This is surprising given that the Presbyterian Church in New Zealand has often been portrayed as a transplanted version of Scottish Presbyterianism. The church's own published history, for example, states that during the nineteenth century it 'was quite simply described by contemporaries as the "Scotch Kirk", a transplantation of Scottish religion and culture'.[93] None the less, there is considerable evidence to suggest that Irish Presbyterians played a very significant role in the church, especially in the North Island. Whereas Presbyterianism in the South Island tended to be dominated by the Scottish Free Church traditions of the Otago settlement, its development in the North Island owed much to a diverse set of influences. Peter Matheson has convincingly illustrated the weaknesses of interpretations that link New Zealand Presbyterianism almost entirely with Free Church traditions. Instead, he argues, 'the Free Church was, of course, by no means the sole influence ... English, Irish, Australian and many non-Free Church Scottish Presbyterians all played a part'.[94] Given the high proportion of Irish-born Presbyterians in the north, it is significant that 'the Free Church of Scotland and, especially in Auckland, the Presbyterian Church of Ireland, were generally recognised as mother churches'.[95] When comparing the component strands of Auckland Presbyterianism, the communicants' roll from St Andrew's Church in Symonds Street provides some indication of this religious diversity. The extant listings contain an equal number of families from the Presbyterian Church in Ireland and the Free Church of Scotland, all of whom worshipped alongside their co-religionists from the mainstream Church of Scotland and other places.[96]

Irish migrants not only constituted a substantial minority of the colony's Presbyterian community, but made a significant contribution to church life. The rapid expansion of the Presbyterian institutions such as churches, schools, libraries and clergy during the 1860s was made possible only with the assistance of the colonial committees of Irish and Scottish churches.[97] Moreover, Matheson has shown that 'an astonishing number of the most vigorous outback and pioneering ministers came from the Irish Presbyterian Church'.[98] Evidence adduced from the induction records of the Presbytery of Auckland provides further support for this claim. A steady stream of ministers who had been ordained and licensed in Presbyteries such as Belfast, Strabane, Londonderry and Coleraine were inducted into the church in the nineteenth and early twentieth centuries.[99] Irish Presbyterianism also furnished some of the most outspoken opponents of ritualism in Christian worship, including Dunedin Ulsterman John Dickson, who attacked 'Romanism' in the Catholic Church and the ritualistic leanings of the Anglican Church.[100]

V

The current state of historical research makes it extremely hazardous to generalise about patterns of settlement among New Zealand's Protestant Irish. None the less, a few broad observations can be made from the available evidence. First, Protestants probably comprised more than one-third of the colony's Irish-born population. Perhaps as many as two-thirds of these migrants were Anglicans and although some emanated from the south of Ireland, most of this group came from Ulster. Irish Presbyterians, on the other hand, would have come almost exclusively from the north. There is some evidence of clustered settlements such as those at Katikati, Pukekohe and Kawakawa, but the Protestant Irish dispersed widely throughout New Zealand. They formed a significant part of the colonial military settlements, the gold rush influx and the assisted immigration schemes of the 1860s and 1870s. So far as we can tell, the timing and destinations of Irish Protestant migration did not differ significantly from their Catholic compatriots.

The crucial difference between Irish Catholics and Protestants in New Zealand lies not in patterns of migration and settlement, but in their adjustment and assimilation to colonial society. Recent historical writing has demonstrated that in some contexts Catholic Irish migrants articulated a politicised cultural identity termed 'ethnicity'. Irish Protestants, on the other hand, seem to have made a rapid transition to new realities and actively participated in the construction of 'the ideal society'. The ease of their adjustment owed a great deal to the fact that they shared the core values of the majority culture within the host society. Their religious traditions brought them into contact with two of the largest groups in nineteenth-century New Zealand: the Presbyterian Scots and the Anglican English. Moreover, their low-church, Old Testament-driven Protestantism fitted in well with the evangelical Protestant tone of the Victorian British world.

The hardening of identities in late nineteenth-century Ireland ensured that many Irish Protestant migrants arrived in the colony well on the way to developing the kind of 'British' identity that proved crucial in shaping settler society. James Belich describes its emergence among the immigrant English, Scots and Irish in New Zealand as 'a cloak you put on when you went out'.[101] Irish Protestants, more than most, wore this cloak willingly and with a well-rehearsed finesse that allowed them to blend invisibly into the crowd.

4
Irish Migration to New Zealand to 1915

Terry Hearn

The dimensions and composition of Irish migration to New Zealand from the beginnings of organised colonial settlement in the 1840s until the First World War is a neglected historical area. Existing studies have tended to rely on literary evidence or inferences from scanty, and often suspect, statistical sources. Moreover, scholars have sometimes failed to recognise that the migrant streams flowing from Ireland, England and Scotland did not constitute a single, undifferentiated phenomenon. In fact, terms such as 'English', 'Scottish', and 'Irish' may obscure more than they explain. I want to establish the broad outlines of the inflow through a detailed analysis of the provincial and county origins of the Irish-born migrants who arrived in New Zealand up to 1915.

The absence of good systematic data bedevils any attempt to chart emigration from Ireland and immigration into New Zealand. The statistics relating to emigration from and immigration into the United Kingdom, published each year in the British Parliamentary Papers, did not separately identify New Zealand until 1906. There are similar problems with the annual returns of the Registrar General of Ireland, which were based on reports given by police at major Irish ports. From 1876 onwards, these show the numbers and county origins of migrants travelling directly from Ireland to New Zealand, but badly understate the numbers involved and exclude Irish-born people departing from England and Scotland for various colonial destinations. The New Zealand immigration data are even less helpful. The extant listings do not distinguish between short-term visitors and long-term arrivals (as do the British data until 1912), and reliable information about migrant birthplaces within the United Kingdom is available only for newcomers who arrived here on assisted passages during the 1871-92 period.

For the purposes of this investigation, I have extracted information from passenger lists and death registers. Although both data sources have limitations, and must be used carefully, they do allow researchers to construct a composite profile of migrant groups. The four sections of this chapter employ one or both of these sources. The first explores basic trends in New Zealand immigration before 1915 through an examination of surviving documentation. The second attempts to construct a detailed profile of Irish arrivals in Auckland from 1840 to 1860. The sections that follow adopt similar methods to investigate assisted Irish migrants to Canterbury (1855-71), New Zealand's assisted inflow between 1871-80 and Irish migration to this country from 1881 to 1915.

I

The ebbs and flows of migration to New Zealand before the First World War fall into a series of well-defined phases. According to the official statistics, about 30,000 people arrived here during the early period of organised settlement (1840-53) and an overwhelming majority came from the United Kingdom. This movement remained sluggish until the discovery of gold in 1861 stimulated a second major phase of immigration. Over the entire period 1861-67 more than 168,000 arrived in the colony, and net immigration exceeded 105,000. The inflow slowed in the late 1860s, but gained momentum during the 1870s when the central government embarked on an ambitious programme of immigration and public works instituted by Julius Vogel. Between the years 1871 and 1880 the total number of arrivals in the colony was almost 197,000, with a net population gain of nearly 137,000. Thanks to a deepening economic crisis, the inflow contracted sharply after 1881 and remained at low levels until the turn of the century. Indeed, from 1888 to 1892 the flow reversed and New Zealand lost, officially, almost 14,000 people, largely to Australia. The final phase covers the period 1900-15 and incorporates the reintroduction of state assistance in 1904, when net immigration amounted to almost 124,000.

Identifying the national or ethnic components of these influxes is a difficult task. Apart from a three-year period in the early 1860s, it was not until 1906 that the British Parliamentary Papers listed separately the numbers emigrating to New Zealand and identified emigrants by country of birth. The data for the period 1860-63 indicate only a small flow from the United Kingdom directly to New Zealand. Those for the period 1906-15 suggest that gross numbers of British migrants departing for New Zealand increased markedly year by year, with the exception of 1910 and after 1913. The numbers of Irish-born emigrating to New Zealand showed some indications of a marked increase only towards the end of the period, although the Irish declined as a proportion of all British-born immigrants arriving in New Zealand. Indeed, from 1900 onwards, New Zealand drew increasingly upon England for its immigrants, with the Scots annually contributing between 14.2 and 18.5 per cent. The data also indicate that the flow of the Irish from the United Kingdom to New Zealand was dominated by males. Altogether, the proportion of males per 100 females was 214:1 in 1906 and 153:9 in 1913, levels that were much higher than for the total Irish outflow from the United Kingdom.

The New Zealand censuses did identify the country of birth of all people resident in New Zealand. The numbers of Irish-born rose rapidly after 1861, reflecting the gold discoveries of that decade and an influx from Victoria that included many of Irish birth, and rose rapidly again after 1874, reflecting the arrival directly from Ireland of large numbers of assisted immigrants. From 1886 the actual numbers began to drop and did so over every inter-censal period from 1886 to 1916. This reflected, among other things, the decline in Irish emigration generally, the ending of assisted migration to New Zealand in 1891, the sharp fall in Irish migration to New Zealand from about 1885 onwards, the consequent ageing of New Zealand's Irish-born and thus a higher rate of mortality, and, possibly, a higher rate of emigration across the Tasman. (It was rare for the Irish to return to Ireland.)

The 1916 census provides some additional details about New Zealand's immigrants, including age, marital status and years of residence. With respect to age, the proportion of Irish-born males aged up to 15 was just 1.4 per cent (compared with 5.9 per cent for the English, 6.4 per cent for the Welsh and 5.4 per cent for the Scots). At the other extreme, those aged 65 years and over made up about one-quarter (24.2 per cent) of the Irish-born, compared with 16.7 per cent of the English, 15.1 per cent of the Welsh and 21.9 per cent of the Scots. So Irish-born males were in general an older group, reflecting the timing of their arrival during the 1860s and 1870s and the contraction in Irish immigration from about 1885 onwards. A similar pattern is apparent in the case of females. With respect to marital status, the 1916 census data indicate that a slightly higher proportion of Irish-born males was widowed (10.2 per cent), compared with other migrant groups and that a significantly higher proportion of Irish females was also widowed (25.8 per cent). The higher rate of widowhood again reflects the older age-structure of New Zealand's Irish-born in 1916 and the arrival of many single Irish females during the assisted immigration of 1871-85. Finally, the 1916 census also includes data relating to years of residence in New Zealand. Compared with English and Scottish migrants, a far higher proportion of the Irish-born population had arrived in New Zealand before 1896.

II

As early as 1841 an unsuccessful attempt had been made to establish an Irish settlement at Kaipara,[1] but the first sizeable group of Irish immigrants to arrive in Auckland, between 1847 and 1852, were the Royal New Zealand Fencibles, intended to augment the province's defences and its labour force. According to Alexander's account, 721 military pensioners arrived, accompanied by 632 women and 1,228 children – a grand total of 2,581.[2] They were settled in four garrison towns on the southern periphery of the Tamaki isthmus: Otahuhu, Onehunga, Howick and Panmure. Of 460 men for whom country of birth was given, 62.8 per cent had been born in Ireland, 28.6 per cent in England and just

7.4 per cent in Scotland. Most of these men were aged from 44 to 49 years, most were married and many had had varied service careers, having served in the East and West Indies, Australia, India and in the Mediterranean. The Irish pensioners were drawn from throughout the Ireland, 30.6 per cent from Leinster – particularly Queen's and Dublin; 24.0 per cent from Munster, particularly Cork, Tipperary, and Limerick; 27.1 per cent from Ulster, notably Armagh, Tyrone, Cavan and Fermanagh; and 18.2 per cent from Connaught, particularly Galway and Mayo.

During the 1850s a second sizeable group of Irish-born arrived in the province from the Australian colonies, in particular, Victoria. A random sample of 500, taken from the *Passenger Lists, Victoria, AUS outwards to New Zealand* for the period 1852-60, indicates that the movement as a whole was dominated by the young, single males attracted largely by the discovery of gold on the Coromandel. The lists also indicate that the Irish-born made up just 8.0 per cent of the total. A third and comparatively small group arrived towards the end of the 1850s directly from Ireland. From 1855 onwards, through its waste lands regulations, and particularly the Auckland Waste Lands Act of 1858 which established the 'Forty acre system', the Auckland Provincial Council sought to stimulate an inflow of migrants from the United Kingdom (and British North America) by offering land. During 1858 and 1859, emigration agencies were established in England, Scotland and in Ireland – in Galway, Castletown, Newry, Belfast, Strabane, Nenagh, Londonderry and Dublin. Between 1858 and the end of September 1862, 15,206 people arrived in Auckland from British ports, 6,943 of whom held land orders representing 242,300 acres. Of those orders, just 4 per cent had been issued by agents in Ireland. The Auckland Provincial Council also supported a modest programme of assisted immigration, from both Australia and the United Kingdom. Details are few, but passenger lists indicate the presence of some Irish immigrants. The *Nimrod,* in 1860, carried twelve Irish passengers out of a total of 146, the *Blue Jacket* 58 out of 227, and the *Avalanche* twenty-one out of 113.[3]

I prepared a more detailed profile of Auckland's Irish immigrants, both self-paying and assisted, by constructing, from the registers of deaths, a population of 2,318 individuals born in the United Kingdom and who arrived before 1860. The following discussion is based on those of Irish birth, a total of 643 people. Just over 40 per cent of the Irish-born arrived before 1850, reflecting the arrival of the Fencibles, while another 23.2 per cent arrived in the three years 1858, 1859 and 1860, almost certainly reflecting the attraction of the province's land regulations. Of particular interest is the fact that the Irish made up 27.7 per cent of the total born in the United Kingdom, compared with their 23.9 per cent share of United Kingdom's 1851 population, so that they were slightly over-represented among Auckland's British-born immigrants. The contrast with the *assisted* flows arriving in South Australia over the period 1836-40 and in New

South Wales in 1841 is sharp. South Australia recruited a mere 7 per cent of its migrants in Ireland, but New South Wales 66.3 per cent.[4] In terms of age, the Auckland arrivals included only small numbers of children under 15 and adults over 45, most (62.6 per cent) immigrants falling into the 20-39 age group. By contrast, migrants who arrived in New South Wales in 1841 included substantially more aged up to 14 years, a heavier concentration in the 18-29 age range, and a much smaller proportion aged 30 and over.

With respect to the balance between the sexes, Auckland's Irish arrivals, particularly in contrast to the English, were relatively balanced with a sex ratio of 108.8 males per 100 females. This equality was one of the most striking aspects of all Irish emigration during most of the nineteenth century. Finally, a high proportion of the Irish males (62.7 per cent) was single on arrival in Auckland, compared with a much lower 39.9 per cent in the case of females. Of those who had married before reaching New Zealand, a good proportion had done so in the Australian colonies. Some 10.8 per cent had married in England and Wales, reflecting the fact that some soldiers chose not to return to Ireland after their discharge, and the movement of many Irish to England especially after 1845. The data may well suggest that at least some, having made a first move overseas, were disposed to make a second and longer move, this time to New Zealand. A small proportion had married in either India or Ceylon, reflecting the presence of soldiers in the sample population. Details of religious allegiance are available only for the person officiating at the funeral service, but they indicate that 27.5 per cent of those born in Ireland were Anglicans, 8.8 belonged to the Presbyterian Church and 56.4 per cent to the Roman Catholic Church; the balance was made up largely of Wesleyan-Methodists.

The matter of religious affiliation bears closely on that of ethnic and regional origins. Munster and Ulster were appropriately represented in the Irish flow to Auckland, but Leinster was significantly over-represented, while Connaught was under-represented. Very similar proportions of the Irish arriving in Auckland and New South Wales came from Ulster and Connaught. On the other hand, the flow into New South Wales was dominated by those born in Munster, while Ulster contributed similar proportions in each case. By the 1850s, the early nineteenth-century domination of Irish emigration by the Ulster-born had begun to give way to migration from the rest of Ireland.

Just ten of Ireland's counties supplied two-thirds (67.2 per cent) of Auckland's Irish immigrants: in Leinster, Dublin; in Munster, Cork, Kerry, Limerick and Tipperary; in Ulster, Antrim, Armagh, Londonderry and Tyrone; and County Galway in Connaught. When the contributions made by each county to Auckland's inflow is compared with its share of Ireland's native-born population in 1851, it is clear that those born in Antrim, Dublin, Limerick and Londonderry were over-represented. This pattern differed quite markedly from that of the Irish inflow into New South Wales in 1841. The poorest, most remote and most agricultural province, Connaught, was the least well represented. Leinster, the wealthiest and least agricultural province, was the second least represented, the migrants being 'mostly derived from the middle range of counties of Ireland'.[5] In short, the Irish migration to Auckland, comprising largely self-paying immigrants, was quite distinct from the assisted flow that arrived in New South Wales in 1841.

Members of the Church of Ireland ('Anglican') were drawn predominantly from Leinster, followed by Ulster; almost one-fifth of the Church of Ireland members came from Munster. The southern province also furnished a majority of the Roman Catholics, although one-third came from Leinster and almost one-fifth from Ulster. A large majority of the Presbyterians came from Ulster.

When the occupational backgrounds of the fathers of Auckland's Irish intake over the 1840-60 period are analysed with respect to religious allegiance, some further interesting patterns emerge. Whereas only 27.3 per cent of the Roman Catholics were farmers (allowing for the usual imprecision attaching to that term, especially in the Irish context), 31.2 per cent of the Anglicans and 48.9 per cent of Presbyterians were associated with the land. On the other hand, whereas only 0.7 of all Church of Ireland adherents came from labouring backgrounds, 9.7 per cent of the Roman Catholics did so. Further contrasts appear with respect to the 'white collar' and 'other' categories. Whereas 16.3 per cent of Church of Ireland adherents came from white collar backgrounds, only 4.5 per cent of the Roman Catholics did so, and whereas 15.6 per cent of the former came from the category 'Other', only 8.7 per cent of the Roman Catholics did so. The category 'other' included, for those belonging to the Church of Ireland, military officers and soldiers. These patterns find a further expression in regional origins. Ulster provided the largest proportion of those with farming backgrounds, while Leinster provided the largest proportions of those from the labouring, 'white collar' and 'other' categories.

So the Irish inflow into Auckland over the period 1840-60 was a complex movement. The inflow appears to have had five components: first, a Roman Catholic stream, originating largely in Leinster and Munster and coming predominantly from farming and labouring backgrounds, with a smaller and similar flow from Ulster; second, an Anglo-Irish stream, originating particularly in Leinster, professing allegiance to the Church of Ireland and coming largely from farming, white collar and 'other' backgrounds; third, a smaller stream originating largely in Ulster, professing allegiance to the Church of Ireland and coming in particular from farming backgrounds; fourth, a smaller stream, also originating largely in Ulster, and coming from farming backgrounds, but expressing allegiance to the Presbyterian Church; and, fifth, a small stream whose members professed allegiance to the Church of Ireland and who originated largely in three counties of Munster, namely, Cork, Limerick and Tipperary.

III

The provincial councils and governments established in 1853 acquired a control over immigration which they exercised until 1871, when central government largely took over responsibility. Canterbury was particularly active in recruiting immigrants in the United Kingdom, partly to augment the labour force and so stabilise wages, and partly to stimulate social and cultural development. Accordingly, emigration agencies were established in a number of places, including the West Country and Ireland, and between 1857 and 1868 immigration from the United Kingdom added a net 19,412 people to the Canterbury population of 6712, three-quarters of the immigrants receiving aid from the provincial government.[6]

Immigration into the province has been the subject of a number of studies. Stevan Eldred-Grigg dealt with the matter briefly, noting that the assisted greatly outnumbered free migrants, that the majority were English and that, of the remainder, the most numerous were the Irish, who had taken full advantage of the nomination scheme introduced during the 1860s. 'In the event,' he noted, 'it [nomination] proved a godsend to the poor, and was soon being attacked as "a means of introducing too many Irishmen". By 1865 no fewer than two-thirds of the female nominees landing in Canterbury were girls from Tipperary, Clare and Roscommon, come to join their families in the new land'.[7]

Irish migration to Canterbury was analysed more fully by Lyndon Fraser.[8] For the period 1855-76 more than half of the 5,134 Irish newcomers whose place of origin was recorded came from Ulster (53.3 per cent), the largest numbers emigrating from Antrim, Tyrone, Armagh and especially Down, with a substantial minority emanating from Belfast and industrial towns such as Portadown and Lurgan. Munster was under-represented among the assisted migrants (27.3 per cent), while about one-fifth of the total inflow was made up by Leinster and Connaught (10.8 and 9.6 per cent respectively). In the south-west, only Kerry ranked in the first five counties sending to Canterbury, with Clare, Cork and Limerick contributing fewer migrants than might have been expected. It should be noted that the period 1855-76 includes immigration under both the provincial and the general governments.

Given that the Canterbury passenger lists included only assisted migrants, Fraser constructed another population, of 1,434 Irish *Catholic* immigrants whose deaths were registered in Christchurch from 1876 to 1918. Analysis revealed that, for the 1855-71 period, an increasing proportion came from Ulster. The proportion coming from Leinster declined over the same period, that from Connaught rose, and that from Munster remained stable. In short, Munster and Ulster supplied an increasingly large proportion of those Irish Catholic immigrants who arrived in Canterbury over the years 1855 to 1871. Nearly half of Fraser's sample could not be traced to existing passenger lists, leading him to suggest that these people travelled independently from Great Britain or elsewhere, especially Victoria and New South Wales. Some of these people had joined the gold rushes to Australia, Otago and the West Coast before finally settling in Christchurch. That many of these Irish-born settlers had moved a number of times was evident in the fact that nearly two-thirds were married when they arrived in New Zealand, and that, of that number, about one-third had married elsewhere than in Ireland.

With respect to age, Fraser's data indicated that over the years 1855-71, the proportion of children aged up to 14 remained fairly stable, whereas the proportion of single adults rose from 43.2 per cent in 1855-61 to 64.9 per cent in 1866-71, the proportion of married adults declining accordingly. The proportions of males and females among the single adults remained relatively steady, males accounting for about 55.0 per cent. It should be noted that, in this analysis, single people included family members aged over 14. With respect to occupational backgrounds, Fraser found that an increasing proportion (60.0 per cent in 1866-71) had fathers who were farmers. Those whose fathers were engaged in the 'skilled trades' declined from 21.4 per cent in 1855-61 to just 11.9 per cent in 1866-71, while those whose fathers were engaged in 'semi- and unskilled' occupations increased from 15.4 to 21.5 per cent.[9] Irish Catholic migration to Canterbury seems to have been a family-oriented chain movement, drawn largely from rural Munster and Ulster, and supported and reinforced by the nomination system.

IV

National Archives holds, for Canterbury, a comprehensive set of passenger lists detailing all assisted migrants. They are listed under three categories, families and children, single men and single women, with details of name, gender, age, county and occupation. With respect to county, migrants were asked to give their 'county where born and where living lately', which means that estimates of geographical origins are likely to be only approximate. It is important to bear in mind that the Canterbury passenger lists include only assisted migrants and not those who made their way independently to the province. Silcock[10] used these lists of assisted migrants in his study of migration to Canterbury, but I have employed them to offer a more detailed analysis, including analysis by families and children, single females and single males. In terms of the proportions born in England, Scotland and Ireland, the English-born dominated the family groups, the English and the Irish the single females, while single males were drawn more or less evenly from all three countries. In terms of their share of the United Kingdom's total population in 1861, the English and Welsh were under-represented, the Scots considerably over-represented and the Irish formed a proportionate share.

Almost two-thirds (65.4 per cent) of the Irish families arrived during the period 1861-66, which included the peak gold rush inflows. Interestingly, the total number of female household heads exceeded that of males, reflecting the presence of substantial numbers of single and widowed female heads, and those joining husbands already in New Zealand. With respect to age, most were concentrated into the younger age groups, 74.8 per cent of male heads and 74.9 per cent of female heads being under 40, while both sexes were considerably younger than their English and Scots counterparts. Exactly a third of all Irish families consisted of husband and wife, and 62.7 per cent of parents and children. The balance consisted of a single spouse and children. With respect to family stage, young married couples and married couples in the early stages of the family life cycle predominated. Childless couples and those with children aged under 10 years, accounted for 67.3 per cent of all families. The accompanying children were mostly young: 73.3 per cent were under 15 years and the great majority were under nine. Interestingly, 12.0 per cent of the Irish families contained children all of whom were aged over 10 years but under 20 years, suggesting that the Irish family stream had three distinctive components: young and childless couples, couples with young children and couples with considerably older families.

Single men are those not otherwise included as members of family units, although they may have travelled to New Zealand with other family members, largely siblings or cousins. Of 910 for whom a country of birth was given, 32.4 per cent were born in Ireland. The peak arrival years were 1863, 1864 and 1870, although the Irish inflow actually began in 1861, two years before single English and Scots males began to arrive. Most were young: over 90 per cent were under 30, with 60 per cent between 20 and 24. In the case of single women, a sample of 1,023 was drawn from those who, like their male counterparts, travelled independently of their families, although often in the company of siblings or cousins. Of those for whom a country of birth was given, 39.1 per cent came from Ireland and the peak arrival years were 1866, 1867 and 1870. Most (95.2 per cent) were under 30, with almost a third younger than 19.

Agricultural labourers made up 67.8 per cent of the assisted Irish adult males, much higher than in the case of the English, but slightly lower than for the Scots. The group included gardeners, farm labourers, shepherds and ploughmen, the last two being prominent among the Scots. The second major group were 'labourers' followed by those with pre-industrial skills; these two groups accounted for 18.8 and 9.8 per cent respectively. Those with pre-industrial skills were much more important among the English (29.8 per cent). In brief, the Irish (and the Scots) were drawn very largely from agricultural occupations, the English from both agricultural and pre-industrial occupations.

Occupations were detailed for only forty-six female heads of households: sixteen were engaged in general domestic service, seven as cooks and housekeepers, six in needlework and five in both farm and laundry work. In the case of the single women, 75.6 per cent were listed as domestic servants, although that term was loosely applied and the category certainly included many who were prepared or qualified to work as domestic servants. Three other categories – outdoor service/farm work, cooks and housekeepers, and needlework – accounted for a further 20.2 per cent.

Irish families came largely from Ulster (68.8 per cent), although within the province the contribution varied markedly by county: Down was the most important single source, followed by Antrim and Armagh. On the other hand, Cavan, Donegal, Fermanagh and Monaghan together supplied just 12 per cent. Munster was the second but very much smaller source. Ulster provided a smaller but still significant proportion of the single females, the most important counties again being Down, Tyrone, Antrim and Armagh. The province of Munster supplied 24.2 per cent, mainly from Tipperary, Kerry and Limerick. Notable is the much higher proportion of single women coming from Connaught: County Galway alone supplied 13.4 per cent of all Irish single women assisted to migrate to Canterbury. In the case of single Irish men, the importance of Ulster is again apparent, the province supplying almost 56 per cent of this group. Again, four of the nine counties dominated the flow: Down, Antrim, Tyrone and Armagh. In Munster, the single largest source was Tipperary and in Connaught, Galway.

Keith Pickens investigated the origins of Canterbury's nineteenth-century population, using a variety of records, including the *Cyclopaedia of New Zealand* (Canterbury) and the records of the Registrar-General of Births, Deaths and Marriages.[11] With respect to places of birth, his data suggest that the Irish-born were drawn from two main areas: 46 per cent came from the northern counties of Donegal, Antrim, Londonderry, Tyrone, Down, Fermanagh and Armagh, and a further 21 per cent from the six southern counties of Clare, Tipperary, Limerick, Waterford, Kerry and Cork. Galway contributed 6 per cent and Dublin City and county 5 per cent. Pickens notes that, on the basis of the 1861 census results, the northern counties were over-represented in Canterbury's population and the southern counties under-represented. That over-representation owed a great deal to the immigrant recruitment programme conducted by the Canterbury Provincial Government.

V

Emigration from Ireland continued at relatively high levels after the Great Famine. The number of departures fell temporarily during the prosperous years for Irish agriculture from 1874-78, but regained intensity in the late 1870s when poor harvests, evictions and declining prices for farm products stimulated the flow of emigrants. Like the Famine exodus, the outflow after 1870 was dominated by people from rural areas and included almost as many women as men. Many post-famine emigrants left as individuals rather than as families. They were younger, lacked marketable skills, and included a high proportion of single women from counties in the west of Ireland.[12] Despite the existence of some anti-Irish sentiment in New Zealand,[13] the immigration authorities appear to have tried to ensure that the Irish were recruited in proportion to Ireland's share of the United Kingdom's total population.[14] According to the data published in *Statistics of New Zealand*, over the 1873-80 period, 89,590 assisted immigrants were born in the United Kingdom, and 24,636 or 27.5 per cent of them were Irish, significantly more than Ireland's 16.7 per cent share of the 1871 British population. The following analysis of the 1870s is based on random samples drawn from the passenger lists of ships that arrived over the period 1871-1880, so deals with *assisted* rather than all immigrants. Most immigration from Ireland did depend on government assistance, but smaller and possibly distinctive flows of Irish-born immigrants may have been missed.

When random samples were drawn and analysed for families, single men and single women, a number of features emerged. First, the timing of departure varied among the three groups. Over half of all families (55.1 per cent) departed during 1874 and 1875. Although 40.3 per cent of all single men also left during those two years, considerable numbers went each year for the remainder of the decade, with the exception of 1880. Single women began to emigrate to New Zealand in larger numbers somewhat earlier than either of the other two major groups, and their departures were more evenly distributed through the decade. The second major finding related to sex ratios. Fitzpatrick notes that the most distinctive feature of Irish emigration from 1871 to 1921 'was the virtual equal contribution of both sexes', most other major international flows being dominated by men.[15] The data for New Zealand suggest a slightly different picture, with males significantly outnumbering females. Third, the flow was dominated by single people. If accompanying children are excluded from the total, 77.5 per cent of the adults were single and single males alone accounted for 45.0 per cent. This high proportion reflected a decline in the emigration of Irish families to New Zealand after 1875. The small number of families and the clear dominance of single people differentiates the Irish emigrant flow quite sharply from the English and Scottish streams. Fourth, ages varied quite markedly, in particular according to marital status, from 33.1 years for married males and 30.3 years for married females, to 22.8 years for single males and 21.4 years for single females. Fitzpatrick's analysis indicated that, in general, for the period 1871-1921, emigration from Ireland was dominated by the 20-24 age group, that is, by people who had entered the labour market but not the marriage market and for whom emigration offered the promise of employment followed by marriage.[16] In that respect the data relating to New Zealand's assisted Irish immigrants of the 1870s offer matches Fitzpatrick's profile.

The fifth major feature related to family structure and life cycle stage. Just over 28.0 per cent of assisted Irish families were childless. Another 5.4 per cent, classified as 'married, with children, spouse absent', consisted largely of wives and children joining husbands who had migrated to New Zealand sometime previously, including some who had arrived on the goldfields during the 1860s. The balance consisted of married couples with children. With respect to stage in the family life cycle, most were in the early and middle stages of the family life cycle: 27.3 per cent had children all aged under 10 years, and 32.2 per cent had some children aged under 10 and some over 10 years. That distribution was reflected in the ages of the accompanying children, 60.5 per cent being aged up to nine years.

The final major feature relates to occupation. In his account of Irish emigration from 1871 to 1921, Fitzpatrick notes that the great majority of emigrants were returned as 'labourers' if male and 'servants' if female. Most came from farming rather than landless backgrounds, farmers' children who could not expect to succeed to occupancy or marry into land. Even by the turn of the century, labourers accounted for some two-thirds of occupied male emigrants.[17] My analysis of the 'Vogelite' migrants examined the occupations of male household heads, single males and single females. There were just eight female heads of households, most of them described as domestic servants. Male household heads show a greater occupational distribution than single males, a reflection of their greater age and experience. Nevertheless, the two categories 'agricultural labourers, shepherds and gardeners' and 'labourers' accounted for 75.7 per cent of all male household heads. By way of contrast with single men, however, 8.8 per cent of male household heads were described as 'farmers or graziers'. These men included members of the 1875 and 1878 parties from Ulster who settled on the Katikati Special Settlement. A further 13.4 per cent fell into the class 'Occupations with relatively little technical change', mostly in the building, metal and clothing (which included footwear) trades. Just 1.5 per cent in the class fell into the class 'Occupations with relatively great technical change' and 0.5 per cent in the category 'White collar'. Of the single men, 92.3 per cent were listed as agricultural and general labourers. Similarly, single women were concentrated into just two classes: 8.3 per cent fell into the category 'Agricultural labourers' and were dairymaids, while 87 per cent were described as 'Servants' and were largely domestic servants with smaller numbers of maids and cooks. The occupational character of the Irish immigrants differed quite markedly from that of the English and Scots, both of which drew considerably fewer migrants from the traditional rural sector.

The data provided by the passenger lists also allows for an analysis of immigrant birthplaces. In his survey of Irish emigration, David Fitzpatrick notes that emigrant origins varied according to destination, so that for the period 1876-95 Irish migrants to the United States tended to come from the counties of

Connaught which had tiny potato gardens that could no longer provide subsistence, many Irish speakers, few Protestants, large agricultural populations, low farm valuations per capita, few off-farm employment opportunities and which had lost unusually large numbers of agricultural labourers since the Famine. England and Scotland drew the bulk of their Irish emigrants from the counties of the eastern and southern coastal belts which were relatively prosperous and urbanised but had endured both industrial recession and restructuring. Canada drew its predominantly Protestant migrants from Ulster, but relied as heavily on the more 'backward' and agricultural counties of the north (such as Donegal) as on industrialised Belfast. Australia drew its Irish emigrants disproportionately from the southern midland counties stretching from Clare to Kilkenny, with a secondary cluster in southern Ulster, counties in which the growth of pastoralism was displacing rural labourers.

The flow to New Zealand, by contrast, was a hybrid of the Canadian and Australian flows, drawing largely from both Munster and Ulster, with an increasing bias towards northeast Ulster towards the end of the nineteenth century.[18] Each of Ireland's three major sources of unemployment in the late nineteenth century was thus associated, to some degree, with a distinct stream of emigration: the destruction of the potato economy of the west with the movement to the United States, recurrent unemployment arising out of industrial recession and restructuring in the northeast with the movement to Britain, and the spread of grazing with the movement to Australia. Fitzpatrick argues that '[t]he characteristic regional distributions of emigrants to each country pointed towards different facets of Irish society, and remained strikingly consistent over long periods despite wild fluctuations in the volume of emigration.'[19]

Two of the key factors involved in sustaining these distinctive emigration streams were the flow of remittances and nominated emigration. Such data as are available indicate that, over the years 1871-75, New Zealand money orders remitted to Ireland amounted to £50,000 and for the period 1876-80 to £73,000.[20] Nominated immigration, by which residents in New Zealand could name relations and friends for free or assisted passages, created migration chains. Seán Brosnahan describes one chain migration, facilitated by government assistance, which saw the transplantation of 'a whole section of East Kerry society' to Kerrytown in South Canterbury.[21] The stream of assisted Irish immigrants coming to New Zealand in the 1870s had two major components. The first originated in Munster – natives of that province were significantly over-represented – and the second came from Ulster, which contributed 40.9 per cent, so that Ulster natives were also over-represented. Conversely, Leinster and Connaught provided small proportions of the flow and were both significantly under-represented. The flow drew unevenly on the counties within each province. Within Munster, Counties Kerry, Clare and Limerick provided proportionately more emigrants than their respective shares of Ireland's 1871 population. Within Ulster, four counties – Antrim, Armagh, Londonderry and Tyrone – dominated the flow, contributing 25.2 per cent of the emigrants compared with their 15.5 per cent share of the 1871 population. Counties that were significantly under-represented included County Dublin in Leinster, and County Mayo in Connaught. These conclusions are supported by the emigration data (which include, it is assumed, both assisted and self-paying emigrants) collected by the Registrar-General for Ireland from 1876 onwards. It is interesting to note that, over the years 1876-80, Ulster provided 33.7 per cent of New Zealand's Irish immigrants but just 20.9 per cent of Australia's. For both countries, Munster supplied the bulk of the migrants, 53.0 per cent in the case of Australia and 50.8 per cent in the case of New Zealand, but Australia drew much more heavily upon both Leinster and Connaught. In short, the New Zealand's inflow of the 1870s drew upon two distinct segments of Irish society. Data on religious affiliation would almost certainly reveal that the flows from both provinces, but especially Ulster, included several distinct streams, much as characterised the inflow into Auckland Province during the period 1840-60.

VI

Irish migration to New Zealand from 1880 to the outbreak of the First World War has attracted little detailed investigation. The data collected by the Registrar-General for Ireland indicate that the Irish flow to New Zealand reached its peak in 1881: after that, numbers declined to just eighty-seven in 1888 before staging a modest recovery until 1891. From 1892 onwards, numbers were at low levels and did not begin to show any marked increase until 1906, reaching a pre-war high of 272 in 1909. Because the data do not include those Irish migrants who departed from Scotland and England or those who migrated first to Australia before finally settling in New Zealand, Donald Akenson prepared another set of estimates which suggest that net Irish immigration reached 1,655 in 1883 and 1,538 in 1884 before declining and indeed reversing in 1888 and 1890. For the period 1891 to 1920, Akenson offers an estimate of total gross immigration which suggests, first, that direct migration from the United Kingdom remained at low levels until 1904, numbers then generally increasing until 1914; second, that indirect immigration also increased from over the years 1904-14; and, third, that indirect migration (largely from Australia) accounted for the majority of Irish immigrants over the entire 1891-1920 period. From his estimates, Akenson concluded that Irish immigration contracted sharply over those years, coinciding with the end of assistance programmes. Again, on the basis of the Registrar-General's data, he indicates that New Zealand's Irish immigrants continued to come largely from Ulster and Munster (together with County Galway in Connaught). The flow from the south and west declined sharply after 1891; as a source, Ulster then dominated, with Counties Antrim and Down being especially important.

Fraser sets the migration of Irish Catholics to Christchurch over the period 1855-1918 in the larger context of emigration from Ireland. He created a population of 1,434 Irish Catholic immigrants whose deaths were registered in Christchurch between 1876 and 1918. Analysis of place of birth indicates that 44.2 per cent had been born in Munster, notably in County Tipperary; Connaught supplied just 14.4 per cent, although Galway was an important county source; Leinster contributed 17.3 per cent, although Dublin was significant; and Ulster provided 26.1 per cent. Fraser's data suggest that the relative importance of the provinces changed between 1872 and 1879 and after 1880: the proportion provided by Ulster and Munster declined, that by Leinster and Connaught increased. The result was that, in the post-1880 period, Ulster, Leinster and Connaught each supplied about one-fifth and Munster just over one-third. It must be emphasised, of course, that these statistics relate to Christchurch's Irish Catholic immigrants and not to all Irish immigrants, although it is interesting to note that a significant, if declining, proportion of the 1,434 Irish Catholic immigrants was born in Ulster.

Fraser went on to discuss other characteristics of the post-1880 inflow, notably gender balance, ages and marital status. Many of the single adults travelled with other family members, including parents, which suggests that the Irish Catholic migration to Christchurch in the post-1880 period may have been dominated by families. With respect to socio-economic background (based on the occupation of the immigrants' fathers), the data for this period indicate that 60.8 per cent had fathers who were farmers, 19.9 per cent were 'semi- and unskilled', 9.9 were skilled tradesmen and 8.8 per cent were 'proprietors, officials, etc.'. The rural character of the Catholic Irish flow to Christchurch seems clear. Fraser concluded that '[t]he movement to Canterbury involved groups of people related by kinship ties or common origins who made their way through a set of social arrangements in which people at the destination provided assistance, aid, information, and encouragement to newcomers'.[22] As a result, the family migration chains forged linked not merely selected counties with Canterbury, but also specific villages and parishes within those counties, among them Headford and Tuam in Galway, Nenagh in Tipperary, Ballycastle in Antrim, Tralee in Kerry and Fermoy in Cork.

Because a significant proportion of Irish migration to New Zealand was indirect, the data collected by the Registrar-General for Ireland should be treated with some care. Data are limited, but those for New Zealand from 1906 to 1915 indicate that those emigrating directly from Ireland always comprised fewer than half of all the Irish emigrating to New Zealand. So an analysis of the character of Irish migration to New Zealand during the period 1881-1916, based on the Irish statistical series, may offer a limited, partial and even biased picture of the total Irish flow. It should be noted that the available data do not give any indication of the length of time those departing from Great Britain had actually spent in England or Scotland. Many of those recorded as having left Ireland for

Great Britain may in fact have been on their way to New Zealand. If the Registrar-General's data for 1881 to 1915 are analysed in five-yearly periods, the figures show that direct migration numbered 3,766 for 1881-85, only 294 in the period 1896-1900, before recovering to 825 for 1906-1910 and 800 for 1911-1915. With the sole exception of 1881-85, New Zealand's share of all persons leaving Ireland was less than 1 per cent in every five-year period.

The Registrar-General's data also suggest that significant changes took place in the migrants' provincial origins. From 1881 to 1895 the two main contributors were Munster and Ulster, continuing the pattern established during the 1860s. Leinster made important contributions during the first half of the 1890s, but Connaught's was always small. During the period 1896-1915 Ulster became the single most important source of New Zealand's Irish arrivals. Munster's share began to increase from 1905 onwards. The data suggest that the availability of state assistance, reinstated from 1904 onwards, exerted some influence with respect to provincial origins. The data also indicate that just eleven of Ireland's counties contributed a very large proportion of New Zealand's immigrants. In Leinster, Dublin was the single most important contributor, although the proportion fluctuated widely from year to year. Five of the six counties in Munster were important contributors, Waterford's contribution being small although relatively more consistent. For Clare, Cork, Kerry, Limerick and Tipperary, the contributions fell into two main phases, from 1881 to about 1895, and from about 1905 to 1914. The Ulster migrants were largely drawn from just three counties: Antrim, Down and Londonderry. In each case the contributions fell into two main phases, from 1881 to the early 1890s, and from about 1900 to 1914. County Antrim was the major contributor. In Connaught, only County Galway made a significant contribution, notably from 1881 to 1899.

When, on a provincial and county basis, the proportion of migrants in the flow to New Zealand is compared with the county distribution of Ireland's native-born population, it becomes clear, first, that natives of Leinster were under-represented in every five-year period between 1881 and 1915, especially from 1895 onwards, with the same being true of all counties with the partial exceptions of Carlow, Kings and Wexford; second, natives of Munster were over-represented until 1895 and then under-represented through to 1915, the counties following a similar pattern, with the exception of Cork, which was consistently under-represented, and Waterford, which was generally over-represented; and, third, natives of Connaught were consistently and increasingly under-represented, and this was true for all counties from 1886 onwards. On the other hand, natives of Ulster were consistently over-represented when their share in the flow to New Zealand is compared with their share of Ireland's total population. That over-representation held for all five-year periods with the sole exception of 1891-95 when there was a short-lived surge of immigrants from Leinster and Munster. Not all of Ulster's nine counties were over-represented. Antrim, Cavan, Down,

Fermanagh, Londonderry and Tyrone were generally over-represented, whereas Armagh, Donegal and Monaghan were generally under-represented. In short, the data suggest that natives of Ulster, and in particularly of Counties Antrim, Down and Londonderry, were significantly over-represented throughout most of the 1881-1915 period and especially from 1896.

In order to include all the Irish-born, both assisted and self-paying, and those who moved directly and indirectly, who arrived in New Zealand over the period 1881-1915, a random sample of arrivals was extracted from the registers of deaths. Of the sample population of 426 individuals, one-third (33.9 per cent) arrived between 1881 and 1885, the numbers then declining through to 1891-95 before recovering slowly. The trend paralleled quite closely that revealed by the Registrar-General's data. The information extracted from the registers also indicated that females made up 43.2 per cent of the inflow, a proportion which corresponds closely to Fitzpatrick's estimate that, over the period 1896-1907, females made up less than two-fifths of the Irish flow to Canada, Australia and New Zealand. When analysed in terms of five-year periods, the numbers of males and females were evenly balanced until 1896-1900 when a marked change occurred and males significantly outnumbered females. In age-specific terms, the imbalance was increasingly marked in the 20-29 age group. That imbalance distinguishes the flow to New Zealand from Irish migration as a whole. When the gender balance is examined for each of the four provinces, it becomes apparent that that change was attributable largely to the immigrants from Ulster: the flow from Antrim (including Belfast), Londonderry and Down was dominated by young males.

Just 27.0 per cent of the arrivals were married, so that flow to New Zealand appears similar to the Irish outflow as a whole. The proportion of married adults rose quite sharply, however, towards the end of the period, although single people continued to dominate. Ulster furnished the highest proportion of males and females who were married, so that both the growing proportions of males and of married people in the Irish flow to New Zealand after 1895 were associated with the shift towards Ulster as the single most important provincial source. Of those who had married before arriving in New Zealand, just over half had done so in England, which may suggest that New Zealand drew some of its Irish immigrants from among those who had been living in England for some years. A further 31 per cent of those who had married outside Ireland before emigrating to New Zealand did so in Australia, a finding which suggests that, after 1900, the inflow from Ulster was balanced by an inflow of Irish Catholics from across the Tasman. A small proportion had married in Scotland, so that New Zealand may also have drawn upon those who had previously moved there. In other words, data relating to place of marriage suggest that, from 1881 to 1915, New Zealand took in Irish-born immigrants from four major sources: largely Ireland itself, but with important streams from England, Australia and Scotland. With respect to age, a very small proportion of the arrivals was under 14 years and 65 and over. For both males and females, those aged 20-24 formed the single most important age group, consistent with the larger outflow from Ireland.

With regard to the provincial and county origins of the 1881-1915 arrivals, just 6.3 per cent had been born in Connaught, while Leinster provided 13.8 per cent, Munster 31.5 per cent and Ulster 48.4 per cent, thus continuing the established pattern. When arrivals are analysed in five-year periods, however, it becomes clear that an increasing proportion was born in Ulster. The proportion born in Munster fluctuated considerably, from 37.2 per cent in 1886-90 to just 20 per cent in 1911-1915. The proportion contributed by Leinster also fluctuated; Connaught was consistently a minor contributor. So the important change in the Irish migration stream to New Zealand from 1881 to 1915 was the declining importance of Munster. These trends continue to accord reasonably well with the Registrar-General's data. For 1901-1905 and 1906-1910, and then largely for Munster and Ulster, there are contrasts between the estimates derived from the Registrar-General's data and those derived from the registers of deaths. The former suggest that a lower proportion of New Zealand's Irish immigrants during those two periods had been born in Munster and, correspondingly, a higher proportion in Ulster. Given that the decade embraced a major influx of people from the Australian colonies, the data suggest that the direct flow of migrants from Ulster was balanced by an inflow of Munster-born from the eastern Australian colonies. If that were so, then the inflow of the Munster-born from the Australian colonies continued a process established during the gold rush influxes of the 1860s. It would also show how the ethnic composition of New Zealand's British-born population was influenced by earlier flows to Australia and by the changing economic relationship between Australia and New Zealand.

The single most important county source was County Antrim in Ulster. Antrim, which included Belfast, provided 17.0 per cent of New Zealand's Irish immigrants over the period 1880-1915. Some fluctuations notwithstanding, the county's contribution increased during the period, so that by 1911-15 Antrim supplied half of all Ulster-born immigrants and 27.1 per cent of all Irish immigrants. Three other counties within Ulster were also important sources: Londonderry, Tyrone and Down. In Munster, two counties were especially important, Cork and Kerry, which supplied 6.9 per cent, and Limerick, Clare and Tipperary also supplied significant proportions. Otherwise only County Dublin in Leinster and County Galway in Connaught made important contributions. In brief, just eleven counties supplied 74.9 per cent of all the Irish immigrants who arrived in New Zealand over the period 1881-1915.

In terms of religious affiliation, provincial and ethnic origins,[23] of 347 immigrants, Roman Catholics made up 54.8 per cent, Presbyterians 22.5 per cent and Anglicans 15.3 per cent; the balance represented other Protestant groups. The small flow from Connaught was almost entirely Catholic. The same was true of Munster; just 5.0 per cent of these migrants were Anglicans, which indicated that any continued outflow from the Protestant communities of the province, notably northern Tipperary, was not directed towards New Zealand. Leinster, on the other hand, presented a different picture: 12.5 per cent were Presbyterians, 27.5 per cent were Anglican, and 55.0 per cent were Roman Catholic. Ulster differed again, with 21.1 per cent belonging to the Anglican church and 21.8 per cent to the Roman Catholic Church, but 42.9 per cent to the Presbyterian Church. So although New Zealand drew on all three ethno-religious communities in Ulster, it drew particularly on those of Scots ancestry. The proportion of all Irish immigrants professing allegiance to the Roman Catholic Church declined through the period, making up 57 per cent in 1881-85 but 37.5 per cent in 1911-1915. Conversely, the proportion belonging to the Church of Ireland increased from 11.9 per cent to 21.9 per cent, and those to the Presbyterian Church from 25.9 to 28.1 per cent. Such changes were consistent with the growing importance of Ulster as the most important provincial source of New Zealand's Irish immigrants, and suggest that New Zealand drew increasingly on those of English ancestry, although those of Scots descent and Presbyterian affiliation remained the single most important ethno-religious group drawn from Ulster after 1896. Interestingly, there were some gender differences in affiliation: whereas 9.8 per cent of all Irish females who arrived in New Zealand over the 1881-1915 period belonged to the Anglican church, 19.4 per cent of the males did so. The gender-specific ratios indicate that males who were Anglicans significantly outweighed females so that the flow from Ulster after 1896 appears to have consisted of an increasing number of young men with affiliations to the Church of Ireland.

The final major finding relates to occupational background. Almost two-thirds (65.2 per cent) of the Irish-born who arrived in New Zealand between 1881 and 1915 were drawn directly from agricultural backgrounds, only small proportions coming from the pre-industrial and industrial sectors. Some interesting changes took place, however, notably after 1896, with a decline in the proportion drawn from agricultural backgrounds (from 71.1 per cent in 1881-85 to 53.1 per cent in 1911-15). The share drawn from those with the pre-industrial or craft occupations remained relatively steady (at about 12 per cent), but that drawn from those with industrial occupations increased quite sharply (from 0.9 per cent in 1881-85 to 10.2 per cent in 1911-15). The share drawn from white collar backgrounds rose from 3.5 per cent in 1881-85 to 6.1 per cent in 1911-15, and from 'other occupations' from 4.4 to 14.3 per cent respectively. These shifts coincided with the emergence of the more highly industrialised Ulster as the major source of New Zealand's Irish immigrants.

VII

An analysis of Irish immigration that relies solely on either assisted or self-paying immigrants will, in all likelihood, produce a partial, even distorted picture of Irish emigration to New Zealand. The character of the total Irish inflows of the 1860s and 1870s very probably differed somewhat from that suggested by an analysis of the assisted immigrants alone. Second, it appears that the provincial and county sources changed quite considerably through the nineteenth century to 1915. Leinster was an important source of Auckland's Irish immigrants, and the same was probably true for Canterbury, where members of the Anglo-Irish gentry played a prominent role in that settlement's founding. Otherwise, Leinster appears as a minor contributor to the New Zealand flow, and Connaught was consistently so. On the other hand, Munster's contribution varied considerably, from a low of 18.4 per cent in the case of Canterbury's assisted immigrants over the 1855-71 period to a high of 42.2 per cent for the 1870s. Finally, Ulster was consistently a major source, although its contribution varied from 29.6 per cent in the case of Auckland to a 59.2 per cent for Canterbury.

A third conclusion, based on a comparison of the Canterbury and New Zealand assisted inflows, is that the availability of state financial aid and the geographical distribution of recruitment agencies and recruitment activities significantly influenced immigrant provincial and county origins. The Canterbury effort was directed in particular towards Ulster, whereas the New Zealand government's effort was less regionally focused. Once migrant flows had begun from particular counties or parishes, remittances and nominated immigration played an important role in sustaining those patterns. The character of the Irish flow to Australia, certainly in the period up to 1860, and especially to New South Wales in 1841 and to Victoria during the 1850s, played a major role in shaping that of the migration to New Zealand. Had gold not been discovered in both Australian colonies and later in Otago and on the West Coast, Irish migration to New Zealand may have remained relatively insignificant and, almost certainly, of a rather different provincial, county and ethno-religious mix. The analyses presented above indicate that any characterisation of Irish migration to New Zealand as comprising two components, one 'Celtic', southern and Roman Catholic, and the other English or Scottish, northern and 'Protestant,' is misleading and oversimplified. The evidence with respect to Auckland and to New Zealand as a whole after 1881 indicates clearly that the Irish flow consisted of a number of components differentiated by ethnic origins or ancestry, religious adherence, social class, occupations and provincial and county origins. Although the demographic character of Irish migration to New Zealand shared many of the features such as age, gender, balance, marital status and occupation of the Irish diaspora as a whole, they did differ in some respects and in some periods. Major gaps still remain in our understanding of Irish migration to New Zealand, but it is clear that the complexity of the various migrant streams that arrived in this country up to 1915 mirrored and embodied the complexity and diversity of Irish society.

5

The Irish on The Otago Goldfields, 1861-71

Terry Hearn

Until quite recently, comparatively little was known about the size, timing and character of the Irish migration flow to New Zealand during the nineteenth century. Studies by Donald Akenson and Lyndon Fraser have partially remedied that deficiency.[1] Nonetheless, the inflows into New Zealand as a whole and, especially, to the goldfields of Otago and the West Coast during the 1860s, have remained practically uncharted. This chapter uses a combination of sources to examine the Irish influx into Otago during that decade, an influx which began with the discovery of an extensive and profitable goldfield in Gabriel's Gully in May 1861.

I

There had been a short-lived rush to the Lindis Pass in inland Otago in 1861, but it was Gabriel Read's discovery of gold later in the same year that proved decisive in establishing the extent, accessibility and payable nature of gold in New Zealand. Read's discovery was closely followed by those of Horatio Hartley and Christopher Reilly in the Clutha River, and by William Fox and others in the Wakatipu Basin. Both Fox and Reilly were Irishmen. Fox, who was born in 1826 or 1827, went to sea, was on the Californian fields about 1850, then on Victorian fields and turned up on Otago's Tuapeka field in 1861, played a major if not precisely determined role in the Arrow discoveries. We know much less about Reilly. Anecdotal evidence suggests that he was born in Dublin, where he may have attended university, and returned to the city before his death in 1887.[2]

These discoveries stimulated a massive migration to Otago. By December 1861 there were an estimated 14,000 people on the Tuapeka goldfield, a figure that declined sharply to an estimated 7,000 during the severe winter of 1862. With the Dunstan discovery of August that year, the inflow from Australia accelerated again and by November there were at least 10,000 on the Otago fields. Further discoveries, in the valley of the Manuherikia and in the Mount Ida district, saw numbers swell to about 19,000 by May 1863 and 21,000 by

September of that year. Vincent Pyke, the secretary of the Otago Provincial Government's Goldfields Department, initially estimated a peak population of 23,850, later amending that figure to between 22,000 and 24,000.[3] That peak was probably reached in February 1864. Thereafter, the goldfields population contracted, as miners and others joined the April 1864 rushes to Wakamarina and then to the West Coast. The December 1864 census recorded only 15,651 people on the Otago goldfields, the total number declining to around 12,000 by April 1865 and 10,900 by November 1865.

II

The gold discoveries stimulated three major inflows into Otago, the first originating within New Zealand itself, the second in the Australian colonies, and the third in the United Kingdom. Data relating to all of these flows are limited, but indicate that the peak migration years were 1861, 1862 and 1863, with a sudden contraction in 1864, reversing in 1865, and recovery for the remaining years of the decade, albeit at very low levels. The patterns for the United Kingdom and Australian immigrants show some interesting contrasts. More than 68,000 people arrived from Australia over the years 1861-63, although that total probably understates the actual numbers of newcomers. The migratory flow contracted very sharply after 1863: there were small inwards movements from Australia in 1864 and 1865, but these were more than offset by a loss of migrants returning across the Tasman. The remaining years of the decade saw only small movements into Otago and very modest net gains. In general, the migrants from Australia were more mobile than their United Kingdom counterparts, who were fewer in number and likely to have arrived during the peak years 1862-64. This flow contracted and did not reverse subsequently, and the net flows maintained a higher and steadier pattern until the end of the decade. After 1864, in terms of the numbers involved, migrants from the United Kingdom were much more significant than arrivals from Australia.

A source recently made available by the New Zealand Society of Genealogists, namely the *Passenger Lists Victoria, AUS outwards to NZ* (Parts Two and Three), permits a more detailed reconstruction of the inflows from Victoria, the single most important Australian source for the Otago goldfields. The news of Gabriel Read's May 1861 discovery was followed, two months later, by the first major influx of people from Victoria. Between August 1861 and August 1864 around 59,000 people arrived in Otago, most entering through the ports of Port Chalmers and Dunedin and a small number disembarking at Bluff. The first rush embraced the months from August 1861 to July 1862; the arrivals reached a peak in September 1861, followed by two smaller peaks in December 1861 and January 1862, before declining as the winter advanced. The announcement, in August 1862, of Hartley and Reilly's major discovery stimulated a second major inflow up to July 1863; once again, the numbers fell as the weather grew colder. A third and considerably smaller inflow arrived over the next 12 months.

Analysis of a random sample drawn from the passenger lists indicates that 56.7 per cent of all arrivals were English, 17.9 per cent Scots, 17.7 per cent Irish and 0.4 per cent were Welsh; the remaining 7.3 per cent was made up of all other nationalities (especially Germans). The rushes were thus predominantly a British phenomenon. If the analysis is confined to those born in the United Kingdom, then 61.1 per cent were English, 19.3 per cent were Scots, 19.1 per cent were Irish and 0.4 per cent were Welsh. In 1861 the English made up 63.0 per cent of the total British-born population, the Welsh 4.0 per cent, the Scots 10.3 per cent and the Irish 22.7 per cent, so the Victorian passenger lists suggest that the Irish were under-represented in the Otago rushes. The preponderance of men among those flocking to the province meant that the proportions of males who were English, Scots and Irish closely approximated each national group's share of the total British-born influx. The same was not true of the very much smaller number of women who participated in the rushes: Scots females were over-represented, the English and, particularly, the Irish under-represented.

My sample included 510 people who gave their country of origin as Ireland. A very large proportion, more than 90 per cent, were male, with females making up just 6.7 per cent of the Irish who arrived during the rush years. Like their West Coast counterparts, most of the men were 25 and older: 40.7 per cent were aged between 25 and 29 years, 24.7 per cent fell into the 30-34 range, and the balance of 17.1 per cent were 35 and over. Altogether, single men made up almost nine-tenths of the inflow; fewer than one-tenth married. The passenger lists also reveal 'travelling status': 86.1 per cent of the males were single men travelling alone. Married men travelling by themselves made up 5.9 per cent, married men travelling with wives 1.3 per cent, and married men with wives and children just 0.6 per cent. So, the Irish male inflow was characterised by a marked lack of both children and the aged, a predominance of single men and a preponderance of those in the younger working age groups. The data suggest that many of the young men who flooded into Otago from Victoria had arrived in Australia as comparatively young children or were relatively recent (post-1855) arrivals. It is possible that, in both cases, these young men were finding it difficult to get into a contracting and increasingly company-dominated and capital intensive Victorian mining industry. The discoveries in Otago (and on the West Coast) proved immensely attractive to this young, energetic and mobile segment of Victoria's population, especially at a time of economic recession in that colony.

Of the small number of Irish females who participated in the rushes, a much lower proportion (52.9 per cent) was single and a much higher proportion (47.1 per cent) married before their arrival. The age distribution also differed for women: 35.3 per cent were under 14 years, while 58.8 per cent fell into the 15-34 age range. Most of that group were aged from 25 to 29 years. Although a majority of the females were either children or married women, 14.7 per cent were single women travelling alone. Irish emigration to Victoria during the 1850s included many young single women who had decided to follow their Irish menfolk, and it seems likely that at least some followed the Irish miners across the Tasman. It should be noted, however, that the numbers involved were small and that single Irish female participation in the Otago gold rushes requires much more detailed investigation. It is also interesting to note that, as the peak of each of the two major rushes passed, both the sex composition and the age distribution changed, with many wives and families arriving to join husbands and fathers.

British data relating to emigration from Britain and Ireland to New Zealand during the nineteenth century are also limited, but one British parliamentary return offers some insights into both the origins and directions of the migratory outflow from the United Kingdom for 1860-63.[4] The return provides numbers of migrants leaving for North America, South Africa, the separate Australian colonies and New Zealand, by nationality. My estimates exclude the category 'not distinguished', which ranged from 4.6 per cent to 13.3. per cent for New Zealand throughout the period. Whether this lack of classification affected one nationality more than another is not known. The proportion selecting New Zealand ranged from 4.1 per cent of all emigrants in 1860 to 9.4 per cent in 1862. At the same time there were major differences among the three national groups. New Zealand took 12.2 per cent of the English-born in 1862. On the other hand, Scottish emigrants were particularly inclined to choose New Zealand over the entire period, taking 30.6 per cent in 1860, 27.2 per cent in 1861, 37.3 per cent in 1862 and 29.2 per cent for the first six months of 1863. Those proportions exceeded the figures choosing all other destinations, including British North America. It is striking that, according to this return, the numbers of Scots-born emigrating to New Zealand exceeded the number of English born. The Irish pattern was quite different: only a small proportion selected New Zealand, but a very large majority decided to sail to the United States, with Victoria being the only other relatively important destination.

Within Australia the preferred destinations were New South Wales and Victoria, with Queensland attracting a growing proportion from 1861. The numbers migrating directly to New Zealand were small, but they increased from 1861. Those selecting New Zealand also increased, from 5.4 per cent in 1860 to 12.9 per cent in 1862, although the result for the first six months of 1863 suggests that the tide of Irish emigration had again turned to Victoria and Queensland. For the entire period 1860-63, the English made up 42.4 per cent of those emigrating directly from the United Kingdom to New Zealand, the Scots 44.3 per cent and the Irish just 13.3 per cent. A comparison with each group's share of the United Kingdom's population in 1861 indicates that the English- (especially) and Irish-born were under-represented, and the Scots markedly over-represented. Clearly, New Zealand's Irish intake largely made its way through Victoria, so it will be useful to consider briefly the character of the Irish who landed in Australia between 1841 and 1860.

III

Almost 23,000 migrants left Ireland for Australia during the Famine decade of 1841-1850, and during the 1850s the number rose to 101,541, so that by 1861 the Irish formed 15.4 per cent of Australia's population. In Victoria the Irish formed 24.0 per cent of the colony's British-born population in 1857 and 26.1 per cent four years later. A recent study of the great migration to New South Wales in 1841 indicates that of the 20,000 assisted migrants two-thirds had been born in Ireland. In terms of regional origins, 30.1 per cent were from Ulster, 19.0 per cent from Leinster, 9.5 per cent from Connaught and 41.4 per cent from Munster. Counties Tipperary and Fermanagh were over-represented, followed by Clare, Galway, Limerick and Tyrone, and then by Cavan, Donegal, Kilkenny, Antrim, Armagh and Wicklow. In this major flow, single females outnumbered single males. Most newcomers were aged between 15 and 29 years, while about two-thirds (67.6 per cent) were Roman Catholic (although only 37.9 per cent of those from Ulster were so). Most of the men were employed in agriculture or labouring, and most of the females in domestic service or agriculture.[5] Of those assisted to New South Wales and Victoria during the 1850s, two-fifths came from Clare, Tipperary and Kilkenny, thus continuing the pattern established during the early 1840s. This pattern remained stable for several decades, despite repeated efforts by colonial officials to attract more northern Protestant settlers.[6]

The Irish also made full use of nomination schemes, thereby reinforcing the established flows. Patrick O'Farrell has argued that the gold-seekers of the 1850s 'formed a solid numerical base for nominations for assisted passages, and remittances of passage money in subsequent years'. He estimates that 85 per cent of the Irish who arrived in Victoria in the 1850s and 1860s were single, many being brothers and sisters, cousins, relations and friends of earlier arrivals. Munster was 'overwhelmingly the source of Irish-Australian immigration from the 1840s to the 1880s, the period of the greatest number of arrivals'.[7] David Fitzpatrick indicates that there were two regions prone to sending migrants: the primary source was a cluster of south-midland counties stretching from Clare and Limerick eastwards to Tipperary, King's and Kilkenny, and a secondary cluster centred on Cavan and Fermanagh in southern Ulster.[8] The provincial and county origins of Australia's Irish were to influence strongly those of New Zealand and, in particular, of Otago and the West Coast.

IV

Few traces remain of the many thousands of men who arrived, mined or laboured and then departed from the province, other than a simple listing on an application form for a mining privilege, or the indelible signs of their industry etched into Otago landscape. We know very little even about those who did remain. When Irishman Patrick Talty of St Bathans died in 1913, it was simply noted that his wife and family had died many years ago, that he had lived alone and that he had been found dead in his hut. Moreover, the widows of many miners could not be traced. Some left the goldfields to join children scattered throughout New Zealand, some (being frequently younger than their dead husbands) remarried, others returned to Australia, some died with few apparently knowing more than the barest details about them (this was particularly true of those who died childless).

To determine the nature of Irish migration to the Otago goldfields, I used a variety of source materials to create a population of 1,364 goldminers who arrived in the province during the period 1861-71.[9] Of these men, 38.3 per cent had been born in England and Wales, 30.1 per cent in Scotland, and 31.6 per cent (431 men) in Ireland. In a pattern reflecting that of gross immigration from Australia and from the United Kingdom, the great majority arrived on the goldfields in the years 1861 to 1863, and most of the remainder in 1864 and 1865. There were no marked differences among the three national groupings, although a higher proportion of both the Scots and the Irish miners arrived in 1861, reflecting the fact that many were drawn from the Victorian goldfields. There was also a slight tendency for the arrival of Irish miners to be spread through the decade, with smaller peaks in 1864-65 and again in 1869-70.

The Irish miners who arrived on the Otago goldfields during the 1860s were somewhat younger than their English and Scots counterparts. Most (83.1 per cent) were aged from 20 to 39, with 50.6 per cent being between 25 and 34. The median age of the Irish was 27 years, but 30 for the English and 29 for the Scots. The evidence suggests that the Irish miners fell into at least two major groups: those who had arrived in Australia in the early 1850s with their families and who in their early twenties joined the rushes to New Zealand; and men in their early twenties who arrived on the Australian fields during the second half of the 1850s.

Most of these newcomers (78.1 per cent) were unmarried at the time of their arrival and the Irish were more likely to be single than their English and Scots counterparts. Just 17.9 per cent were married; the marital status of the balance is unknown. When the place of marriage is established for those who married before reaching New Zealand, only 31.5 per cent had married in Ireland, while 63 per cent had married in Australia. These proportions were much higher than those for English and Scots miners. That contrast probably reflects the more family-oriented character of the English and Scottish migratory movement on the one hand, and, on the other, the young, single person-dominated character of the Irish migratory movement of the early 1850s to the Victorian goldfields. Almost 91 per cent of the Cornish miners who arrived in New Zealand already married had done so in Cornwall, while of those Irish miners born in Munster (Clare, Cork, Kerry, Limerick and Tipperary), most had married in Australia. Again in contrast to the English and Scots miners, the great majority of the Irish miner marriages had been contracted after 1850, and the Irish were considerably older at marriage than their English and Scots counterparts. One consequence was that almost a third (32.3 per cent) of the Irish miners had been married within a year of their arrival in New Zealand, and a total of 67.9 per cent within five years. The corresponding figures for the English were 15.4 and 42.3 per cent, and for the Scots 15.5 and 40.8 per cent respectively.

Altogether, Munster supplied 43.0 per cent and Ulster 37.7 per cent of the 337 Irish miners in the sample. When compared with the provincial shares of Ireland's total native-born male population aged 20 years and over in 1861, it is apparent that both the Ulster- and Munster-born were over-represented. Both Leinster- and Connaught-born miners formed a small proportion of those who settled in Otago. In brief, the data indicate that the gold miners of Otago drew disproportionately on the migrant streams from Munster and Ulster. Eight out of Ireland's 32 counties, five in Munster and three in Ulster, supplied 63.7 per cent of Otago's Irish miners. In Munster, Tipperary, Clare, Cork, Limerick and Kerry supplied 40.9 per cent, and in Ulster, Antrim, Down and Londonderry furnished 22.8 per cent. With the exception of the Cork contingent, those born in the other seven counties were all over-represented among Otago's Irish miners. That was particularly true of those born in Clare, Tipperary, and Londonderry.

Of the three major nationalities, a considerably higher proportion of the Irish (45.2 per cent) did not have families before arriving in New Zealand; the per centages for English and Welsh-born were 35.0 and 29.0. These per centages are consistent with those for the year of marriage. There is also some evidence to suggest that the wives of Irish miners were more likely to have travelled with or joined their husbands soon after their arrival on the goldfields. This may reflect the fact that many of these women had reached the Victorian goldfields sometime earlier. On the other hand, many married Cornish miners migrated alone and only later, sometimes many years, sent for wives and families.

Details of miners' occupations before they reached either Australia or New Zealand are scarce. Obituaries show that many had been employed in agricultural pursuits, mining or seafaring. Death certificates, however, do provide the occupation of the *father* and, despite some imprecision, the pattern is clear. A large proportion of the Otago miners came from agricultural backgrounds, although the proportion varied from a comparatively low 33.3 per cent for the English/Welsh, to 47.7 per cent for the Scots, and a very high 75.9 per cent for the Irish miners. These per centages can be compared with the proportion of each country's total workforce employed in the agricultural sector in 1871: 19.1 per cent for England, 26.9 per cent for Scotland and 58.1 per cent for Ireland. That distribution suggests that the miners were drawn disproportionately from agricultural backgrounds. Although the period 1853-72 is often described as the 'Golden Age' of British agriculture, a period of rising prices, rising rents and rising farmer incomes, it also embraced major changes in the agricultural workforce, not least in Ireland. The very high proportion of the Irish miners drawn from agricultural backgrounds is consistent with the contraction in the number of small holdings, the transition from cereal to pastoral production, the change from manual to horse-powered agriculture during and after the Great Famine, and the consequent growing emigration of the sons and daughters of small farmers.

V

What of the Irish women who settled on the goldfields of Otago and married miners (of all nationalities)? To answer this question, I will focus on 400 United Kingdom-born wives who arrived up to 1871.

When the year of arrival is analysed in terms of national origins, some interesting patterns emerge. Whereas only 3.2 per cent of the Irish arrived before 1861, 10.7 per cent of the English did so, while 43.9 per cent of the Irish arrived over the years 1862-64, compared with 47.4 per cent of the Scots but only 26.8 per cent of the English. This suggests, among other things, that a large proportion of the Irish women were drawn from the Victorian goldfields and thus from the inflows of the 1850s.

In terms of age, only 1.9 per cent of the Irish wives were under 15 years when they arrived in New Zealand, compared with 10.7 per cent of the English and 12.8 per cent of the Scots, a further indication that a good many of the English and Scots women who married miners had arrived in the colony as young children before the discovery of gold in 1861. The very small proportion of Irish females aged under 15 years reflects the very small inflow of Irish before 1861. Nevertheless, the English wives were generally significantly older on arrival: 23.2 per cent were over 35, compared with 9.8 per cent of the Scots and a mere 5.1 per cent of the Irish. Conversely, whereas 49.1 per cent of the English were aged between 20 and 34, the comparable figure for the Scots was 62.4 per cent and for the Irish 79.5 per cent. The contrasts are quite marked and reflect, in particular, the character of the Irish migratory flow to Victoria during the 1850s and the importance of Victoria as a source of both miners and those who married them.

Whereas 71.8 per cent of Irish miners were single on arrival in New Zealand, a considerably lower 59 per cent of those Irish women who married miners were single. That proportion married was, however, much higher than in the case of English wives. The result for the Irish-born is significant, given that few of these women were under 15 years when they came to the colony. The data suggest that young, single Irish women were a particularly mobile group, as important an element in the mid-nineteenth-century migratory streams, including the gold rushes, as their male counterparts. The evidence suggests that, as in the case of the Victorian rushes, young and single Irish women followed their countrymen onto the goldfields, many proceeding directly from the United Kingdom as either provincial or central government-assisted immigrants.

With respect to place of marriage, the pattern is similar, of course, to that for those miners who married before arriving in New Zealand. Whereas 67.2 per cent of English- and Welsh-born wives married in England, and 70.5 per cent of the Scots-born married in Scotland, the comparable figure for the Irish was only 20.9. Conversely, 76.1 per cent of the Irish-born married in Australia, compared with 25.9 and 29.5 per cent for the English-Welsh and Scots-born respectively. Major contrasts also emerge with respect to the year of marriage: whereas 37.9 per cent of the English- and Welsh-born had married before 1854, the corresponding proportion for the Irish-born was just 2.9 per cent. On the other hand, 89.7 per cent of the Irish married between 1855 and 1864. Such differences point again to the distinctiveness of the Irish migratory flow to Victoria during the 1850s and the importance of Victoria as a source of Otago's Irish goldfields settlers.

The distribution of birthplaces for the Irish wives differs in two main respects from that of their miner husbands, with proportionately fewer being born in Ulster (30.5 per cent compared with 37.7 per cent) and proportionately more being born in Connaught (15.3 per cent compared with 5.6 per cent). The two main provincial sources, however, remained Munster and Ulster. In Ulster, most had been born in Antrim and Londonderry, while in Munster, Clare, Cork, Limerick, and Tipperary were the most important sources. In Connaught, Galway was the birthplace of 11.0 per cent of the wives of Otago's gold miners. The pattern of female representation also differed from that of the miners: the pattern was similar for Leinster and Munster, but Ulster-born females were under-represented and those born in Connaught marginally over-represented.

It is clear that the pre-1871 Irish women came largely from agricultural backgrounds, although the proportion was lower than in the case of their male counterparts, comparatively more having fathers with pre-industrial skills. The occupational backgrounds of the English wives were similar to those of the English-born miners, with a slightly lower proportion being drawn from agricultural backgrounds, and a slightly higher proportion from those described as 'occupations with relatively little technical change', notably mining, a reflection of the presence of a large number of Cornish on the goldfields. The occupational background of the Scottish wives quite closely approximated that of their English counterparts, but it differed from that of the Scottish-born miners, with fewer coming from agricultural backgrounds, and more from 'occupations with relatively little technical change' and 'occupations with relatively great technical change', differences consistent with the more marked urban origins of these women.

VI

Contemporary and much later literature tends to present the gold rushes as spontaneous, unplanned and unorganised, with populations that were cosmopolitan and dominated by young, single, footloose males. Many of the miners moved from rush to rush, constituting an international army whose movements and activities were practically unrestricted. There are no totally reliable estimates of the number of people involved in the gold rushes of the nineteenth century, and few records survive, but in each case some remained to carry on the mining industry, settle on the land and build new communities.

With respect to the Irish flow onto Otago's goldfields, a number of conclusions can be drawn. First, it is clear that two major migratory streams, the first and largest from Victoria, and the second from the United Kingdom, converged on Otago. Second, the rather limited evidence available suggests that the two streams differed, possibly quite markedly. Certainly, unlike the inflow from the United Kingdom, the Australian stream contained many Irish men, mostly young and single, the veterans or the sons of veterans of the earlier Victorian rushes. Third, the gold rush influx as a whole exhibited a quite distinctive regional mix. For the English, the counties of the south-west, and notably Cornwall and Devon, were the single most important source, while the Scots were drawn more widely, but with a significant proportion born in the Highlands and Islands. The Irish-born were drawn largely from Ulster, notably Counties Antrim, Down and Londonderry, and from Munster, in particular Counties Clare, Cork, Limerick, Kerry and Tipperary. The birthplaces of the Irish women tended to follow, with the addition of Galway, those of the Irish miners. For these men and women, the discovery of gold offered new opportunities, new hopes, the prospect of immediate low-risk and low-cost gain despite the vast distances to be travelled, and the certainty of temporary discomfort or even privation. Fourth, most of the miners were concentrated into the prime working age groups, with the Irish tending to be a little younger than their English/Welsh and Scots counterparts. The women were generally younger on arrival in New Zealand than their husbands. Fifth, most of the men were single when they arrived. Those Irish men who had already married before arrival did so largely in Australia; the same was true for Irish women. Finally, most of these young Irish men and women who arrived in Otago during the 1860s were drawn from an agricultural background, and that was entirely consistent with the expulsive forces at work in the districts of their birth.

The gold rushes greatly stimulated what before 1861 had been a very small inflow of Irish into New Zealand as a whole and Otago in particular. They established complex migratory links between Otago and Victoria, while ensuring that the earlier Irish influx into Victoria strongly influenced the character of the later flow into Otago. They appear also to have established the provincial and county sources of New Zealand's Irish immigrants, a pattern that was to persist until about 1890, when a growing proportion was drawn from Ulster. The rushes brought many men and women from those parts of Ireland, in particular Munster, which had experienced the Great Famine and which were continuing to undergo marked social and economic changes, among them a redistribution of land, the replacement of tillage with pasturage, de-industrialisation as the Irish textile industry contracted, and the transformation of those social customs that had otherwise supported family and community stability. The fact that the influx into Otago consisted of so many young men and women, although consistent with the outflow from Ireland for much of the nineteenth century, reflected the powerful forces transforming rural Ireland. The fact that many arrived through Victoria meant Otago acquired an influx of new settlers, many of whom had already acquired considerable colonial experience and who were prepared to employ that experience in helping to shape a new society in New Zealand.

6

Irish Migration to the West Coast, 1864-1900

Lyndon Fraser

John Noonan Callinan left his family home at West Gragan, County Clare, for the last time in 1863. His departure coincided with an agricultural depression that brought severe financial hardship to rural communities throughout Ireland.[1] Yet the immediate cause of his emigration was his father's death earlier in the year. Michael Callinan (1790-1863) bequeathed a large tenant farm of ninety acres to his eldest son, Patrick, so leaving Ireland was the best option for those who did not inherit.[2] John's eldest sister, Catherine, had been sent to join relatives and friends living at Ballarat in the Australian colony of Victoria. A younger brother, Michael, followed three years later and settled in west Melbourne, where he developed a substantial contracting business. The passage of other family members awaited the arrangement of Patrick's marriage in 1860, the payment of their sister-in-law's dowry and his succession to the land. The death of Michael senior opened the way for a further reduction in the size of the family household at West Gragan. John's voyage to Victoria aboard the *Eastern Empire* in mid-1863, and the later arrival of his mother and three younger siblings on the *White Star*, completed a complex process that involved the transfer of land at home and the transplantation of non-inheriting children abroad.[3]

No account of John Callinan's subsequent movements in Australasia survives, although it is clear that he chose not to remain permanently in Melbourne. Parish records show that he married Bridget O'Neil, a farmer's daughter from Newmarket, County Tipperary, at the Roman Catholic Chapel in Euroa on 2 January 1871. The couple made for the prosperous agricultural district of Kyneton later in the year and their eldest child, Catherine, was born there in 1872.[4] Although the available evidence is ambiguous, it seems likely that the presence of kinsfolk in Westland may have encouraged them to seek new opportunities across the Tasman. The Callinans landed at the flourishing port-town of Hokitika in 1874 and settled in an isolated hinterland community some distance from Goldsborough. Bridget gave birth to two more children – Kate and James –

during their sojourn on the diggings and must have found life onerous in the wretched conditions of the mining camp. After several years of struggle, the couple abandoned the Waimea and shifted north to Brunnerton, where John found steady work as a coal miner. Three decades of continuous residence in the small mining township were broken only by an unsuccessful stint at hotelkeeping in Westport, which ended in bankruptcy in 1902. This misadventure prompted John's return to wage labour at Brunnerton and later in Greymouth. It was here that he remained, outliving his wife and two eldest children before dying at Kotuku in April 1933. The funeral attracted 'a numerous attendance of friends', many of whom travelled 'from the country districts' to witness the burial of an Irish tenant farmer's son in the Catholic section of the Kararo cemetery.[5]

John and Bridget Callinan were among several thousand Irish men and women who settled on the West Coast of New Zealand's South Island during the nineteenth century. Like the Callinans, most of these newcomers made their way to the region from the Australian colonies and many belonged to expatriate social networks that extended back and forth across the Tasman. Despite the importance of these connections, the West Coast Irish have attracted little attention from scholars exploring the various diasporic communities scattered throughout Australasia.[6] There has been no detailed treatment of their story and we still await a regional equivalent of Malcolm Campbell's fine-grained portrait of the Irish in south-western New South Wales.[7] Yet the same mechanisms that bound the parish of Clonoutly to Boorowa and Dromore to Illawarra, also connected Burawn with Charleston, Kilrush with Kumara and Skibbereen with Addison's Flat. The Irish pattern of settlement was largely a self-perpetuating phenomenon that sustained a complex web of linkages stretching from Nelson Creek to Ballarat, and from south Westland to distant parishes in County Clare. Like their contemporaries who emigrated to eastern Australia, the West Coast Irish constructed enduring ties of kinship and acquaintance that enabled them to appropriate a new environment and build a strong and assertive expatriate community.

This chapter examines the broad dimensions of Irish migration to the West Coast during the period 1864-1900.[8] It seeks to determine the key demographic features of the movement and to amalgamate these findings with recent work in Irish-Australian studies. In my view, an understanding of the West Coast migrant saga is incomplete unless its close historical connections with the Australian colonies are taken into account.[9] The analysis that follows is in two parts. The first section, a close investigation of the migratory currents that flowed into the West Coast from various points of origin, shows that the Irish migrant stream comprised heterogeneous strands, which differed according to age, gender, regional origin, religion and marital status.[10]

The second section explores the relative influence of informal social networks in shaping key aspects of the migration process.[11] The significance of these institutions in attracting settlers to nineteenth-century New Zealand has been challenged by Miles Fairburn, who argues that migrants ventured here 'alone or as members of their immediate families and thus left behind their blood and affinal relationships'.[12] According to Fairburn, a lack of continuity with Old World kindred ties is indicated by the rarity of transplanted communities, a chronic shortage of females, small numbers of elderly kinsfolk and relatively modest levels of chain migration.[13] These factors, he suggests, ensured that New Zealand received a larger proportion of bondless individuals than other new societies.[14] Fairburn's emphasis is a useful corrective to idealised notions of community in New Zealand immigration history, but his account fails to grasp the transnational nature of informal social networks that stretched social relations across large distances. On the West Coast goldfields, Irish men and women were not inevitably severed from their Old World associations. Rather, newcomers relied on expatriate neighbours, friends and kinsfolk for material assistance and companionship during their transition to a new environment. This pattern held true regardless of a person's time of arrival or social background and provides strong evidence for the persistence of Old World social ties among the region's Irish population.[15]

I

North America was a much more attractive prospect to nineteenth-century Irish men and women than travelling to the distant Australian colonies.[16] In the 1850s, the average cost of an unsubsidised fare on the southern route was three to five times higher than that for a transatlantic crossing,[17] and the length of the voyage made the recently settled colonies less accessible than Britain or North America.[18] These competitive disadvantages were partially offset by the policies of colonial governments, which offered extensive subsidies to attract migrants from the British Isles. State financial assistance was a crucial distinguishing feature of Irish movement to the colonies. It broadened the scope of immigrant recruitment and enabled politicians and administrators to impose some degree of control over the selection of newcomers.[19] Colonial officials attempted to choose government-assisted passengers from England, Wales, Ireland and Scotland in proportion to each nationality's representation in the United Kingdom population. At the same time, they made strenuous efforts to achieve the Wakefieldian prescription for an even balance of the sexes by extending preferential terms to single women.[20] But there was strong competition for migrant labour in Britain, and recruitment agents sent out substantial contingents of Irish passengers when other 'British' settlers were unavailable.[21] This infusion of 'undesirables' provoked considerable anxiety in the colonies, where it sharpened anti-Irish sentiment and led to persistent complaints about the size and quality of the Irish intake.[22]

Almost one-third of a million Irish ventured to Australasia between 1840 and 1914, along with 40,000 or 50,000 Irish felons transported into penal exile in eastern Australia at imperial expense from 1788 to 1853. Relatively few elected to go to the colonies during the Great Famine, when more than one million people fled Ireland for safer havens abroad.[23] But the discovery of gold in 1851 led to an influx of nearly 100,000 Irish migrants, doubling the number of arrivals between 1836 and 1850.[24] This spectacular increase continued into the early 1860s before it slowed temporarily, regaining momentum from the mid-1870s until the beginning of the next decade. Thereafter, the intensity of Irish movement to Australia slackened to become a relatively minor flow.[25] In global terms, the colonies accounted for about one-fourteenth of all the Irish-born living abroad in the later nineteenth century. Australian census returns from 1891 show that more than two-thirds of the expatriates had settled in Victoria and New South Wales, compared with about one-fifth in Queensland. Much smaller numbers were living in South Australia, Tasmania and Western Australia.[26] Irish migrants constituted nearly one-quarter of the foreign-born component nationally in the same year and were second only to the English-born as a source of Australia's immigrant population.[27]

Irish migration to the West Coast differed in several major respects from the corresponding movement of free immigrants to the Australian colonies. First, throughout the nineteenth century, the migrant stream contained an overwhelming preponderance of males. This was largely a consequence of timing, in that the gold rushes (1865-68) took place at the same time as colonisation and did not follow the introduction of agriculture or extensive pastoralism, as in New South Wales and Victoria. In addition, the Coast's gold, coal and timber were extractive industries based on heavy manual labour.

An equally striking contrast with the Irish-Australian experience is that most newcomers were already seasoned colonials, many of whom had spent considerable periods in other New World settings. The extensive mobility of individual migrants is vividly illustrated in the case of Murtagh Doyle, a publican's son from Coolesholl, County Wexford, who emigrated to the State of New York and joined the US Army at Buffalo in 1857. When the American Civil War broke out in 1861, Doyle fought with the 8th Regiment of US Infantry and received an honourable discharge for 'loss of sight' near Berlin, Maryland, in 1862. Notwithstanding this debility, he immediately enlisted in the US Marine Corps and served on both the USS *Union* and USRS *Vandalia* for the remainder of the conflict. After his term of service expired, Doyle returned to Ireland and married Susan Cassidy, a farmer's daughter from Kilcavan, at the Catholic Chapel of Tomacork, County Wicklow, on 27 November 1871. Seven years later the couple and their three children sailed to Lyttelton on the *Opawa* and the following year, 1879, moved to Greymouth where Doyle pursued his trade as a baker.[28] The more modest migration paths of Robert Patterson from Killyleagh, County

Down, and Daniel Sheedy, from County Cork, included extended sojourns on the Otago diggings and were more representative of Irish movement to the region. Both men began their careers on the Victorian goldfields before joining the rushes to Gabriel's Gully in 1861 and south Westland four years later.[29] Colonial experiences such as these provided newcomers with an extensive repertoire of skills and resources that helped them to adjust to a harsh and unfamiliar environment.

Colonial officials were much less influential in determining the characteristics of the region's migrant stream than in the Australian colonies. State financial assistance certainly played an important role in attracting newcomers to the West Coast during New Zealand's immigration drives of the 1870s, but the main impact of government recruitment policies occurred circuitously, through decisions taken by selecting agents working on behalf of the eastern Australian colonies or the three main South Island provinces. Typical in this regard was Limerick-born Patrick Bourke and his younger sister, Catherine, who obtained assisted passages to Port Chalmers aboard the *Timaru* in 1882. Also on the voyage was Margaret McGirr, an eighteen-year-old from County Tyrone, whom Bourke later married at St Patrick's Church in Greymouth on 19 November 1887.[30] Like many other government-assisted passengers arriving on the West Coast, all three resided for several years at their original point of destination before leaving to rejoin kinsfolk and friends. In each of these cases administrative decisions taken elsewhere contributed towards further Irish immigration into the region and ensured that some of the preferences of colonial selecting agencies were reflected in the distinctive make-up of the local population.

Despite these differences in timing and composition there were striking similarities between Irish migration to the West Coast and to the eastern colonies of Australia. Nowhere was this more apparent than in the strong presence of expatriates. Census figures show that the Irish component of the West Coast's foreign-born population was about one-quarter for the years 1864 to 1900, a proportion that closely matched the comparative per centages recorded in 1901 for New South Wales, Victoria, and Queensland.[31] The Irish-born contingent reached its peak at the height of the gold rushes and then declined in both absolute terms and as a per centage of the entire population. Newcomers maintained a rough parity with their English-born counterparts until late in the century and consistently outnumbered continental European and Scottish-born migrants by more than two to one. Generally speaking, Irish men were more likely than their foreign-born counterparts to settle on the goldfields or in newly opened agricultural districts.[32] Irish women, on the other hand, were proportionately more likely to live in urban boroughs compared with most other nationalities, except the Australian-born. As a result, the predominance of males was counterbalanced in the three major towns of Westport, Greymouth and Hokitika, where the sex ratios of the population approached those characteristic of the wider diaspora. There were some important local variations. In the counties of Grey and Westland, for example, Irish migrants comprised the largest foreign-born group at each census between the years 1878 and 1906. But the overwhelming impression is that newcomers dispersed widely throughout the region on their arrival and did not cluster together in localised concentrations. It is difficult to escape the conclusion that the West Coast Irish were a diverse 'charter group' with a powerful role in defining the nature of the society they were creating.[33]

What were the geographical origins of the region's Irish population? The rural southern midland districts of Clare, Limerick, Tipperary, King's and Kilkenny provided more than two-fifths of all emigrants from Ireland to the West Coast and their preponderance strongly indicates the Australian antecedents of the inflow. This is particularly evident in the case of Clare and Tipperary, which dominated Victoria's intake and contributed the largest share of newcomers in absolute numbers and relative to their respective populations. An important secondary concentration developed around the highly urbanised north-east Ulster counties of Antrim, Down and Londonderry, an area that contained Protestant majorities and a rapidly expanding industrial sector. The most convincing explanation for the north-east's prominence is that the West Coast acquired part of its Ulster component through earlier recruitment campaigns undertaken by the provincial governments of Otago and Canterbury. Both provinces conducted mobilisation drives in Ulster and the connection is further strengthened when one considers that two-fifths of all the northerners had arrived in New Zealand before 1865. Altogether, emigrants from Ulster comprised about one-quarter of the inflow, while Connaught and several Leinster counties were under-represented. This disparity is further accentuated by the fact that most of those from the western province emanated from a single county – Galway – with Dublin, Kilkenny, King's and Meath accounting for three-fifths of all Leinster-born migrants. Along the western seaboard, Kerry and Donegal established close associations with Westland during the early stages of colonisation and may have contributed a number of bilingual Irish speakers. There is also evidence to suggest that certain key parishes or districts with strong Australian connections, such as Ballyvaughan in County Clare and Nenagh in County Tipperary, were particularly inclined to send emigrants to the region. These findings are broadly consistent with Murray McCaskill's pioneering analysis of Westland tombstone inscriptions, which reported 'a notable regional concentration' for Ireland based around the six adjacent counties of Tipperary, Kerry, Cork, Limerick, Clare and Galway.[34] But the region also received substantial infusions from north-east Ulster and can be pictured as a hybrid of the Australian and New Zealand emigrations.

The balance of religious affiliations of Irish migrants to the West Coast closely resembled the patterns found in Irish society as a whole. Roman Catholics comprised about three-quarters of the total influx throughout the nineteenth century and this proportion increased markedly after the mid-1870s, reflecting the prevalence of chain migration among the southern Irish, who encouraged relatives and friends to follow them to the colonies. For some migrants, no information on denominational association can be found in the extant listings. In some cases, an unfortunate combination of sudden death, difficult terrain and distance from churches conspired to prevent religious practitioners from officiating at all funerals. Elsewhere, these silences no doubt indicate that the deceased did not attend church. In an 1874 report to the Marist Vicar-General, for example, the parish priest at Reefton, Michael Cummins, lamented that all around the district

> there are little digging townships with a Catholic population – but too far and the way too difficult for them to meet in one place for mass – as Boatmans & Larrys – neither of them have chapel or school as yet – Lyell – central place, second in importance ... is a fearful place both naturally and supernaturally speaking – the people are drunken, immoral and boisterous, no proper hotel, no chapel, no school and nothing done towards either ... it is full of nominal Catholics of all nations and deserves no other name than little hel [*sic*]. There is much good to be done, but the large and dangerous rivers and frost and snow melting, where with two and three feet wide tracks, we have to ride 1700 feet above a river or precipice, render it difficult for me to attend to all alone.[35]

It seems likely that the data understates the true proportion of Roman Catholics among the Irish-born. In the first place, this group was more inclined than other denominations to settle in the isolated goldfields communities. Evidence from parish returns for Ahaura and Greymouth show that poor communications prevented priests from reaching Catholics in remote districts regularly and forced them to construct a series of stations in private homes.[36] Second, the figures tend to obscure the long-term impact of the post-1880 immigrants, most of whom were Catholic and still living at the end of the century. We can safely assume, however, that the Catholic-Protestant breakdown exceeded that for the New Zealand province of Canterbury (37/63) and generally mirrored the eastern Australian colonies of Victoria (70/30), New South Wales (71/29) and Queensland (72/28).[37]

A notable feature of the available documentation is the degree to which Roman Catholics were disproportionately over-represented among the emigrants from north-east Ulster relative to their share of the area's population. Altogether, Catholics accounted for almost two-fifths of all those born in counties Antrim and Down, whereas Presbyterians comprised only one-quarter of the inflow even though this group were the most numerous in both places. In Ulster between 1861 and 1911, the Catholic population declined by about 29 per cent compared with a 16 per cent decrease among Presbyterians and a 6 per cent fall in the number of Church of Ireland (Anglican) adherents.[38] Ulster Anglicans were over-represented on the West Coast in proportion to the North's non-Catholic population, but the Church of Ireland provided relatively fewer emigrants from the southern provinces than might have been expected. Among Westland's Protestant population, the Anglican element was notable for its strong representation in larger urban centres, such as Greymouth and Westport. In addition, more than one-half of all Anglican men and two-fifths of their Presbyterian brethren had arrived in the colony before 1865, compared with only one-third of Catholic males. This data provides support for the view that the unrestricted flow of migrants to the West Coast from Australia was dominated by 'South Irish country Papists', while the population received substantial numbers of northerners through immigration schemes operated by provincial administrations in Otago and Canterbury, which favoured migrants from north-east Ulster.[39]

An examination of sex ratios among Irish migrants to the region indicates a number of significant local variations. The inflow from County Dublin, for example, contained a disproportionate number of married couples and an almost equal balance of the sexes. Counties Tipperary, Limerick and Clare, on the other hand, were more typical in terms of the respective per centages of men and women. Male dominance was greatest among emigrants from the north-east Ulster counties of Antrim and Down, which contributed a smaller proportion of women to the diaspora than other places in Ireland between 1851 and 1920. Yet the ratio of males to females from each county (5.50:1 and 7.00:1) considerably exceeded the comparable dimensions of the wider outflow (1.31:1 and 1.50:1). On the West Coast, Ulster men outnumbered their female counterparts by 3.54 to 1; the sex ratios were much less skewed for the southern provinces.

The exceptional excess of emigrant males from north-east Ulster is difficult to explain. Presumably it owed something to the socio-economic pressures generated in rural Ulster, which favoured the consolidation of holdings into commercial farms and the concentration of the region's linen industry in the factories of Belfast and its adjacent towns at the expense of cottage manufacturing in the countryside. Although the north's urban/industrial growth provided opportunities unavailable elsewhere in post-famine Ireland, the region could not absorb all the disinherited farmers' children, unemployed rural artisans or farm labourers displaced by these processes. Moreover, some forms of employment stimulated by economic expansion were more accessible for women, making overseas destinations more attractive for males than short-distance migration to the northern industrial towns. The high rates of male emigration that accompanied the decline of Ulster's population by one-fifth between 1851 and 1911 were unique in the context of the post-famine exodus. It is significant that most of the Ulster men who made their way to the West Coast chose to leave home during a period of relatively high emigration from the northern province in the 1850s. Emigration from Antrim and Down increased by 114 and 36 per cent throughout the decade, compared with a decrease of 44.5 per cent in total emigration from the whole of Ireland.[40] The prominence of single males was therefore accentuated by the nature and timing of their departure from Ireland, as well as the disparity of the sexes typical of a goldfields population.

Another important finding from this study is that more than half of all Irish females (53.1 per cent) who settled on the West Coast in the nineteenth century had married elsewhere before their arrival.[41] This preponderance of married women counterbalances the misplaced focus in local histories on the lives of prostitutes and colourful individuals such as Barbara Weldon and Bridget Goodwin.[42] By contrast, four-fifths of adult males were single when they reached the West Coast and a substantial number remained unattached until the end of their lives. Of all the migrants who married outside New Zealand, more than half did so in Australia. About two-fifths had taken their vows in Victoria, while those who formed unions elsewhere in New Zealand were overwhelmingly inclined to celebrate marriages in Otago. Most surprising, however, is the number of couples who married before they left Ireland (38.7 per cent). In a study of Irish family life in Victoria, Chris McConville has plausibly suggested that these folk may have challenged the 'exacting tyranny' of Ireland's inheritance rules by arranging improvident unions.[43] In these cases, he argues, the promise of an assisted passage to the colony served as a form of punishment for people who had openly defied the complex demands of rural Irish society. Similar tensions in the workings of post-famine Ireland's dowry system have been documented by David Fitzpatrick and Kerby Miller,[44] but currently there is insufficient evidence to test the adequacy of this hypothesis for the West Coast Irish. Nonetheless, the extant listings show that a previous marriage in Ireland was an experience shared by one-quarter of all women and about one-twelfth of the men.

Broadly speaking, these newcomers were considerably older than their counterparts who left Ireland for various global destinations during the nineteenth century.[45] In total, the West Coast received almost twice the proportion of people aged between 25 and 34 found elsewhere in the diaspora.[46] Equally striking is the fact that about one-quarter of all the migrants were over 35, compared with one-tenth of their compatriots at home. This trend is strengthened when one considers that the figures used in this analysis record the age of migrants on arrival in New Zealand and do not reflect the local reality, where a considerable minority would have made their way to the West Coast after having arrived elsewhere in the colony. In terms of religion, these patterns show little variation among males but there are significant differences by denomination for women. Whereas the median age of Anglican women was 28.5 years, Roman Catholics were on average three years younger (25.3) and marginally less likely than the Protestant cohort to have been married when they arrived on the West Coast.

Obtaining information about the socio-economic background of the newcomers is a more hazardous undertaking. Probate files contain few references to prior social status, and data from other sources is fraught with ambiguity. Such is the case with death certificates, which required officiating doctors or coroners to complete standardised forms recording fourteen items, including the name and occupation of the deceased person's father. Some local registrars appear to have been reluctant to enter these details in their inventories and the occupational titles used lack any real consistency. These problems are made worse by the common tendency for Irish rural labourers and assisting relatives to describe themselves as 'landholders' or 'farmers', no matter how tenuous their connections with the landed property.[47] Despite these limitations, the source materials do provide a broad indication of the pre-migration background of the West Coast Irish and allow us to construct a plausible interpretation of their meaning. Of the 1104 people for whom reliable information can be ascertained, a high proportion (65.9 per cent) were the disinherited offspring of Irish tenant farmers for whom rural society offered few opportunities. The children of agricultural labourers, on the other hand, were badly under-represented (9.0 per cent) relative to their numbers in the Irish population and compared with the corresponding figures for Catholic Irish immigrants living in the province of Canterbury (22.6 per cent).[48] Denominational differences are particularly evident in relation to adherents of the Church of Ireland. Compared with Roman Catholics or Presbyterians, the Anglican component included a larger number of people whose fathers were professionals (7.7 per cent) or proprietors (17.7 per cent), and considerably fewer had been engaged in farming or menial occupations (52.3 and 6.9 per cent). Nonetheless, the wider picture is clear and backs up anecdotal evidence that suggests the West Coast's Irish population came from '[the] well-to-do classes at home', with a pronounced bias towards the sons and daughters of small and middling tenant farmers.[49]

In summary, then, Irish movement to the region was highly selective in terms of age, gender, county origin, religion and marital status. Altogether, Irish migrants comprised about one-quarter of the West Coast's foreign-born population between the years 1864 and 1900. The regional origins of the inflow were quite distinctive, centring upon a cluster of southern rural districts with strong Australian connections. An important secondary concentration around north-east Ulster featured a disproportionate number of Roman Catholics, as well as a chronic excess of emigrant males. Although single men dominated the West Coast's intake in absolute numbers, more than half of all Irish women had married before emigrating. In addition, migrants of both sexes were considerably older than their compatriots who ventured elsewhere, and most had served extensive colonial apprenticeships in other global destinations. Finally, the balance of religious affiliations among the West Coast Irish closely matched that of the eastern Australian colonies and included a similar proportion of newcomers from rural backgrounds.

II

Age, gender, family structure and economic circumstances played an important part in shaping the movement of Irish men and women to the West Coast, but the role of associative networks based on friendship or familial ties is less clear. A major study of Catholic Irish migration to nineteenth-century Canterbury suggests one avenue of enquiry.[50] The source materials used in this analysis show that the eastern province's migrants were made up of clusters of people bound together by acquaintance and kinship ties, who came to the colony at a critical stage in their lives. Australian historians have documented similar patterns of chain migration and solidarity in several different locations and one scholar has identified personal relationships – along with state paternalism – as a major determinant of Irish emigration.[51]

To what extent were these kinds of interpersonal connections influential among the West Coast Irish? Although the absence of detailed population records makes it impossible to answer this question with any degree of certainty, some useful information on migrant network patterns can be abstracted from nomination files when these sources are combined with other documentation. The bills system operated by the central government in the 1870s formed part of a 'two-tier' recruitment policy governing state-assisted migration to New Zealand.[52] Under these regulations, colonial residents could nominate family and friends in the United Kingdom and Europe for a subsidised passage by paying a substantial contribution towards their fare. Although deposits for classes other than female domestic servants amounted to one-third of the full price for a nominated migrant, this sum still compared unfavourably with the cost of an unassisted steerage ticket to North America. Thus even the standard contribution for single men, which ranged from £4 to £6 throughout the decade, represented a major outlay for sponsors in terms of funding and organisation. In short, the nomination process was neither free nor unconstrained.[53] Rather, it constituted a major source of private funding for immigration to New Zealand and considerably reduced state expenditure on recruitment campaigns by shifting some of the responsibility for selecting new migrants to local receiving networks.

A close analysis of Westland's surviving inventory shows that Irish settlers made extensive use of the bills system to bring relatives and friends to the colony.[54] Altogether, Ireland received nearly two-thirds of all nominations sent from the region during the period 1872-73. Of these, more than half went to Munster with counties Clare, Limerick and Tipperary accounting for about two-fifths of the total. An examination of individual forms points to the existence of localised migration chains connecting Westland communities with specific points of origin such as Ennis (County Clare), Castlegregory (County Kerry) and Birr (King's County). It is also noteworthy that Irish sponsors recognised a wider range of relatives and friends than other nationalities and were much more

John Noonan Callinan of West Gragan, County Clare, emigrated to Victoria aboard the Eastern Empire *in 1863 and settled on the West Coast in the mid-1870s. He is pictured standing to the immediate right of his daughter, Kathleen, who married Richard Rogers at Greymouth on 24 July 1906. (Courtesy of Brian Nolan)*

A Limerick-born labourer, Patrick Bourke, met Margaret McGirr of County Armagh on the Timaru's *voyage to Otago in 1882. The couple were married at St Patrick's Church, Greymouth, on 19 November 1887. This photo shows the Bourke family in 1902: (L to R) Back: Kate (1896–?), Patrick, Jr (1892–1973), Margaret (1895–1982). Middle: Frank (1891–1976), Margaret (née McGirr, 1862–1919), Jack (1898–1979), Patrick, Sr (1856–1945). Front: Alice (1900–1991), Mary Ellen (May, 1904–1969). (Courtesy of Ron Patterson)*

Michael Flanagan of Tobertoby, County Louth, sailed from Liverpool to Melbourne with his brother, Patrick, in 1857. He spent time at various destinations in eastern Australia, the West Coast and the United States, before returning to Ireland at the request of his father in 1890. 'Instead … of the lad of seventeen years you last saw,' Michael warned him, 'you will meet a grey old man of fifty'. Michael Flanagan to John Flanagan, 20 May 1890. (Courtesy of Donald Murphy)

Below: *Margaret Anne Kilpatrick (1837–1922), a native of County Armagh, sailed to Auckland on the* Indian Empire *in 1862 with her husband, David, and infant son, William. The daughter of Robert Reid, a teacher at Balleer, Margaret wrote several letters to family and friends in Ulster. (Courtesy of Alan Kilpatrick)*

Left: Alice Gilmore (1857–1934) emigrated from County Down to Auckland in 1876 aboard the SS Bebington. *(Courtesy of Alice Gemming)*

Right: Elizabeth Ferguson (1860–1943) and her sister, Hessie, arrived on the West Coast as assisted immigrants from County Armagh in 1884. Elizabeth later married Robert Ayson and lived at Balclutha. *(Courtesy of Lorna Neame)*

Ellen Piezzi (1849–1922) from County Kilkenny ran the Helvetia Hotel in Goldsborough with her husband, Julius. Ellen married Dennis Maher in 1883, seven years after Julius's sudden death, and moved to Wellington where she continued her involvement in the hotel trade. This photograph shows Ellen (centre right) at the bar of the Panama Hotel in Wellington: (L to R) Tom Walsh, Ellen Maher, Ellen (Piezzi) Maher, Guiglio Masciorini. *(Courtesy of Teresa O'Connor)*

Left: The Green Ray's Gaelic specialist, John Patrick Tohill (Seaghan O'Thuatail), came from a staunchly Fenian family in Napier. He went to Dunedin to evade conscription and managed to avoid detection when the newspaper's office was raided by police in 1918. *(Courtesy of the Tohill family)*

Above right: Henry (Harry) Tohill. Unlike his brothers, John and Frank, Henry Tohill could not evade the military authorities. He served time in jail for avoiding the medical examination that formed one part of the conscription process. *(Courtesy of the Tohill family)*

Right: Carte de visite-sized reproductions of sketch portraits of the 'Irish Invincibles', featured in a Weekly Irish Times supplement, 3 March 1883, were sold in Dunedin by W.R. Frost and Co.

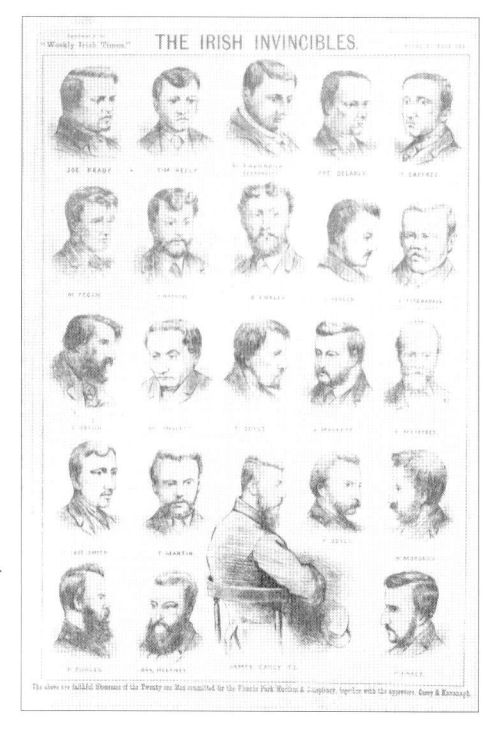

This Dunedin group appears to be wearing the Maoriland Irish Society's badge: 'a harp with a cross scroll "Dia Saor Eire".' (Courtesy of the Tohill family)

Right: *James Bradley probably inspired the founding of the* Green Ray. *He may have also been a member of the Irish Republican Brotherhood and the organisation's Supreme Council. This photograph was sent home to relatives in Ireland. (Courtesy of Catherine Craig)*

This photograph shows a Catholic procession at the fiftieth jubilee of the Dominican Sisters' school in Dunedin in 1921. An Irish Republican flag is openly displayed on the building to the upper left of the image. Angry letters to the newspaper by 'Loyal' Protestant citizens made much of this flagrant demonstration. *(Courtesy of the Dominican Sisters)*

Below: *Patrick Cody and sons, Riversdale, c. 1914: (L to R) Luke, Patrick Jr, John, Patrick Sr, Michael, Laurence. Daniel Cody is absent. (Courtesy of Patrick Cody)*

John Charles Troy and his wife, Catherine, 1952. Troy was secretary of the Wellington branch of the Maoriland Irish Society and reputedly organised an 'underground railway' to assist Irish military evaders escape the country during the First World War. He emigrated to New Zealand in 1914 and came from a staunchly nationalist family with branches in Fermoy and Limerick. His uncle, William, was a friend and colleague of Charles Stewart Parnell, as well as a member of the Irish Republican Brotherhood. Leaders of the organisation were regular visitors to the Troy household. (Courtesy Tom Troy)

Below: *Delegates to the 'Unity Conference' of 1885 which resulted in the formation of a national Hibernian organisation: (L to R) Back: R. Lloyd (New Headford), P. Hoskins (New Plymouth), M.A. Neill (Wanganui), J. O'Brien (Auckland), J. Morrison (Blenheim), M. Bohan (Wellington). Front: P. Leahy (Christchurch), G.J. Sellars (O.C. District), J.A. Reardon (Napier & Hokitika), R.P. Lonargan (Christchurch), S. McGreevy (Waipawa).*

A group of Wellington Hibernians on their special day, 17 March, around the turn of the century.

Greymouth Hibernians proudly pose with Archbishop Mannix of Melbourne during the prelate's 1924 visit. Bishop Brodie of Christchurch sits to his left.

inclined to extend their munificence to potential emigrants of the same generation.[55] More surprising is the fact that nearly three-fifths of all the Irish nominees were single women. Presumably this distinctive preference was a response to the perpetual shortage of domestic servants on the West Coast.[56] The notion that local Irish exploited the bills system to import suitable numbers of marriageable females is also attractive, but without better supporting evidence this explanation cannot wholly account for the discrepancy. Overall, it is apparent that Irish settlers gained some measure of control over the selection of further migrants during the 1870s through the elaborate machinery of government nomination schemes. The arrangement and payment of deposits for kinsfolk, neighbours and friends was a carefully planned exercise that led to the same kind of 'reiterated self-replication' evident in the Australian colonies.[57]

The complex process of negotiation that accompanied the practice of nominating relatives and friends to the colony is revealed in correspondence with colonial administrators. Mary Neylon of Addison's Flat, for example, sought a refund of £5 from the central government for the passage of a County Clare farmer, David Clune, who had 'refused to Immigrate and has likewise written to me to that effect'.[58] On the other hand, the father of Annie and Bridget Halley forbade his daughters to take a nominated passage deposited by their sister in Greymouth and insisted they travel to the colony from California. An Auckland immigration official established that the two siblings had travelled

> from Ireland by way of New York, and thence to California en route for Auckland, but under whose direction, or at whose cost they professed to be wholly ignorant, and they had no papers of any kind to shew. They stated that they were nominated by their sister resident at Greymouth, and were told by fellow passengers that the Government would send them on from Auckland. When this was declined, their friends at Greymouth, I am informed here, paid their passage (10 pounds) per *Lady Bird* south.[59]

The relative frequency of comments such as 'declines no reason' and 'gone & left no address' on cancelled bills are much less revealing about the degree of co-operation between families in Ireland and their connections in Westland.[60] Yet the possibility that recipients of nominated passages might decline the opportunity of deliverance in the New World does not seem to have deterred Irish nominators. Some correspondents like Edward Duffy enthusiastically expressed their desire to bring out 'friends' from Ireland.[61] Others were sufficiently confident in their dealings with the bureaucracy to propose alternative arrangements to existing regulations. John and Maurice O'Connor of Greymouth, for example, nominated large numbers of kinsfolk from County Tipperary during the early 1870s. The town's immigration officer, James Wylde, considered these newcomers 'a superior class' and noted the O'Connors were

> desirous of sending for other members of their family, who having capital, wish to settle here, and would bring a considerable number of ordinary Immigrants with

them. They have not sufficient means to pay the full amount of, say, second class passages and leave them sufficient for establishing them in the Colony, and they will not come amongst the ordinary immigrants. Under the circumstances Messrs O'Connor apply that free passages may be granted them under the usual regulations, but that they shall be allowed to come as second class passengers by paying the difference to the Agent General or to the ship owners ... I think it desirable to give every encouragement to these people, as there already here are an excellent class of settlers and I have every reason to believe will induce a large stream of Immigration from the part of Ireland from which they come.[62]

In another case, the New Zealand nomination system was reshaped to accommodate familial connections in eastern Australia. Ellen Connell, proprietress of Westport's City Hotel, paid a deposit for the passages of her sister, brother and father, who sailed to Nelson on the *Mataura* in 1875. After the vessel's arrival, she removed all three to lodgings in the town and proceeded to arrange their departure for Melbourne aboard the *Albion*. Nelson's immigration officer, Charles Elliot, reported that Connell's father had no idea that he was expected to continue on to Victoria and, in fact, signed a promissory note for £16 to cover the costs of his voyage.[63] In her own testimony, Ellen Connell claimed he 'went to Melbourne to see more children of his and he and brother intend comming [sic] back to me', while her sister, Johanna, remained in Westport. Furthermore, her financial circumstances were such that an immediate payment of the outstanding fares would cause severe hardship.[64] Subsequent letters in this chain of correspondence indicate that Ellen Connell's actions were not intentionally fraudulent.[65] Instead, it seems likely that she did not fully comprehend the significance of political and administrative boundaries in framing colonial immigration policies. Johanna Connell's eventual departure 'to keep house' for her father in Melbourne and Ellen's willingness to reimburse the state for passage money owed by relatives forcefully remind us that familial obligations regularly extended across the Tasman.

The function of informal social networks in structuring the flow of migrants into Westland and south-west Nelson is further illuminated by information taken from probate records. An examination of surviving testaments from the West Coast for the period 1865-1910 suggests that Irish movement to the region was a collective rather than individual enterprise.[66] Although some newcomers travelled independently, a substantial majority relied on kinsfolk and friends for information, advice and material assistance during the process of migration and settlement. This pattern held true even for the most restless migrants and found expression in the executorships created by Irish testators.

One the most critical decisions facing a person making a will was the choice of suitable executors who could be relied upon to administer the estate and carry out the wishes expressed in the testament. It is significant that among single Irish males, more than three-fifths of all testators chose to appoint expatriate neighbours or acquaintances as executors of their estates. A substantial minority, almost 20 per cent, entrusted kinsfolk with this responsibility, while many made use of local storekeepers, priests or merchants in joint partnership with friends.

The testamentary preferences of widowed adults closely matched those of single men in terms of property management.[67] Bridget Houlahan of Dillmanstown, for example, named a parish priest, Matthias McManus, and an Irish Catholic storeman, John Crowley, as joint trustees and guardians of her three infant children.[68] Similarly, Leinster-born James Jones considered his executors, Bernard Ward and Patrick Dee, sufficiently trustworthy to administer his property for the benefit of his brother and 'such of my children as [they] shall in their absolute discretion think fit'.[69] The wills of married men, however, are less revealing. Altogether, about two-thirds of this group named wives as executors of their estates, with slightly more than half entrusting this duty to wives alone. In cases where testators chose to exclude their spouses from this role they constructed executorships that re-created Old World social ties. Nonetheless, even these men showed great willingness to bequeath all of their estates to their wives and most provided widows with sizeable powers of disposal over property.[70] This finding raises the intriguing possibility that Irish women enjoyed a higher status in nineteenth-century Westland and south-west Nelson than their contemporaries in the province of Canterbury.[71]

These patterns of executorship underline the importance of contact among ex-neighbours and relatives, yet the principal concern of those who left wills was the final disposition of their worldly property. In this regard, the probated estates of unmarried men contain some of the best information on immigrant social ties. These testators did not have to balance as many competing interests and were usually better placed to extend their generosity to distant kinsfolk and friends. Altogether, in nearly three-quarters (71.6 per cent) of the extant probates, single males directed bequests to persons outside their immediate families. Siblings featured in about three-fifths of the wills, while non-kin were referred to in more than one-third.[72]

A common theme that emerges in these testaments is the frequency with which friendships and family ties extended across the Tasman. James Quillinan of Capleston, for example, named William Noonan and Richard Dunphy as trustees and executors of his worldly affairs. He bequeathed his hut and personal possessions to an acquaintance, James McCaffrey, and directed that a sum of £10 be applied for the benefit of Reefton miner, Peter McDonnell. Quillinan devised one-third of the residuary interest in his estate upon a niece, Alice Hayes of Ballarat, and his executors were instructed to divide the remainder equally between a second niece, his sister and brother-in-law, all of whom lived in Geelong.[73]

A significant minority of testators also endowed relatives in Ireland when naming their legatees. Kerry-born Thomas O'Rourke stipulated that all his property was to be sold and a sum of less than £80 set aside 'in connection with my wake and funeral and the erection of a suitable tombstone and railing around my grave'. He willed £20 to procure masses and granted the remainder to his three siblings in Gurtduff.[74] In a similar vein, Richard Bayley bequeathed the residue of his estate 'unto my sister Mrs Isabella Comerford formerly of Finnoe, Borris O Kane, Tipperary, Ireland, now probably of Dublin' and, in the event of her death, to the children of his brother, Henry, of Finnoe House.[75] Case studies such as these highlight the continuing importance of familial obligations in Ireland for the West Coast's Irish population and show that inheritance sometimes entailed the transfer of considerable material resources to those at home.

Perhaps the most striking evidence relating to interaction between expatriate neighbours, acquaintances and kinsfolk is found in documentation generated by intestacy cases.[76] In accordance with colonial laws, those seeking to administer the property of people who died without leaving a will were expected to find sureties and to furnish sworn affidavits in support of their petition. Probate courts also required successful applicants to provide an inventory of the deceased's belongings and a detailed account of all disbursements made under the administration of the estate. Tipperary-born John Clerehan died at Maori Creek in 1896 leaving property worth £352. His eldest brother, Patrick, who lived in Melbourne, stated that John had corresponded regularly with him since his arrival on the West Coast in the mid-1860s. He was survived, too, by another brother, Daniel, and a sister, Anne, both of whom were also living in the Victorian capital. Patrick's son, Roderick, applied successfully to the Supreme Court in Greymouth for letters of administration to the estate of his deceased uncle and secured an expensive bond with the assistance of a Maori Creek storekeeper, Jeremiah O'Donnell, and Martin Shanahan of Greymouth.[77]

By contrast, the will of Croninville miner Patrick Donovan could not be found after his death in 1891. In a sworn affidavit, his working mate, Dennis Collins, claimed he was 'born next door' to the deceased in the townland of Burawn, County Cork, and had 'known him since my early childhood'. The two men had not been separated during their sojourn in the colonies and used 'a common purse'. In addition, Donovan made frequent visits to Charleston and always stayed in the Collins's household. On one occasion, he contracted a severe illness and executed a will in the presence of Westport's parish priest, Father Thomas Walshe, Charleston journalist Patrick Kittson and Cork-born labourer William Mullins. Collins's wife, Alice, who nursed Donovan during his convalescence, carefully related the contents of her former patient's testament. He bequeathed all his mining property at Croninville to her son, James, and devised the residuary interest of the estate upon Dennis Collins. In his religious dispositions, Donovan willed £10 to Reverend Father Walshe 'for the celebration of Masses for the repose of his soul' and asked Alice Collins 'to see that his wishes were carried out'. The Westport Supreme Court was sufficiently impressed by this supporting affidavit to grant the probate for Donovan's estate to her husband.[78]

Ulster-born Alexander Mitchell, on the other hand, drowned in a remote section of the Waimea River where there were 'no grave yards, no roads and no other means of carriage of [his] remains ... than on men's shoulders'. Documentation surrounding an application by his two surviving brothers for letters of administration to Mitchell's estate shows that he emigrated from the family homestead at Ballinaskeagh, County Down, in 1846. After landing in Quebec, he made his way to Dundas where he secured a clerkship in a local foundry. Mitchell disliked this position intensely and told his father that he would rather 'beg for work everyday than be confined the way I have been this summer'.[79] He tried his hand at harvesting in the company of an ex-neighbour and claimed to have earned 'a good deal more money' than from his previous engagement. Yet he complained bitterly that a lack of capital prevented him from purchasing suitable farmland in Canada. Mitchell made repeated appeals for financial assistance from home and his own correspondence combined expressions of filial piety with reproaches about 'odd and disrespectful' letters received from Ireland.[80] These requests became more desperate when he borrowed money to purchase a small farm in Woolwich, Canada West, and faced mounting pressure from creditors. Despite this dispute with his family, Mitchell continued to take part in deliberations about further emigration by relatives and acted as a patron for new arrivals. During the winter of 1850, he employed 'a little daughter of Ann jane [*sic*] Porters' as a housekeeper and assured his father that he would find work for the son of an old acquaintance: 'I will take an Interest in his welfare so far as in my powers or any person in the neighbourhood. If James wishes to work for me i will give him more than he can get from another and if not where ever he works i will see his pay is sure'.[81] A combination of hard times and bad debts eventually broke his resolve to remain on the land and he joined the exodus of 'new chums' bound for the Victorian goldfields in 1853.

Mitchell did not correspond directly with kinsfolk in Ireland during his sojourn in the Australasian colonies but maintained some degree of contact by sending newspapers to family members. More importantly, he was able to draw upon a network of expatriate acquaintances who provided much-needed companionship in the New World and sustained connections with home. A former neighbour, Richard Megaffin, for example, wrote to Mitchell's parents from Ballarat and assured them that their son 'was doing well and in Good Health – he wished us to Remember him to his Friends'.[82] Mitchell seems to have relied on old companions after he had relocated his carting business in Invercargill and extended his operations to the Waimea diggings in South Westland. His family received periodic reports about his progress from returned Australian and New Zealand migrants, whom he had instructed to call on them. Like other intestacy records, Mitchell's case documents the persistence of Old World social ties in several different locales and suggests that interaction with expatriates formed an essential part of the Irish experience on the West Coast.

The persuasiveness of this interpretation is reinforced by an illuminating exchange of letters between the expatriate Flanagans and their connections in County Louth. At the centre of this correspondence was the eloquent goldminer Michael Flanagan, who emigrated to Melbourne in 1857 and eventually returned home to work his father's farm after lengthy periods in the eastern Australian colonies, the West Coast and California. Although Michael's colonial experiences were marked by extensive mobility, the nineteen surviving letters in this series affirm the enduring significance of family and neighbourhood networks in structuring the migration process. His enthusiastic account of a reunion with an elder brother in Queensland must have provided some consolation to an 'Uncle Priest' in Ireland:

> About the end of August last I left Melbourne for this colony to join Pat from whom I had a letter a few days previous to me leaving in which he gave a rather favourable account of the diggings ... The time passed well enough during our journey the nights being pretty cool compensated us a little for the fatigues of the day under the nearly perpendicular sun. On the thirteenth day from our leaving the coast we got a first glimpse of a curiously made up little township composed of bark and slabs and this was the diggings. I was over a week on the diggings before I found Pat. One day I was wending my way amongst the bark and slabs which compose the township and I saw advancing before one curious looking bushman and as I came close and got a nearer view I found I saw the face before not untill he put out his hand and began laughing did I fully recognise the man I was in search of. Pat was a good deal changed since I last saw him before. His appearance would nearly put one in mind of a Maori. The sun of Queensland browned him very much but the climate did not disagree with him. He was in perfect health, but he looked rather thinner than when I last saw him and although New Zealand seems to have agreed well with him during the three years he was there he did not look three years younger after all. There were two Clougher men along with him when I met him who were his mates one of these was the young man who came out along with Dick Sheridan – Pat Kirk.[83]

Significantly, Michael Flanagan emphasised the importance of companionship as a prerequisite for 'getting on' in Australasia:

> The friendship of any true friend and especially one who had influence would certainly be a great benefit to any young man in a strange country but to the friendless and the lonely and to those who do not possess the natural gift of being bold and <u>shameless</u> and who have not plenty of what in the colony is called "cheek" it is hard, very hard to obtain a footing amongst a class who make money by means which I would live a poor man all my life rather than descend to.[84]

The intricate system of intelligence that connected rural Irish households to distant West Coast settlements and their busy expatriate networks was vividly illustrated during Michael's residence in Charleston. After Louthman Patrick

Kirk died in a street brawl, his mother appealed to Flanagan for help in retrieving her son's estate. Bridget Kirk's heart-rending petition served as a powerful instrument of moral persuasion:

> poor Patt was the quietest child I ever rared it is little I though the day he left Clougher that I would never see him again ... when Patt father heard he heard it on Monday and he died in 10 days after he died on the 16 of febuary and he never wore in better health he was at mass the Sunday before he heard so you must think that was a trial to lose my husband and son in 3 months there is nothing breaking my heart but to think of him being without the Priest fare from home.[85]

The explicit nature of her instructions to 'get the money' deposited by Patrick in the Bank of New South Wales and the admission that 'it was bad enough to lose him self and not all his Property' were unusual recitations in the context of Irish-Australian correspondence.[86] Such directness suggests that the letters were an act of desperation by a vulnerable and dependent widow rather than a blatant expression of avarice.[87] The impact of her appeal was no doubt enhanced by the collaboration of Michael's 'Uncle Priest', who advised his nephews to 'do your best to have every thing right. Yet do it prudently without making an enemy for yourselves'.[88] The voices emerging from these letters show that the moral and material obligations prescribed by Irish society 'did not lapse through separation'.[89] The renewal of contact with home and the replication of Old World networks in Westland and south-west Nelson consoled migrants and eased their adjustment to unfamiliar terrain.

III

What conclusions can be drawn about the nature of Irish migration to the West Coast of New Zealand's South Island between the years 1864 and 1900? In the first instance, the geographical origins of the region's migrant stream were quite distinctive, showing a marked bias towards key centres of Australian emigration such as Tipperary, Clare and Limerick in Munster, Galway in Connaught, and King's and Kilkenny in Leinster. This pattern is hardly surprising given that the physical isolation of the West Coast from the rest of the South Island helped turn the region into 'an economic dependency of Victoria' during the mid-1860s and made its capital, Hokitika, 'a Trans-Tasman suburb of Melbourne'.[90] Yet the movement also featured an important secondary cluster based around the north-east Ulster counties of Antrim, Down and Derry – an area that had strong connections with the provinces of Canterbury and Otago. Chain migration among the West Coast's expatriate population ensured that these originating localities remained predominant throughout the period. Whatever their origins, an overwhelming majority of newcomers came from a rural, small-farming environment in Ireland. They were considerably older than their compatriots arriving in the great emigration ports of Liverpool, New York, or Sydney and they possessed markedly different levels of experience acquired during an extended colonial apprenticeship. By Irish standards, these expatriates were multi-skilled and extremely resourceful. Most had spent a long time working in Australia and this learning phase was an ideal preparation for the hardships of everyday life on the West Coast.

The composite profile of Irish migration to the region closely resembled Australian patterns in terms of religious affiliation, socio-economic status and proportional representation. Like their counterparts in south-western New South Wales, for example, these newcomers encountered a cosmopolitan environment without entrenched power bases.[91] The Irish-born were a numerically strong charter group whose members participated actively in the colonisation process and in the formation of local community life. Although it is true that the West Coast's Irish intake differed from the corresponding movement to eastern Australia in several respects – the preponderance of single males, the disproportionate number of married women and the dominance of privately financed immigration – the crucial function of Old World social ties in influencing migration suggests underlying similarities with Australian patterns of settlement and adjustment. The selective re-creation of kinship and neighbourhood networks provided an important source of companionship, material assistance and information for recent arrivals on the goldfields, and helped to preserve notions of familial duty prescribed by Irish society. Distance may have strained or even broken allegiances anchored in Ireland, as the Mitchell correspondence shows, but the evidence seems to indicate that migrants constructed complex webs of association which extended across the Tasman in both directions and stretched as far as distant rural households in the Burren of Clare. Although this conclusion must remain provisional, the close links of mobility and kinship that tied the West Coast Irish to the colonies of Victoria and New South Wales suggests that their experiences also need to be incorporated into the narratives of Irish-Australian history.

7

'In Prospect of a Happier Future'
Private Letters and Irish Women's Migration to New Zealand, 1840-1925

Angela McCarthy

In 1876 eighteen-year-old Alice Gilmore accompanied her brother, John, on the SS *Bebington* bound for Auckland and reunion with their brother Andrew, who had settled at Tauranga two years earlier. By contrast with many vessels during this period, which made the journey in about three months, the SS *Bebington* endured an uncharacteristically 'long & unpleasant voyage' of 160 days. This was followed by five weeks in quarantine at Motuihe Island, due to death and illness. When Alice Gilmore eventually set foot in Auckland she told readers at home on the Ards Peninsula, 'I can say very little as yet but it is here as it is every where. Some has a good word & some a bad one'.[1]

Only one of Alice Gilmore's letters has apparently survived, but correspondence from her brothers John and Andrew provide fleeting glimpses of her progress in the colony. The year of their arrival, John Gilmore optimistically informed his parents that 'Alice has a good chance at her trade'.[2] One year later he noted that 'Alice is still busy at her business and seems to do well'.[3] In 1878, however, Andrew jested that 'Alice has shifted from us and left John and I to cook for ourselves. She prefers the Company of a strange man. She got married in January last to a Mr James Fenton'.[4] Alice and James Fenton eventually had seven children and lived at Te Puke, in close proximity to her two brothers. When Alice died on 12 May 1934, at 76 years of age, her obituary hailed her as 'a woman of strong personality' who 'could tell many interesting experiences of the early days.'[5]

Personal letters, such as those written by the Gilmores, are a valuable source of information about the migration experience. As Patrick O'Farrell has argued, they provide 'an intimate insight into what the migrant actually thought and felt, expressed without constraint, and with the honesty and candour appropriate to close family situations'.[6] More recently, David Fitzpatrick has highlighted the consolatory and functional significance of private correspondence. In his research into personal accounts of Irish migration to Australia, Fitzpatrick uncovered 111 letters in 14 sequences and explored the 'personal journey' of each individual migrant through a combination of local and family sources. Personal letters, he suggests, were 'a tool for sustaining solidarity among separated kinsfolk'.[7]

Yet an influential strand in the study of emigrant correspondence has stressed the disruptive impact of the migration process and the themes of loneliness and alienation. In a major study of the Irish in North America, for example, Kerby Miller concluded that '[a]cute homesickness pervaded the letters and journals of most post-Famine emigrants'.[8] Similarly, Patrick O'Farrell has suggested that the Irish 'brought their kinship mentality to Australia, where it gradually crumbled and fell apart, declining into a residual social atomism marked by separation, isolation, loneliness and eventual alienation of society's individual parts.'[9] This interpretation has been reiterated most recently in Porter and Macdonald's collection of extracts from nineteenth-century female correspondents in New Zealand. They claim that migration was 'inherently destabilising' and that '[p]eople tore up their old connections'.[10] Miles Fairburn, in his analysis of nineteenth-century New Zealand, has also argued that 'the dearth of kinsfolk' led to loneliness and atomisation.[11]

The experiences of Alice Gilmore and migrants like her raise important questions about the interpretations made by historians who have too easily assumed that mobility inevitably led to weak kinship networks. Reliance on extracts with minimal biographical content has contributed to migrant experiences being interpreted out of context. This chapter, which surveys the responses of Irish women to their voyage out, work experiences and new surroundings, is based on a close reading of forty-six surviving letters supplemented by a range of genealogical sources.[12] My central argument is that kinship ties played a critical role in Irish female migration to New Zealand and helped to overcome feelings of loneliness or alienation. Along with evidence of extensive familial bonds, reports from migrants contained positive assessments of colonial life and suggest that these newcomers made a relatively easy adjustment to New Zealand society.

I

Historians have given a number of explanations for the emigration of Irish women, including a desire to improve their opportunities for employment and marriage abroad.[13] Recent commentary has linked both motives by suggesting that they pursued economic gains in order to increase their marriage prospects.[14] The personal testimonies of migrants such as Agnes Lambert, however, illuminate the more pressing, private factors which could trigger migration. In January 1860 eighteen-year-old Agnes departed from Liverpool on the vessel the *Red Jacket* and within four weeks of her arrival at Auckland gave birth to a son. Reflecting on the circumstances of her departure seventeen years later she resignedly mused, 'I have Been an outcaste from you all But I Forgive him that was the cause of it all as my father ought to have forgiven me.'[15] Time had apparently mellowed Agnes's father for, in response to this letter, Agnes was informed that he 'will die contented since he knows yoa are still alive.'[16]

Letters from other family members also yield clues about the decision to leave Ireland. The departure of Margaret Kilpatrick, for instance, may have been influenced by her husband David, whose choice of New Zealand took precedence over the potential reunion of Margaret with her sister Martha in Canada. As Martha revealed after the Kilpatricks' emigration to Auckland on the *Indian Empire* in 1862, 'What freak could possess David Kilpatrick to start for N.Z. If he wished to make money faster, he might have tried Canada, or some place within the bounds of Christendom but to start on a 10 months voyage, speculating, what an idea, and only think I don't know yet what Kilpatricks they are'. That Martha had anticipated reunion with her sister is clear: 'I used to think when R. J. would marry I would send for M. A. but that freak is ended. All hopes of ever seeing her seems now blasted.'[17] Brigid Dawson, on the other hand, appears to have been successful in delaying her family's departure to New Zealand from County Armagh. Although her husband, Peter, had prior colonial experience and urged his family to emigrate from Armagh, Brigid's uncertainty appears to have temporarily prevailed. As she confided to her sister in 1924, 'I am sorry at that we did not come out here sooner or that I kept Peter back so long from coming for it was myself done it, as he was at me all the time to say I would come'.[18]

Like the Gilmores, Kilpatricks, and Dawsons, most correspondents emigrated to New Zealand with other kinsfolk and often rejoined busy expatriate networks in the colony. We may surmise that the presence of Old World acquaintances helped new arrivals adjust to colonial life and prevented them from penning emotional responses to their departure. The letters of non-migrants, on the other hand, conveyed immense grief about the dispersal of their families. From Balleer, Margaret Kilpatrick's mother poignantly confessed that 'there is one long heart rending thought that troubles me. That is I fear I never will see you in this life.'[19] Ann McCleland's departure from County Londonderry for Wellington in 1840 provoked her mother to movingly write of 'the deepest heartfelt sorrow and distress of mind & bodey that it is possible for one of my age & constitution to bear. I suffered after you went away grieving night & day about you. I hoped that you would have perhaps ruid & changed your mind when you would go to Liverpool but alas to my sorrow you went on leaving me to grieve your absence.' Elizabeth McCleland also revealed that other family members were 'in great grief about you when you went away'.[20]

Irish correspondents in North America reciprocated the anguish expressed by their loved ones in Ireland and conveyed 'deep sorrow at leaving home and kin'.[21] By contrast, Irish women travelling to New Zealand provided practical rather than emotional responses to their departure, possibly to assist potential migrants in their decision-making. Alice Gilmore, for example, described the cramped and stifling conditions endured by steerage passengers on the SS *Bebington* during the long crawl through the tropics:

> I never was sea sick nor no other sickness not even a headacke. Only once or so during the hot weather. We were six weeks in the tropics. It was said she did not move the length of herself. It was very uncomfortable especially at night. There was only two side hatches & no portholes in our compartment & 54 people. We could not bear any cloths on us. I & a few other never slept any during that six weeks. There was only one other girl that was not sea sick besides me.

Another Ulster Protestant, Bessie Macready, vividly described a storm encountered during her voyage to Canterbury on the *Pleiades* in 1878. She recalled 'the roaring of the wind, the rattling of things all around us. The creaking of the timbers and dashing of the sea against the ships side was enough to strike terror into a stout heart'. Despite her fear, Bessie displayed courage:[22]

> After breakfast the storm having abated a little one of the officers took me to the poop and the sight that presented itself to me was truly grand. The sea was covered with little hills as it were as far as the eye could reach and each of these topped with white spray and constantly in motion. Now and again the sea would fall in one part, then a number of these hills would come together forming one great peak which would then break the spray rising to a great height and when the sun shone on it presenting all the colors of the rainbow. A feeling of admiration and awe came over me when I looked at it. The Officers said I was brave to come on deck at such a time.

Other letters writers recounted similar kinds of social interaction between female passengers and crew members. On the SS *Bebington*'s voyage to Auckland in 1876, Alice Gilmore noted that 'There was no deaths in the single girls & only 1 married man leaves a wife & 4 children. The sailors sub[s]cribed & gave her £20. I believe the goverment is to provid for the children & she go to service but she's going in another line of service. She is to be married to one of the sailors in Auckland in a few days.' Margaret Kilpatrick informed Armagh readers that the ship's captain 'used to send down porter to me and say it was for they mother of "that fine little Irish man"'.[23] Although Protestant writers frequently declared their Irishness,[24] Alice Gilmore was careful to distinguish herself from a contingent of non-Ulster migrants aboard the *Bebington*:

> The most of the passengers was South of Ireland the roughest & worst class of people I am sure ever come here before & nearly all R.C. If you had only heard them praying when the thought the were in danger when she used to be rolling about. All the crowd belong to her said the never sailed in one lurched so much. The was a great many never seen a ship before till the left Ireland & the were in the greatest state if there was a sea come over her. Ever you seen prayin to the Holy Mother & all other Half way subitutates & the next day if she ran any studdy like came dancing & singing & cursing & sweering & carry storyes & tell lies to the superintendent on

thire shipmates. I am as frightened of dying I am sure as any other body but I was always reconciled to my lot. I thought that if she went down I might as well go home in a quiet state as In a fuss. It would be all one at our Journeys end.

The crew's behaviour on emigrant ships was sometimes less than savoury and occasionally involved the sexual harassment of female passengers. Writing to his parents in Balloo, County Down, in 1861, James McIlrath described the gallant intervention of a fellow passenger in defending female honour, an episode that reveals the vulnerability of female migrants: 'That night a sailor would kiss two girls by force. A man interfered. The sailor took his knife and said he would have his life on the spot. If not he would befor he reached Melbourne. The man met him the next morning. He struck the sailor and put the pipe he was smoking down his throat. He died in a few hours.'[25]

Such incidents reinforced the necessity for the strict segregation of the sexes during the passage. Alice and John Gilmore, for instance, endured intermittent contact aboard the SS *Bebington*:

> There was no communication between male & female at least there was none allowed. I could only speak to Jonny twice a week that was Monday & Tursday from 30.3. PM till 4. PM. That was not much & sometimes not at all for the would not believe that we were brother & sister. The often told me in our compartment that I had run off with him but the were convinced at last. He got to cross if I laughed at any of the sailors as we could do no more & it was only for laughing sake.

Few correspondents reported on shipboard activities undertaken to relieve the monotony of the voyage. However, by 1924, when Brigid Dawson sailed to Wanganui with her family on board the *Athenic*, the entire journey was completed in about six weeks. She revealed that

> 'the children enjoyed it for there was still something new every day that occupied there time and kept them in fun but I was beginning to think the time long myself. No doubt its a long journey six weeks and a day night and day and had nothing to do only sit about that left the time to seem longer. From to much work to no work abal kilt [*about killed*] me.'

After arriving in New Zealand, Brigid Dawson promptly re-established her domestic routines and told her sister that 'there is no slavery or work only to cook and wash and the clothese are never dirty for washing like at home.' Comparing her situation in Wanganui in 1924 with conditions in Armagh, Brigid was thankful to have 'no worry or trouble about crops or how they will be saved or hens or eggs or Turkeys.' Other letters document the contribution of Irish women to the successful management of farms. From Foxton, in the Manawatu, Catherine Sullivan informed her brother-in-law that she milked four cows while 'Nellie milks 83 cows besides all the dry cattle … [and] Bridge milks 35 cows'.[26]

Single Irish women were usually employed as domestic servants or shopkeepers in the colony. Bessie Macready, the orphaned daughter of a Belfast teacher, worked in both occupations. Three years after her arrival, she provided her cousins with a 'short sketch' of her progress in the province of Canterbury:

> Well for the first sixteen months I remained with Aunts in the Bays, which is a delightful place but not a place to progress rapidly. In fact it was a losing game with me while there. About that time a friend of Aunts offered me the entire charge of a shop in Lyttelton which I accepted and was there for a year and a half and many a weary time I spent there, business dull, long hours, and innumerable little trials ... However I was gaining something and that enabled me to bear up in prospect of a happier future.

That future included taking charge of a villa in Christchurch in which Bessie claimed to be 'very comfortable just now. I have got a nice girl for a servant and am attended to like a lady'.[27]

Some Irish women made extensive use of kinship networks to obtain employment. Abigail Gilmer, for instance, arrived in the colony as a domestic servant, having been nominated by her cousin, William Gilmer, in 1884. His brother, Samuel Gilmer, employed Abigail, but William learned upon his return to Mullaghanee in County Monaghan that her work practices left much to be desired:[28]

> I could do nothing for her. She - would not be satisfied till *till* she would get to Henry as my work was of such a nature there was two much confinement connected with it and went to Henry. I told her when leaving [*omitted:* she] should be carefull - I would take her back when I was going to Wellington. Before sending her to Henry I put her in the laundry. Of course I seen at once it was no good that her intention was to do as little as possible. Well that did not trouble me as far as her work was concerned but I found that she did not come out here to work for me. Well I kept her for twelve months and paid her regular every month but no thanks nor no improvement in the girl only dying with laziness and far extravagant as regarding her clothing was something awefull. So she went to Henry and Henry and her only agreed a few weeks so Sam Hill offered her big wages so she went there and I have not heard from her since. I fear there is no good and before her. In fact I could not have done more for her. Perhaps strangers might suit her best. At all events let her have a trial of them.

Sam Hill obviously held a different opinion of Abigail, for they married the month that Samuel Gilmer composed his letter!

Like the Gilmer brothers, Kilkenny-born Ellen Piezzi became a prominent hotelier in the colony. However, her husband's premature death, combined with the precarious nature of West Coast life, prompted Ellen's bleak portrayal of conditions at Goldsborough: 'I had a great many losses this year. Pepel gone true the cort turning *o*nsolvent. I lost a fine cow £15 wurt [*worth*] in a hole in the bush. I canot get any of my old acounts in. The pleas is so poor. The bisness Was Never quarter so bad before.'[29] Nevertheless, she remained resilient. She obtained another hotel and told her brother-in-law, 'I am dooing prity fare traid at present'.[30]

Occasionally, Irish women were hindered in their household duties by illness. At these times, husbands provided essential support. Margaret Kilpatrick, for example, praised her husband's diligence in carrying out domestic duties after she had broken her arm. 'David', she claimed triumphantly, 'was cook, housemaid & every thing'.[31] Similarly, Agnes Lambert explained that her marriage to a widower with several children was substantially enriched by her partner's conduct: 'My husband is verry kind to me and keeps me well and the Girls are verry kind to me thank God for it.'[32] Ellen Piezzi's marital advice to her sister-in-law in 1878 was probably influenced by the recent sudden death of her husband:[33]

> Love yor husband as you love yor one flesh. Respect him ten times beter than yorself. Obey him in [*every*]thing he tell you to do*or* No mater What he tell you too. Doo it for he Nose best What is the bes to bdone and he Never Will tell yto doo rong. Be kind to him and regoice At his fut step coming home to you for it sweet voice is Like [?a] bell too yor Ere.

> Keep in yor one house and good distand with yor Naberes [*neighbours*] and dont Let them No [*know*] any thing About yor husband or yor one bisness. Never tell any thing about him to any one. Keep yor one sakret [*sacred*] and you Will be come good Wife.

The warmth of marital relations must also have eased the adjustment of Irish women to colonial society.

Correspondents in Ireland were particularly eager to receive information about colonial marriages. For instance, Maurice Keane in Waterford urged his sister Mary to provide the pertinent details about their sister Bridget's marriage in Otago: 'We are glad to hear from you but we are troubled about Bridget untill we know more about her in your next letter as I expect to have in a couple of weeks more if you'll keep to your promise as you said. I hope you'll give us all particulars about her & where her husband is from for there are many heartys around here. We would like to know where he is from. Now dont dissapoint us Mary in telling us all.'[34] In response to these kinds of enquiries, many correspondents were careful to stress the desirability of marriage alliances based on Irish birth. Thus, Catherine Sullivan happily reported the weddings of her Irish-born daughters at Foxton: 'Maggie and Bridge married two brothers named Spelman. They are Irishmen. Katie is married to an Irishman from Limerick'. Although another daughter married a Protestant, Catherine declared he was 'a good a husband as ever woman got.'

The retrospective announcement of Alice Gilmore's marriage was made by her brother Andrew. Although she had wed a fellow Ulster migrant, he chose to justify his sister's choice by emphasising the groom's economic status:[35]

> He is a carrier. He came here from Sydney New South Wales, Australia about 5 years ago. Him and I have been intimate friends since we knew one another. He left County Antrim about the year 1859 near Randalstown – only a boy then. He holds an ordinary position. He has 8 draught horses, 2 saddle horses, keeps 5 horse waggons

and three horse drays on the road. Has a store and butcher shop 45 miles up Country – small block.

Case studies such as these underline the importance of kin networks in shaping marital outcomes among Irish settlers in New Zealand.

Information about children featured prominently in the letters exchanged between Ireland and New Zealand, but there is little evidence that Irish correspondents considered their offspring 'encumbrances'.[36] Instead, letter writers frequently emphasised the emotional and practical support that children provided to their mothers. Writing from Tonduff in County Antrim to her daughter Rose Gamble at East Taieri, Catherine Colgan happily contemplated, 'Maggie will be a great big girl now. She will be able to do a lot of work for you now.'[37] Likewise, Margaret Kilpatrick proudly described her daughter as 'a fine woman & a true helpmeet' and claimed that 'God has blessed me with good children. Every bodey says the are models. This is no Ireish blow, but a fact.'[38] Widowed hotelkeeper Ellen Piezzi related a touching episode describing her son's attempt to comfort her with his reassuring words, 'dont crie mama dident god take my papa frome us. Such a dear little boy he is'.[39]

Ellen Piezzi's concern for her children extended to anxiety about their education. In particular, she feared the effects of a mining environment on them. Ellen therefore sent her eldest daughter away to boarding school to 'be taugh her fathers langus and musick and brought up insely [*immensley*] better than be around the [*erased:* by] publick house door'.[40] From Antrim, Catherine Colgan expressed delight that her colonial grandchildren 'are at school and the are learning so well'.[41] Higher education was also admired. According to Bessie Macready in Christchurch, 'young ladies go in quite as strongly for education as do the gentlemen'.[42]

Apart from providing their children with benefits, Irish migrant women were also expected to support their parents and siblings. As Maurice Keane forcefully reminded his sister Mary: 'My mother is out of the barrack now. She could not remain there any longer. She is not well since she threw up the blood. She hardly have any appetite at all but now I am asking you to try and assist her for you know very well she needs it and it is time for you to think of her now if you will ever think & I hope you wont be so false hearted as not to do so.'[43] Migrants who failed to send letters or money to their parents were often chastised. William Lysaght, for instance, bitterly criticised his cousins: 'Is it not an awful shame to say that Patsy or Kitty dont write. The three of them have their mother working for Her living now in her old age. If they had the least shame in them they would not allow such a thing'.[44] Likewise, Mary Anne Gilpin rued her sister's silence: 'She never wrote to me yet. Indeed mother thinks her very unkind. Never answered their letters'.[45]

More critically, colonial correspondents were expected to supply advice and encouragement to potential migrants. Maurice Keane, for example, implored

Mary to provide a passage for his two brothers: 'Dear M send James his passage at once if you can as he is too willing to go out there for there is no work for him here and it would be a charity for you to send for him & bring him out of this place & write to John and ask him would he like to go out for we dont know what he's going to do at present and it would be better for him if he would do something & go out of this place'.[46] John Keane also asked his sister 'to let me know what sort of a country is New Zealand for my trade. If its any way fair I would wish you to send for me & If not you ought to send me a help to send me to America or else to buy tools and work at home'.[47]

Elizabeth McCleland also sought information about the colony. She requested her daughter Ann to 'tell us some of the perticulars of the treatment of the Voyage & how you came on since what you ar doing & where you worship on Sunday. Also the customs and maners of the people the Climate produce trade laws & prospects of this new Coloney.'[48] Elizabeth's request for information was deliberate, designed to evaluate the potential of the colony for the emigration of Ann's siblings. As Elizabeth indicated the following year:[49]

> if you like that place and think it anserable I will on your account be content to let Nancy and Jean Both go to you and strive to be content myself if I know that you are content. So you may think of the feelings of a Mother to you My Dear Daughter when I would let your two sisters go to you to make you hapy for if I thought you happy yourself I would rest satisfied about you.

Elizabeth told her daughter Ann that sister Nancy 'intends to goe to you If you give her the least encouragement'.[50]

Margaret Kilpatrick provided specific advice in her recommendation of future migration to New Zealand: 'Servents are much wanted both girls and boys'. She was just as explicit in attempting to dissuade her brother's emigration: 'I would not advise Joseph to come here as he would not stand the work he would have to do'.[51] Agnes Lambert, on the other hand, longed to be reunited with her sisters but tempered her wish with a warning: 'I would like to see some of my sisters out here But if they are doing any way [*erased*: wel] well at home they had Better stay there for this is not much of a place unless you have plenty of money'.[52]

Other correspondents supplied favourable accounts of colonial life. From Auckland in 1862, the year of her arrival, Margaret Kilpatrick requested her brother Thomas to 'go out to Mama and read her this. Tell her she dreamed a very straight dream about this place. The green hill, the great mountain, the sea below, and the Valley beyond it. All is just as she told me. Tell her I am far better than ever I expected I would be.'[53] This perception of the colony as Arcadia was echoed in Bessie Macready's effusive claim upon reaching the colony in 1878: 'The prospect is beautiful. I have travelled over about fifteen thousand miles of water and at last got to the desired haven.'[54]

Although these early impressions may have been consoling devices, both

Margaret Kilpatrick and Bessie Macready continued to praise the colony. Three years after her arrival, Bessie marvelled at 'a beautiful island, with a very fine dry climate, very well suited to my constitution. We have here nine months of splendid summer weather most of it a great deal warmer than the warmest summer day you experience at home & I believe my health has been greatly benefitted by the change.'[55] As for Canterbury's livestock, 'we have very fine fat cows quite as nice as the home ones. You see they were all brought from home at first. Then our sheep are quite as woolly and quite as nice to eat. I believe they are better, they get such nice grazing.'[56] From Auckland, Margaret told her family in Armagh that 'they people at home are onely sleeping. The master is not greater than his servant here. All work, and hard work.'[57] Her good friend Elizabeth Walker queried from Armagh in 1864, 'would you have had the same independence in this country and be happy'.[58] More than forty years later, Margaret acclaimed her physical surroundings: 'I have not told you of our lovely city with its electric trams, & its hot springs & its lovely scenery, & mount Eden, which is close to me 500 feet above the sea. A lovely view from the top.'[59] Fellow Armagh native, Brigid Dawson, likewise enthused from Wanganui in 1924 that 'we have more money that we can call our own than ever we had on our big farm in Cambly. I have money for everything I want, and plenty to eat and drink.'

While their letters contain strident affirmations of contentment and success, a few of the Irish women featured in this study encountered serious difficulties in New Zealand. For example, Catherine Colgan, upon learning of the financial hardship encountered by her daughter and son-in-law in Otago, offered words of reassurance: 'I would wrote to you before this time but I knew you had a little trouble, as we all have our troubles in this world. I trust you & your husband has got it all settled before this time. I was up in Mrs Gambles, 3 weeks ago & she was telling me all about it. She said to me not to be troubled about yous. She said you would be as well off as ever & I trust you will.'[60]

Some hardships arose from the isolation of many small communities in the colony. Ellen Piezzi, for instance, wailed, 'poor me I got no one neder [*neither*] of mey one [*my own*] or Julius nere me but black strangers to spake to god help me'.[61] Ellen's comments were inevitably influenced by the death of her husband. Likewise, Bessie Macready's musings that she was 'a poor weary pilgrim alone' and 'had many, very, very weary days and often longed for the old home & friends',[62] presumably resulted from just the presence of elderly aunts in the colony. Even though Ellen Piezzi and Bessie Macready had relatives in New Zealand colony, Agnes Lambert was without kin. This undeniably influenced her perspective, as did negative colonial conditions: 'I am very lonely. how I woud like some of you out here with me But I Dere say none of you woud come here. You are all to tighter and I am forgoten so I must live and Die alone. I sepose you are all married and Doing well. I am not Doing verry well at present as I am Doing nothing now as Bisonus is very Bad and I have lost a Deal of money.'[63]

That expressions of loneliness were influenced by factors other than the absence of kin is suggested by the construction of similar expressions in correspondence from Ireland. Sarah Reid, for instance, admitted to her sister-in-law Margaret Kilpatrick that 'if I feel lonely I got out for a run on the bicycle'.[64] Another acquaintance of Margaret Kilpatrick's confessed to a 'lonely separation from my children'.[65] The death of loved ones, however, was the most frequent cause of declarations of loneliness from both migrant and non-migrant correspondents. Reflecting on her husband's premature passing Ellen Piezzi sighed, 'i am very lonley after my poor Dead husband and i soo yong'.[66] Elderly widows also voiced their loss including Margaret Kilpatrick, who implored her brother Thomas to 'write again to your lonely sister'.[67] Margaret also learned of her mother-in-law's death in Armagh. As Mary Kilpatrick revealed, 'We feel very lonely since she was always with us and we are now alone'.[68] Likewise, the death of Kate Keane's father in Waterford provoked Kate to reflect, 'Mossie & I were very lonely indeed'.[69]

Reports of death and burials featured prominently in the exchange of letters between Ireland and New Zealand. For instance, in 1902 Mary Keane learned of her father's death in Waterford from her sister Kate: 'We could not be shown greater respect if we had 2 thousand a year for rich & poor flocked to our Fathers funeral. People marvelled at the funeral. It was about 2 miles in length'.[70] Likewise, Winifred Furlong in Auckland was told by her aunt in 1892 that her grandmother 'was buried very respectable & had a very large funeral.'[71] The informant, Mary Shanahan of Kilflyn, County Kerry, tearfully told her niece, 'Oh winnie I cannot really believe that she is gone from me that kind & generous Mother. Oh she was the good Mother to us.'[72] Mary Shanahan also outlined the consequences of her mother's death: 'I am as worn now & as gray from trouble. I had quite enough of trouble before [*erased:* now] this and now my Good Mother her death will kill me.'[73] Upon learning of her grandmother's death, Winifred Furlong sought a personal memento. In response, her aunt Mary Shanahan commiserated, 'I haven't got anything left after her to send you only her Photo'.[74] That same decade, from Lehinch in County Tipperary, Lizzie Strong told her cousin Daniel of his aunt's death: 'She has left a vacent place in the house that never can be filled. But hope God has called her to a happy home beyond the skys' where grief cant reach her more'.[75] For many correspondents, death held the promise of a reunion. As Catherine Colgan revealed, 'I send my love to all my dear children and I hope to meet you all if not in this earth I hope we will all meet in heaven where there will be no parting'.[76] Elizabeth McCleland also expressed the wish that 'we shall one day meet in Heaven where we never have to part'.[77]

Opportunities for earthly reunion were rare, but this did not prevent correspondents from contemplating a return to Ireland. As Agnes Lambert told her sister in 1890, 'I am think of caoming home soun as I can'.[78] Thirty-five years later, and a year before her death, she revealed, 'I would love to go back to Ireland now but of course it is impossible. I was leaving for Ireland some years ago – had my passage booked and luggage aboard but at the last minute had my things taken off and came ashore but now I wish I had gone after all.'[79]

Irish mothers were particularly keen to welcome their daughters home. From Foxford, County Mayo, Cecilia Coghlan revealed, 'It would give me the greatest pleasure to see you in the old house again . . . If you come you may be sure you will get a "Cead Miela Failtha"'.[80] Elizabeth McCleland also offered to welcome her daughter home: 'Dear daughter let me know if you are content in your mind or if you be fretting about being home for I would wish you to tell me your mind for I would have more contentment to know how it is with you and if you be not content let me know and we will assist in sending money to fetch you home.'[81] In 1847, following a stint with her husband in Chile, Ann McCleland eventually did return to County Londonderry, but the couple re-emigrated to New Zealand twelve years later.

II

Donald Akenson has argued that 'emigration was not a passive experience to be born stoically, but an active and energetic strategy for getting on in the world.'[82] The private letters featured in this study support the view that Irish female migrants to New Zealand were historical agents who exploited new opportunities for personal advancement that were not available at home. During the course of their transition to colonial life, these women made extensive use of Old World social ties and maintained close contacts with kinsfolk in Ireland. The persistence of busy expatriate networks in the colony appears to have ameliorated many of the disturbances that accompanied the act of migration. Although some female correspondents articulated feelings of sadness or remorse, these letters cannot be read in isolation as a sign of atomisation. Nor do they support the view that migration was a 'destabilising' experience marked by alienation and loneliness. A period of financial hardship or the death of loved ones, for example, were most frequently the basis for these expressions among migrants and non-migrants alike. The surviving correspondence shows that Irish women responded warmly to New Zealand life and constructed favourable reports to kin of work experiences, marriage prospects and domestic life. Despite the many hardships they encountered in the colony, female letter writers held fast to the 'prospect of a happier future'.

8
'Shaming The Shoneens'[1]
The Green Ray and The Maoriland Irish Society in Dunedin, 1916–22

Seán Brosnahan

Irish issues played an unusually divisive role in New Zealand society between 1916 and 1922. A number of local groups followed events in Ireland very closely in the wake of the Easter Rising of 1916 in Dublin. For some, the struggle for Irish independence represented a threat to the stability of Empire and showed that Irish Catholics were fundamentally unsuitable as citizens in New Zealand, the Great Britain of the South Pacific. For a second group, and in particular the 'lace curtain' Catholic bourgeoisie, the events in Ireland were a potential source of embarrassment. They threatened to undermine a carefully cultivated accommodation between Irish ethnic identity, centred around the Roman Catholic Church, and civic respectability, in the midst of a population with an Anglo-Protestant majority.[2] For yet another group, the rebellion and its aftermath generated hope for the realisation and fulfilment of the revolutionary dreams of generations of dead Irish patriots.

This chapter explores Irish issues in New Zealand politics from 1916 to 1922 through a fine-grained analysis of a small group of 'advanced Irish nationalists' in Dunedin. These men were few in number. They have left little evidence of their activities behind them. We know little of their motivations, the way they worked together, or their long-term achievements. Yet their very presence in the city merits attention because it suggests that there were genuine Irish 'Sinn Féiners' in New Zealand who claimed close connections with 'the martyrs of 1916'. Their radical credentials assured them of a special place in the spectrum of international revolutionary thought and philosophy that fuelled the development of left-wing politics in New Zealand throughout the period under consideration. It seems significant that this brand of militant Irish radicalism developed concurrently with the rise of the New Zealand Labour Party and waning Irish Catholic support for the Liberal Party cause. Yet existing scholarship has focused on the relationship between the New Zealand Catholic episcopacy and the Labour Party, and the 'Irish campaign' run by Labour leaders. It was among working-class Catholics, however, that Labour won its battle for the 'hearts and minds' of New Zealand after 1916.[3]

I

By 1916 there were clearly divergent approaches between the 'ornery Irish' of the lower orders and the 'better class' of Irish, with aspirations to respectability, who had heretofore taken the lead on public platforms when Irish issues arose in Dunedin. Their leadership was readily apparent. It was they who hosted the delegations of Irish nationalist politicians who toured the colonies at regular intervals from the 1870s.[4] Although the Irish campaign for constitutional change through Home Rule retained controversial overtones, it had become an increasingly acceptable cause. Moreover, it was something that gave the colonial Irish an opportunity to demonstrate their patriotic allegiance to Ireland and their commitment to the Empire. The Irish delegations closely followed this line in New Zealand, where they argued that 'Home Rule' within the Empire would strengthen the bonds between otherwise disparate entities.[5] It underpinned the enthusiastic reception and generous financial support accorded to John Dillon and Sir Thomas Esmonde in 1889, to Michael Davitt in 1895, and to Donovan, Redmond and Hazleton in 1911.

Less evident, however, is the level of support within New Zealand for the tradition of Irish nationalism based on the use of physical force. Historians have convincingly demonstrated that traditions of violent resistance to the Anglo-Protestant establishment were deep-seated in rural Ireland.[6] Memories, if not membership, of secret societies such as the Whiteboys or the Ribbonmen must have formed part of the intellectual baggage of many Irish men and women who emigrated to New Zealand. In addition, political prisoners formed a significant minority of Irish convicts transported to Australia. It is reasonable to surmise that some of these men crossed the Tasman Sea and brought their ideas and attitudes with them. We do know that the colonial government was forced to respond to violent demonstrations linked to Irish causes in 1869 and 1879.[7] Moreover, Fenian organisers such as Michael Cody, who toured the country in 1876, received generous financial support from local Irish communities.[8] Despite a lack of documentary evidence, we can assume that some of the New Zealand Irish would have celebrated the activities of O'Donovan Rossa's Fenian dynamiters in the 1870s, and perhaps even the terrorist killings carried out by the 'Irish Invincibles' during the following decade.[9]

The advocates of physical force, chiefly the Irish Republican Brotherhood (IRB) in Ireland and the Clan na Gael and Fenian Brotherhood in the United States, withered away in the 1890s.[10] At that stage the future seemed to lie with the constitutionalists. They recovered from the set-back of the Parnellite split to make real progress towards a transfer of power in Ireland. After 1900, however, there was a quiet resurgence in the IRB. It came as a youthful cohort of revolutionaries drew on the cultural energies unleashed in Ireland by the Gaelic revival and infiltrated two key organisations: the Gaelic Athletic Association and the Gaelic League. Hard-nosed ideologues like Bulmer Hobson and Dennis McCullough developed cells of committed young Republicans in Ulster. Meanwhile, James Connolly was busy fostering a revolutionary spirit among Dublin socialists, and Patrick Pearse developed a mystical vision of a resurgent Gaelic and Catholic Ireland. From this volatile mix of disparate factions and contradictory philosophies grew the somewhat odd combination of forces that fuelled the Easter Rising in 1916. By this time, a handful of Irish revolutionaries had found their way to the colonies, where they played a critical role in forging support for the rebels.[11]

The events of 1916 reverberated around Irish communities in New Zealand. The immediate colonial response of dismay and repudiation mirrored popular reaction in Ireland itself. The Rising was an act of desperation by a tiny minority within the secret and little-known Irish Republican Brotherhood (in whose name a declaration of independence was made). It had such poor organisation and coordination that it was largely confined to central Dublin. There was no chance of military success. Even this sad reality was seized on with enthusiasm by Patrick Pearse, the visionary poet who was the notional leader of the rebellion. He believed that freedom for Ireland would come only through a redemptive blood sacrifice by its patriots. He offered himself up to the altar of martyrdom. The result was the military fiasco foreseen by wiser minds within the IRB, and one more disastrous episode in a long list of failed Irish uprisings.

Although the rebellion was farcical, its ramifications were far more serious in the context of the European war. The IRB had long held, as a basic principle, that Irish opportunity would come from English difficulty.[12] From this perspective, British military engagement was perceived as an ideal opportunity to carry out a successful uprising. On previous occasions, however, rational analysis had weighed against revolution. As well, a secondary principle, that the timing of a rebellion would be decided by the Irish people themselves, served to postpone revolutionary action.[13] In 1916, the Irish public were solidly behind the war effort against Germany. Some 150,000 Irish men had enlisted in the British Army.[14] In addition, constitutionalism gained an upper hand when John Redmond's Irish Parliamentary Party negotiated a Home Rule Bill into British law in 1914. The legislation was to come into force when the hostilities in Europe ended and depended on Ireland's commitment to the war effort.

New Zealand's Irish leaders sat squarely behind Redmond. They were enthusiastic about the prospect of Home Rule after the war. Moreover, they were committed to the war effort for reasons of their own. They saw the war as an unprecedented opportunity to build a more cohesive society. Patriotism would bring an end to the division wrought by sectarian animosities over issues such as the Bible-in-Schools controversy and unify the nation. In short, Irish Catholics would benefit by suppressing their distinctive identity in the interests of national unity under the banner of the Empire. Henry Cleary, the Bishop of Auckland, was the most eminent supporter of an integrationist line. His commitment to the war effort was deep-rooted and personal. He became a military chaplain in 1916 and served with distinction in Flanders. The Catholic weekly, The *New Zealand Tablet*, was also an enthusiastic advocate for this position. The paper's columns were full of war news between 1915-16 and emphasised Ireland's contribution to the point of absurdity. Meanwhile, Catholic families offered up their sons and joined in the patriotic fervour as much as any other group in New Zealand society.

The Easter Rising of 1916 deeply embarrassed local Irish communities, but later events would challenge the 'integrationist' line of their leaders. Initial reaction was swift. A hastily assembled meeting 'fully representative of the Irish in Dunedin' telegraphed its support to John Redmond and to Herbert Asquith, the British Prime Minister.[15] Up and down the country, others adopted a similar line. *New Zealand Tablet* editorials railed against 'The Made-in-Germany Rebellion'. Consolation was found in the small scale of the rebellion and depictions of its leaders as a bunch of 'nobodies' who were unrepresentative of Irish opinion.[16] Thus far, the New Zealand Irish were in step with their host society and the majority viewpoint within Ireland itself. The repressive actions of the British government, however, reversed these perspectives and local Irish opinion began to diverge sharply from the views of the wider community.

In reality, Pearse's punt on the glory of martyrdom had worked. Britain overreacted to the tiny rebellion in Dublin and adopted a heavy-handed response that was unnecessarily punitive. Rebel leaders were executed. There was no mercy. The British-born syndicalist leader, James Connolly, co-opted to the IRB's military council in 1916, was shot in a chair, still badly wounded from the fighting. Seventeen hundred Sinn Féin suspects were rounded up and deported to prison camps in England and Wales. A state of military emergency was declared in Dublin, and an occupation force arrived to 'pacify' the city. It behaved in ways that changed the public mood.[17] As martyrs, the rebels acquired a symbolic potency that could only be strengthened by British repression. Moreover, the imprisoned Sinn Féiners had a superb opportunity to develop their organisation by transforming a motley crew of detainees into cadres of committed members, schooled in the Republican message and in the ways of effective political action. They were released six months later, and returned to Ireland to spread the word.

Irish communities in New Zealand kept a close watch on these developments. Unlike most other groups in colonial society, they were not dependent on the British cable news service.[18] Friends and relatives in Ireland provided an alternative source of information. Another was the Catholic news agencies from which the *New Zealand Tablet* drew a steady stream of detailed reports. One reference point, with an impeccable reputation, was the Marist priest Father

James Watters. Formerly the founding head of St Patrick's College in Wellington, Watters was killed at his school in Dublin by British troops. His death outraged New Zealand's Catholic population and exposed them directly to the severity of Britain's response to the uprising. Further stories, such as the murder of Francis Sheehy Skeffington, served to confirm the suspicion that the British authorities were going too far.[19] There was growing sympathy for the 'innocent victims' of the Easter Rising. This was made public when the Irish Relief Fund was launched in September.[20] Wellington's Hibernian Society, meeting in October, applauded P. J. O'Regan's refusal 'to censure those who gave their lives'.[21] In November, the Catholic Bishop of Christchurch, Matthew Brodie, publicly stated that the 'misgovernment of Dublin Castle' was largely responsible for the rebellion. By this time, Catholic opinion was falling out of step with the general feeling in New Zealand society.

Expressions of support for the Irish rebels became more dangerous when casualty lists grew longer and patriotism intensified. Old sectarian animosities were rekindled in New Zealand and Catholics became a prime target for accusations of disloyalty. Catholic outrage at the brutality of Britain's military response to the rebellion only made matters worse. In mid-1916, a Conscription Bill was introduced into the New Zealand Parliament as the number of volunteers trailed behind the demand for reinforcements. Opposition to conscription drew together a loose alliance of pacifists, socialists and Christians. Labour groups, hitherto plagued by factionalism, found some unity of purpose in the debate over conscription.[22] It was here, on the margins of accepted opinion, that Labour and the Irish found each other. Labour advocacy of the Irish cause, and opposition to conscription, built a bridgehead into the Catholic electorate vote. Once there, Labour was able to broaden its support base by appealing to the working-class concerns of Irish Catholic ethnics. Just as the rise of Labour gave expression to the struggle for political influence by Catholics in New Zealand society, the efforts of Irish Republicans represented a new element seeking to exert influence within the Irish ethnic community.

II

Irish Republicans offered an alternative view of Irish affairs at the very moment that the integrationist line began to unravel. On 5 August 1916, a new organisation held its inaugural meeting in Dunedin. Its promoters described themselves as 'a few clear-thinking young Irish men and women' who wanted to differentiate themselves from the 'self-righteous crawling poltroons' who had sent the cablegrams of support to Redmond and Asquith in May.[23] At first, 'the Irish Club' functioned as a social gathering where Irish musical entertainment and dancing formed a central focus. The organisers' description of club meetings as a 'real Irish Ireland night' was justified by the choice of songs and a congregational rendition of 'God Save Ireland'.[24] Behind the scenes, however, a sharper edge was being honed. The Dunedin Irish Club was forging links with committed Irish patriots around the country and a new national organisation was announced in 1917. Similar groupings formed in Gisborne, Napier, Hastings and Wellington. Together they became the Maoriland Irish National Association, soon shortened to the Maoriland Irish Society (MIS). The Dunedin club was the 'Robert Emmet branch' and its social programme continued throughout 1917. Nonetheless, teaching gained in importance, with lectures on Irish history and the songs of rebellion. In addition, there were indications of a more direct, hardcore involvement in the Irish struggle with close links between club members and 'brethren at Home and in America'.[25] News from other centres was also encouraging. By June, Wellington's 'Thomas Davis branch' was holding fortnightly social gatherings. MIS members in Napier were supporting a 'gallant comrade', Thomas Spillane, during a conscription appeal, and a new branch had been formed at Riversdale in rural Southland.

An intriguing aspect of this new organisation was not who was in it, but rather, who was not. Of all the 'leading' Irishmen who had appeared on the platforms to welcome Irish delegations of earlier years, only Frank Armstrong, a middle-aged Protestant dentist, had an association with the new movement.[26] In Dunedin, priests never appeared at Club gatherings. Their absence signaled a *de facto* condemnation by the established Irish Catholic community. Also absent were Dunedin's 'lace curtain Catholics', the middle-class social achievers whose names appeared on all the various committees for the Hibernians, for the Catholic Federation, for St Patrick's Day concerts and the like.[27] They would not have felt welcome. In 1917, the MIS President, John T. Sullivan,[28] declared that while there were no constraints on membership, 'the Shoneen Irish, the anti-Irish and the Westminster type of Irish would be out of place'.[29] He went on to put it even more bluntly: 'This club is not restricted to professional ladies and gentlemen – indeed we are not too eager whether they join us or not.'[30] These statements tell us something important about the nature of the Dunedin Irish Club. It presented a low-key challenge to an existing leadership cadre in Irish Dunedin comprising Catholic clergy and their 'shoneen' favourites among the laity. But without any surviving first-hand accounts of the club's activities, it is difficult to carry this analysis any further. Like similar groups in Australia, the majority of its members were undoubtedly attracted by the opportunity for social interaction.[31] The vicarious association with a stirring tradition of Irish patriotism was no more than an added interest. The real action was elsewhere.

In the public arena, a new monthly journal lay at the cutting edge of Irish political activity in Dunedin. The *Green Ray* was first published in 1916, independent of the Dunedin Irish Club, but with a similar genesis. It proclaimed itself to be 'the only truly Irish newspaper South of the Line, and the only Republican journal in Australasia'.[32] The editorial line was strong and clear:

against Redmond and the Irish Parliamentary Party; for Sinn Féin and the rebels of 1916. It was, unsurprisingly, opposed to conscription. The efforts of conscientious objectors to evade the authorities were reported with approbation. It professed itself 'purely non-sectarian but intensely Irish National', and strongly disavowed any connection with any other paper, including the *New Zealand Tablet*, which it depicted as the 'slave of the Irish Parliamentary Party'. The journal's main target was less the British or New Zealand governments than the 'wishy-washy, hand-rubbing, knee-bending, beggin-your-pardon Irishmen – creatures termed in old Ireland as the shoneen class'.[33] The *Green Ray's* mission was the shaming of the 'shoneens' and the promotion of Sinn Féin. It pushed the same fusion of Gaelic cultural revival and nationalist politics that had transformed the nationalist movement in Ireland in the decade before 1916. It was a transformation that produced the 'Irish Irelander'. An earlier generation of colonial Irish leadership had not kept pace with these developments. When local support for its champion, the Irish Parliamentary Party, began to collapse, these men were left without a constituency. A small group of emigré Irish republicans, with hard-line credentials as members of the nationalist movement, charged into the breach. The *Green Ray* was born.

An itinerant Irish journalist, Thomas Padraic Cummins, edited the paper. Nothing is known of his early life, but before coming to New Zealand he had been a journalist, teacher and soldier in the United States, Mexico, Argentina and Uruguay.[34] He had mixed with some of the luminaries of radical Irish republicanism, and claimed personal acquaintanceship with both Patrick Pearse and Thomas McDonagh. By the time these former comrades had embarked on the disastrous Easter Rising in Dublin in 1916, Cummins was already in Dunedin. There he worked as a correspondent for the *Truth* newspaper. Tall, dark, and a poet, Cummins was the very archetype of the romantic revolutionary. He was also married with three children. This afforded him a degree of protection from the threat of conscription. It meant he could play a leading role within the *Green Ray* operation, and within the MIS.

The journal's Irish language specialist, John Tohill (Seaghan O'Thuatail), was forced to work 'underground' in Dunedin to avoid conscription. Born in County Tyrone, he had attended boarding school in Belfast before emigrating to Napier with his parents and nine siblings in 1909. His father, John snr, was a leading light in the Napier branch of the MIS. Back in Ireland, the family had had a long association with secret societies such as the Ribbonmen, and more latterly the IRB.[35] In one column O'Thuatail recalled that

> In the winter of 1906 I attended a lecture by Mr Thomas O'Donnell MP, before the Young Ireland Branch of the United Irish League, Belfast, on Thomas Davis ... [who became a] ... personal friend from then on and ... together [we] helped found the 'Dungannon Club' some of whose members have since paid the penalty of death, or are in prison.[36]

Elsewhere he claimed that he knew Pearse, Plunkett, McDonagh and MacBride 'intimately but only met [Thomas Clarke] once'.[37] This, if true, is a pedigree without peer in the context of early twentieth century radical Irish nationalism. It suggests, too, that the MIS may have been a front for IRB activity.[38]

The shadowy presence of James Bradley is yet another indication of an IRB connection in Dunedin. Although he is mentioned in neither the *Green Ray*, nor in MIS reports, one historian has credited Bradley with the idea that launched the journal.[39] We do know that Bradley was from the same district in Ireland as the Tohills, and that the two families were close.[40] Moreover, he was reputed to have been very active in militant republican circles in Ireland, even serving for a time on the Supreme Council of the IRB.[41] James Bradley and his brother Bernard (Ben) sailed to Dunedin before the war, following an uncle who had emigrated earlier. The two brothers were working land at Ferndale, near Mataura, when the National Register was compiled in late 1915. Once conscription came into force, however, they went underground. James spent time in the Dunedin suburb of Mornington before hiding at the Sawyers Bay property of an Antrim-born Anglican, Nat Gordon. He then left for Australia as a stowaway, and remained there for several years.[42] His brother was less fortunate. In October 1917, a warrant was issued for his arrest in Mataura. The following August, he tried to escape from the port of Wellington with five other Irish objectors. They were caught and sentenced to three months imprisonment for attempting to leave New Zealand without a permit. In December, after their release, Ben Bradley was court-martialled for 'desertion' from the Expeditionary Force. He was sentenced to two years in prison.[43]

A Fenian pedigree could also explain the appearance of a branch of the MIS at Riversdale in mid-1917. This was largely the work of one extended family, the Codys, who were among the most defiant opponents of conscription in New Zealand during the First World War. The local patriarchs of the clan were two Galway-born brothers, Patrick and Laurence Cody, who had arrived in New Zealand aboard the *Dilharee* in 1875.[44] They settled at Riversdale and Heddon Bush respectively. Each headed a large family. By 1916, five of Patrick's sons and four of Laurence's were eligible for military service. All were determined that they would not serve the British Crown. Patrick's eldest son, Daniel, left New Zealand for South America early in the war. Laurence's sons, Walter and Thomas, fled the country after the introduction of conscription. The others went 'underground' when they were called up. Between 1917 and 1918, warrants were issued for the arrest of Luke, Lawrence, Michael, George, Walter and Patrick Cody (President of the Riversdale branch of the MIS).[45] Lawrence and Michael went north under assumed names. Both were captured later on and forced to serve time. Patrick and John, who had been granted exemptions to run the family farms, were called up in place of the brothers who had disappeared. When they refused they were tried at a Trentham military court in August 1917.

They each served eight months of their eleven-month sentences.[46] Walter escaped overseas, while George and Luke evaded the police until the cancellation of the warrants for their arrest in 1920.[47]

Why was this one family so defiantly opposed to service to the Crown? Unlike the pacifist objector Archibald Baxter, the Codys left no memoirs.[48] The only contemporary record of their testimony lies in a *Green Ray* report on the August 1917 trial of Patrick and John Cody. Patrick told the Military Court that 'the Sinn Féin cause was his, and as a loyal Sinn Féiner he could swear allegiance to only one cause'.[49] This comment, however, does not explain the depth of the Cody family's 'Fenian' commitment. One possible explanation is that the Southland family was connected in some way to Michael Cody, the 'head centre' of the New South Wales Fenians in the 1870s. Michael Cody had come from the most violent wing of the Fenian movement. He had been the 'centre' of a Fenian circle in Callan, County Kilkenny. In 1865, he was in hiding with the Fenian leader John Devoy, who later described him as 'a man of great determination ... [with] a weakness for punching policemen'.[50] When arrested the following year, Cody put up a fierce struggle and escaped once from custody. Sentenced to twenty years imprisonment, he was transported to Western Australia in 1867 with a party of sixty-two Fenian convicts.

Michael Cody was conditionally pardoned and released from jail in 1871. After spending time on various New South Wales goldfields, he settled in Sydney.[51] With some other ex-convicts, he immediately set about establishing a Fenian 'organisation' on the goldfields of New South Wales, Queensland and the South Island of New Zealand. These recruitment and fundraising efforts were so impressive that Australasia was allotted one seat in the new seven-member Revolutionary Directory established in 1877 by the United Brotherhood, a secret revolutionary wing of the American Clan na Gael.[52] Their finest hour came with their support for the United Brotherhood's expedition to Western Australia in 1876. Six of the still captive 1867 convicts were rescued and sent to freedom in America on the whaler *Catalpa*. Michael Cody played a central role in these events. He had toured New Zealand on a fundraising mission in early 1876, but his subsequent fate is unknown.[53]

In New Zealand, the Cody brothers had arrived from Galway at the beginning of 1875. Available records show no evidence of any family relationship between them and Michael Cody, who is recorded in his convict record as Dublin-born. Nevertheless, when the Codys established the Riversdale branch of the MIS in 1917 they named it the 'John Boyle O'Reilly' branch, unlike the other branches who had chosen names to honour the Protestant Irish rebels of 1798 or 1848. Instead they chose to honour the most famous of the 1867 Fenians transported to Western Australia, and a man who was both a colleague and intimate of Michael Cody.[54]

Fenians of old or no, the Codys were at the centre of New Zealand Irish opposition to the war effort. Given the reputed IRB connections of the Tohills and the Bradleys, and the nationalist pedigree of Thomas Cummins, there were plenty to generate Fenian 'smoke' in Dunedin. If there was also Fenian 'fire', in the form of an IRB sworn circle, this cannot be confirmed from the surviving evidence. One might well ask, however, what such an organisation would have concerned itself with in the context of the New Zealand of 1916-20. One possible answer lies in the help given to Irish conscientious objectors, to evade the authorities and avoid conscription. There were many such men among the officially recorded 2045 defaulters.[56] Together with the pacifists and the socialists, they made up the largest contingent of 'defiant' objectors to military service. If caught and still 'defiant' these men could expect no leniency from the authorities.[57] Evasion was a serious business. Many left their local district and headed for the opposite end of the country. Tim Brosnan, for example, left Owhango in the central North Island as soon as he was called up in January 1917. He headed south and was eventually arrested in Winton at the end of August.[58] Michael and Lawrence Cody fled in the other direction, and were, in turn, arrested at Wanganui and Patutahi (near Gisborne). On the other hand, Jim Bradley chose to lay low in the Dunedin suburb of Mornington, and then at Sawyers Bay. A sympathetic network of friends and relations was vital. Here the Irish fugitives may have had an advantage as the earlier patriotism of Catholic New Zealand was confronted by growing sectarian animosity.[59]

The tale of Cricklewood farmer Gerald O'Connor's midnight flight – on a horse with muffled hooves – illustrates this kind of support within the South Canterbury Irish community:

> Here and there other horsemen joined them. Below Albury an elderly farmer on a black horse came out of the shadows and wished them well and God speed and almost frightened them to death ... by three o'clock they were in Temuka, waiting in a side street for a goods train which passed through at 4 a.m ... From there they caught a train to the West Coast and disappeared into the bush for the duration. The horses that were ridden were planted all over Temuka in the yards of sympathisers or relatives and left to be picked up innocently at some future time.[60]

There is also evidence of a more organised system of assistance to fugitives. Gerald Griffin told a researcher in the mid-1960s that John Troy, secretary of the Wellington branch of the MIS, had organised an 'underground railway'[61] to smuggle objectors out of the country. When travel restrictions were imposed in August 1916, this route became dependent on the co-operation of seamen willing to conceal and look after the stowaways. The exploits of successful evaders, like Jim Bradley, support this contention, as does the capture of Ben Bradley's party of five. A police investigation in 1917 implicates the Dunedin Irish nationalists in such an 'underground railway'. A concerned citizen, H. Butcher, wrote to the military authorities to report that one Bert Ryan was willing to smuggle Thomas McCracken out of the country, and that he had boasted that marine firemen had already helped with the escapes of several other men. A figure of £10 was cited as the cost of the operation. The police investigated the allegation, but when questioned Thomas McCracken claimed that Ryan had simply told him of the escapes and said he was glad of it. The police concluded that Butcher had exaggerated. They also noted that Ryan was 'the alleged editor of the Catholic *Green Ray*'. The chief detective asked for a copy. It was the first time the police had shown any interest in the paper.

Ryan was undoubtedly lucky to escape further investigation, given his close association with the core group of Irish nationalists in Dunedin. Unlike Cummins, Tohill and the Bradleys, however, Albert James Ryan was a New Zealander, born at Waitahuna in 1884 to Irish migrants. Waitahuna had a high proportion of Irish settlers. Throughout Ryan's youth their priest was Monsignor Patrick O'Leary, the most fervently nationalist Irish priest in Otago. When war broke out in 1914, Bert Ryan was living in Dunedin and working as a commercial traveller. He belonged to the MIS from the outset. Ryan became its chief organiser in 1917, and the manager (not editor) of the *Green Ray*. His close shave with the local detectives brought unwelcome attention to the journal, which was sailing close to the line of permissible publishing. From mid-1917 the journal was monitored by the Dunedin police and only its limited availability saved it from official censure.[61] For despite all its righteous thunder, the *Green Ray* was no real threat to the New Zealand establishment. It had a limited circulation and was largely preaching to the converted. Yet the journal gained a significance out of all proportion to its actual readership because of changes in the mood of New Zealand's Catholic Irish population. The 'shoneens' were indeed being shamed.

III

The 'shaming of the shoneens' was not the work of the *Green Ray* alone. In mid-1917, a Wexford-born priest, Father James Kelly, arrived in Dunedin to take over as editor of the *New Zealand Tablet*. The Catholic weekly had begun to alienate readers with its jingoistic war reporting and Kelly was employed to turn the paper around.[62] This mandate became a mission for the ardent Sinn Féin supporter, who sought not only to realign the war reporting, but to 'convert' New Zealand Catholics to the Sinn Féin cause. 'The Sinn Féiners', he wrote in his first Easter editorial, 'died like men, bearing the punishment for the faults of all'. It was an extravagant claim that echoes with Isaiah's prophecy about the sufferings of Christ.[63] Nor was Kelly afraid to attack the enemies of Ireland, and he took a broad view of who these might be. His outspoken comments inflamed sectarian ill-feeling around the country.

In 1917 the possibility that Roman Catholic clergy might be liable for military service under the conscription regulations provoked Catholic anger more effectively than Irish affairs could ever do. Protestant extremists seized on the issue to push their own rabid anti-Catholicism. An explosive situation was brewing and Kelly seemed to take delight in stirring the pot. Irish readers thrilled to the new editorial approach that one prominent Auckland Irishman described as 'taking off the gloves'.[64] The extremes of Kelly's language went far beyond the degree of dissent permitted under New Zealand's war regulations. Outside the Catholic community, the public reacted with outrage. Nonetheless, the government was reluctant to target the official Catholic newspaper, given the tense sectarian situation then prevailing in the country. The *Green Ray* provided a safer target and was shut down in June 1918.[65]

The offending issue (May 1918) commemorated the Easter rebellion, but it was no different from earlier editions in either sentiments or language. Yet its lead article, 'To the Memory of the Dead', was seized upon as an incitement to sedition. A comparative examination of the *New Zealand Tablet* identifies articles with similar phrases and subject matter in every issue. The decision to prosecute the more insignificant publication was clearly political.

At the request of the Minister of Justice, the *Green Ray* had been under police surveillance for seditious comment since March.[66] The *New Zealand Tablet* was added to the surveillance list in June, and copies of both journals were sent on to Wellington. The decision to suppress the *Green Ray* was taken by the Solicitor General. Dunedin detectives descended on the *Green Ray* office on 8 July. Fortunately, the 'fugitive' John Tohill was not present when the police arrived. Thomas Cummins, who was there, admitted that he had written the article in question, while Bert Ryan admitted that he was the manager for the journal. A fortnight later the pair were tried at the Dunedin Police Court and convicted for the publication of a seditious utterance.[67] The judge declared that it 'seemed to him that on every page [of the *Green Ray*] there was a seditious utterance.'[68] He decided to make an example of the men. They were sentenced to eleven months, with hard labour.

At the time, politicians and Protestant extremists insisted that the *Green Ray* was published from the *New Zealand Tablet* offices – to the chagrin of its writers.[69] Much has been made of that association, and particularly so in relation to the Catholic elements of the *Green Ray*. Subsequent historians have viewed the two publications as 'Catholic papers'.[70] While it is true that most of the *Green Ray* writers were from a Catholic background, none were influential in church affairs. Moreover, the newspaper repeatedly attacked the New Zealand Catholic clergy for their lack of leadership on Irish issues. Father Kelly and Thomas Cummins may have had surreptitious meetings at the Crown Hotel,[71] but the *Green Ray* had set its course before Kelly arrived in Dunedin. It was he who chose to follow a similar direction on Irish issues and in his later promotion of socialism. It was most definitely the *Green Ray* that led the way toward Labour. Some of the non-Catholic contributors exemplify the wartime association of Irish issues and socialist politics. Arthur McCarthy, a leading Dunedin socialist, was one such columnist. He wrote a regular column, entitled 'The Workers Realm'.[72] Similarly, Mark Silverstone, a Polish-born Jew and perhaps Dunedin's most radical socialist, supplied articles on international events written from a socialist perspective under his established literary nom-de-plume, 'Diplomaticus'.

The socialist link grew stronger in the wake of Cummins and Ryan's imprisonment. Meanwhile, the *New Zealand Tablet* maintained a studious silence over their case. Discretion was perhaps the better part of valour under these circumstances. The Dunedin branch of the MIS also proved to be weak-hearted. With its hard-core Irish nationalists in prison or 'on the lam', the Club's second-tier leaders were indecisive. Instead of exploiting the opportunity to publicise the cause by appealing the case, they fell back on the traditional Irish fount of wisdom and turned to Father James Coffey for guidance. As Bishop Verdon was ill, he was then the *de facto* head of the church in Dunedin. Father Coffey's advice, unsurprisingly, was to avoid a public 'stoush'. Instead he helped with the organisation of a petition to the Minister of Justice, in which they not only attributed Cummins' seditious article to a moment of 'excessive zeal for the cause of Home Rule for Ireland', but also sought a remission of his sentence in return for a 'bond of good behaviour'.[73] Cummins, in jail, was furious, but he and Ryan did not help matters by dithering over the choice between an appeal and the petition. Fortunately, harder heads in the Wellington MIS stepped into the breach. They employed a well-disposed Napier lawyer, B.J. Dolan, to take over the case, and started a fund to support the prisoners while they served their sentence. Despite repeated requests, the *New Zealand Tablet* failed to take the lead in the advocacy for this appeal. Instead it was the Labour Party weekly, the *Maoriland Worker*, which promoted the fund and published the lists of subscribers between August and December 1918.[74] The sum raised was £440.

The Labour Party leader, and *Maoriland Worker* editor, Harry Holland had been a Sinn Féin advocate since 1916. While he had no Irish connections himself, he had become an expert in Irish history, and wrote and lectured widely on the issue through 1917 and 1918. From May 1918, as a Member of Parliament, he was one of the imprisoned Sinn Féiners' few 'friends in high places'. He wrote regularly to them, and he visited them in the prison at Templeton. Cummins and Ryan were released from jail in April 1919, having served a longer sentence than either the Sinn Féiners interned in Britain in 1916 or the Sydney IRB circle imprisoned in June 1918. They returned to Dunedin and received a rapturous reception from Irish Club members, still staunch in their Irish convictions but paying tribute to the 'Socialists' who had been 'so kind to them'.[75]

By then the war had ended. Although conscription was a dead issue, sectarian sensitivities and Irish issues were becoming increasingly divisive in New Zealand. British propaganda had characterised the war in Europe as a crusade for the 'rights of small nations'. Around the world Ireland's supporters now looked to the post-war settlement as a test of Britain's good faith. The principle of 'self determination' remained the focus of international attention throughout 1919, but Britain once again failed to deliver in Ireland.

Meanwhile, Sinn Féin had grown into a truly national movement (but for Ulster) and won a landslide victory at the polls in December 1918. In 1919 the group began to assert itself as the *de facto* government of a Republic of Ireland, with a parliament – Dáil Éireann – that met in Dublin, and with Eamon de Valera as President. In January Sinn Féin's military arm, the Irish Republican Army, strengthened by the experienced Irish veterans who had returned from the war in France, began the police assassinations. This brought a new struggle in which public opinion, intimidation and guerilla tactics would all play their part. Once more, the British reaction was heavy-handed. It included the deployment of a harsh and repressive mercenary force. The 'Black and Tans' acquired their name from the colour of their uniforms. Their name was soon synonymous with outrageous deeds. By 1920 Ireland was in a state of open warfare.

Once again, the Irish in New Zealand found themselves at odds with the wider community. British sources were unchallenged in their dominance of the news services to the colony. On the other side, Sinn Féin literature was proscribed, and the mere possession of this material was sufficient to bring conviction for sedition. 'Loyal' and 'Protestant' New Zealand was at best primly disapproving, and at worst vehemently opposed to the developments in Ireland. One *Otago Daily Times* correspondent spoke for many when declaring that '[t]here is no room in New Zealand for disloyalists'. Some 200,000 people joined the Protestant Political Association to resist what they perceived as a serious Catholic threat to the Anglo-Protestant establishment in New Zealand. The Catholic Irish, however, had been won to the Sinn Féin cause. These were not just the 'ornery Irish', or the emigré Republicans and their socialist friends. They were mainstream Catholics. They included not only the clergy, but also the 'lace curtain' shoneens. Between 1918 and 1921 there was a remarkable convergence of opinion between these different strands of society. They inclined increasingly to points of view advocated, since 1916, by the radicals. Cummins and Ryan now stood alongside the clergy on public platforms, while 'God Save Ireland' replaced 'God Save the King' at the St Patrick's Day celebrations in Dunedin.

IV

The politicisation of the Catholic community is usually associated with the Irish Self-Determination Leagues that were established by its traditional 'lace curtain' leadership in every New Zealand centre during 1919.[76] Yet the personal diaries of a Dunedin Irish Catholic businessman, Thomas J. Hussey, cast new light on this process. In many ways, Hussey was an archetypal 'lace curtain' Catholic.

The son of Irish immigrants, he gained honours in the Catholic school system and secured a position in an old established Dunedin mercantile firm. He was a talented musician, a keen golfer, and an enthusiastic territorial soldier. He was also a Hibernian, a choir member at St Joseph's Cathedral, an active member of the St Vincent de Paul Society and a member of the Catholic Federation committee. Hussey's name appears in almost every local *ad hoc* Catholic committee established to organise a fundraising bazaar, a jubilee or a special celebration. More often than not, Hussey acted as the Secretary or Treasurer. It was the same with the golf club committee, the Royal Dunedin Male Choir and the Liedertafel. He was a confidante of the Bishops, a friend to the priests, brothers and nuns, a key director on the board of the *New Zealand Tablet* and a neighbour of the prominent Catholic lawyer J. B. Callan. In short, Hussey was not only the very model of the devout Catholic, but also a loyal and valued member of civic society and generally able to reconcile these two dimensions of life.

The Hussey diaries present an insider's view of Dunedin's Catholic society throughout the period. Moreover, Hussey's book-keeping role at the *New Zealand Tablet* gave him a unique view of the challenges faced before and after Kelly's editorship. The diaries show that the circulation of the paper was falling by mid-1916 because of its coverage of Irish affairs. The arrival of Father Kelly in early 1917 began to turn the fortunes of the paper.

The timing of Kelly's editorship coincided with a furore over the possible conscription of Catholic clergy and religious representatives – '*Brother Doody ordered into camp at Wellington This means trouble*' *[27 July]*. The Catholic community rallied behind the feisty new editor. By October Hussey was reporting a record monthly subscription: '*New Zealand Tablet subs coming in strong.*' *[10 October]*. The next month Kelly published his infamous description of Queen Victoria as 'a certain fat old German woman'.[77] There was a corresponding '*Great howdoyoudo*' *[16 November]* in Dunedin. Kelly spent the evening of 25 November at the Husseys' discussing the response. The Presbyterian Synod declared '*that Roman Catholicism is the greatest menace to the Empire in existence*' *[29 November]*. Kelly's enemies were not only outside the Catholic fold. In December Hussey wrote: '*Dr Cleary on warpath Bishop Brodie in Dunedin Will see Dr Cleary does not do for Dr Kelly if I can help it.*' *[6 December]* Kelly survived this episcopal onslaught, but a week later the directors of the *New Zealand Tablet* responded directly. They struck down the proud assertion carried on the paper's masthead since 1872: 'Sole Organ of Catholic Opinion'.

Hussey noted the inaugural meeting of the new Irish Society in Dunedin in August 1916, but he was not a participant. By late 1917, however, he was complaining that the Christian Brothers end of year break-up was not up to standard; there were no Irish items. By January 1918 he was reading Leckie's *History of Ireland* and had spent an evening at Jack Sullivan's. He followed political developments in Ireland very closely as Sinn Féin began to take the fight to the British. Meanwhile, the *New Zealand Tablet* was '*doing famously*' *[25 April 1918]*. A bitter war of words raged between the *New Zealand Tablet* and the *Otago Daily Times*. The suppression of the *Green Ray* in July gave Hussey pause for thought. It was unfortunate that he wrote those thoughts into his diary in code, something he had never used elsewhere. Kelly's increasingly extravagant statements on Irish affairs were of growing concern to the *New Zealand Tablet* Board. By January 1919 things were simply '*Too hot and we will have to define our position [9 January 1919]*'. Kelly resisted all requests for moderation. He pressed ahead with his vigorous advocacy of Sinn Féin and his typical lambasting of his opponents. In Ireland, the guerilla war continued to build and anarchy was increasingly the order of the day. Hussey noted these developments with great concern.

In December 1920 James Whyte, the new Bishop, finally arrived in Dunedin. He succeeded Bishop Verdon, who had died during the 1918 Influenza Epidemic. Whyte, born in County Kilkenny, had spent most of his life as a priest in Sydney. His patronage gave life to the Irish Society, which had reformed as a 'Literary, Musical and Social Society' in July. This time the society had the clerical support which had not been offered to its earlier manifestation. During the 1920s, its meetings always included a lecture from one of the city's priests.

The city's lay leaders were drawn from among South Dunedin's young colonial-born Irish men. Edmund Nolan and Frank Mullin played important roles, with Bert Ryan and Thomas Cummins in the background. John Robinson, another South Dunedin Catholic with strong Labour connections, tackled the Protestant Political Association and other antagonists in a stream of letters to the papers and a series of public lectures on Ireland.[78] The 1921 St Patrick's Day celebrations, organised by the Irish Society, afforded the new Bishop an opportunity on which to raise the flag for Ireland. His comments on Sinn Féin were direct and supportive. He ended by quoting the British Labour Commission: 'the name of England stinks in the nostrils of the whole world', because of the Black and Tan reprisals.[79]

Public advocacy for Sinn Féin had its price. The general public held a quite different view of Irish affairs, and of Sinn Féin. Hussey's diary records the 'loyalist' reaction to these public assertions of Catholicism: '*a lot of recrimination in papers re St Patrick's day celebration*' *[20 March]*. As a result, municipal elections the following month were marked by the '*Great bitterness being shown towards Catholic candidates*' *[15 April]*. One Catholic candidate, Mrs Margaret Jackson, was successful in a minor poll for the Charitable Aid Board but '*Brown's* [John A. Brown, the other Catholic candidate] *Labour members did badly Religious element very strong*' *[28 April]*. May 1921 brought the establishment of the Self-Determination League in Dunedin. Hussey was elected President. Two nights earlier, he had been host to the touring Sinn Féin representative,

Miss Katherine Hughes, during an evening of '*very interesting discussion on Determination*' *[6 May]*. The League proved an uneasy coalition. There were some '*very steamy*' *[21 June]* meetings, but by mid-1921 John Callan, the leading Catholic lawyer, and Dr Milligan were appearing at meetings.[80] 'Shoneen' Dunedin was lining up behind Sinn Féin, but it shared the SDL platform with the socialist Irish of South Dunedin, prominent among them John Tohill, John A. Brown and Jack Robinson.

For Hussey the issue became very personal when his boss Edgar Hazlett, son of a Londonderry Anglican, took exception to his views.[81] He had already become '*very nasty*' *[28 April]* during the local body elections in April. By the end of August, with the Self Determination League in full flight, matters came to a head. '*Great go with E.C.H. over Irish question Offered to resign from firm at 3 months*' *[27 August]*. The traditional reproach against the 'shoneen' Irishman had always been that he put his pocket before his country's honour. If Hussey is viewed as the archetypal 'lace curtain' Catholic, and thus as one of the 'shoneen' Irishman, his offer was a direct demonstration of a 'radical' commitment to Ireland's cause. At the same time, however, the old attachment to 'Home Rule' and an Ireland that lay within the Empire's fold did not die easily. Within the League, men like Hussey and J. B. Callan still promoted the model of Dominion Home Rule for Ireland, even as de Valera and the Dáil Éireann sparred with Lloyd George's government over full sovereign independence.[82] With the signing of the Treaty that established the Irish Free State in January 1922, Hussey was jubilant, '*My pick has come true*' *[9 January 1922]*'. On the local front, however, sectarian difficulties still lay ahead. The year of 1922 brought Bishop Liston's trial for sedition in Auckland and the nasty campaign in Dunedin when state school teachers sought to exclude the Christian Brothers from local rugby competitions.[83] By the year's end, however, Irish issues were more settled: '*Free State an accomplished fact in Ireland People have lost interest in the matter.*' *[14 December 1922]*.

V

With the establishment of the Irish Free State, Dunedin's Irish community stepped back from further agitation over 'homeland' affairs. Independence, however qualified, had finally been won. It was now up to the Irish at home to fight their own political battles.[84] Without this divisive element in New Zealand, 'Irishness' could now sit safely in the field of cultural activity. Political action was an entirely different matter. The years since 1916 had bequeathed a legacy of support for the emerging Labour Party. It had been the sole advocate for Irish independence on the New Zealand political scene. A unified view on Ireland, however, was but one part of this growing alliance. The role of Irish socialists within the Party was of equal importance. They were as committed to the domestic platform of the party as to its international policy.[85] Between 1916 and 1922 these men and women pushed their way forward and became leaders within their communities. In this they owed nothing to their successful integration within the 'establishment'. Quite simply, Labour offered the most to an Irish working-class constituency and deservedly won its electoral allegiance in the years that followed.

9
'The Importance of Being Irish'
Hibernianism in New Zealand, 1869–1969

Rory Sweetman

> He had made up his mind when leaving the old sod not to join any secret society. He had seen his countrymen cast into jail, homes wrecked, and the hearts of aged parents lacerated on account of secret societies, [but] when he saw the members of the Hibernian Society march in procession with their beautiful regalia, he felt his heart rush to his mouth, and his hand stretched out to them.
> *William Kane (District Secretary 1886-1932)*[1]

The Hibernian Australasian Catholic Benefit Society has just celebrated its 130th birthday in New Zealand. The only survivor of a host of lay Catholic organisations which flourished and faded during this time, including the Holy Name Society and the Catholic Federation, it has also outlasted its Australian parent.[2] Accorded only a footnote in our history books, the Hibernians have fallen victim to what Donald Akenson has described as the 'collective historical amnesia' regarding the Irish experience in New Zealand.[3] This is an undeserved obscurity for an organisation which played an important role in the lives of many Catholic families, helping to cushion them from the effects of economic downturns and to provide social support and fraternalism. I have argued elsewhere that the Society's religious dimension, rather than its Irish identity, provides the key to understanding its remarkable longevity.[4] This chapter will examine the kinds of 'Irishness' articulated by the Society during its first century of existence.

I

On 16 December 1869 a group of Irish men gathered in the Brian Boru Hotel at Greymouth. One of a cluster of establishments in the town catering for the hordes of goldminers and their prodigious thirst, the Brian Boru was named after the Irish leader famous for beating the Danes at the battle of Clontarf in 1014. The name made good commercial sense, as there were many Irish men among those who had recently deserted the Otago and Victorian diggings to follow the latest discoveries on New Zealand's rugged West Coast. In 1871, for example, the

Irish-born made up over one-quarter of the newly created Westland province.[5]

The meeting was very much an Irish affair. There was Daniel Sheedy, proprietor of the Brian Boru, Martin Kennedy, the mining magnate, Peter Purcell, Patrick Griffen, and Thomas Joyce, all well-known Irish residents of Greymouth. Most of the thirty men who were initiated that day as members of the Ballarat Hibernian Society would also have been Irish-born, so it was no surprise that the new branch was named after St Patrick, Ireland's national saint.[6]

The key player in the day's activities was Francis H. Byrne, secretary of the Ballarat Hibernian Society, who had recently arrived from Melbourne to spread the gospel of Hibernianism. He had been invited to the West Coast by a group of Irishmen at Addison's Flat, and was on his way there from Hokitika when intercepted at Greymouth. As well as acceding to Martin Kennedy's request, he founded a branch at Charleston before carrying out his initial commission. Byrne then travelled to the Coromandel, another mining centre eager for his services.[7] The seeds he planted soon germinated. By the end of 1873 Hibernians could be found at Auckland, Grahamstown, Ross, Coromandel, Greymouth, Hokitika, Waimea, Queenstown, Charleston, Brighton, Inangahua, Reefton, Christchurch, Oamaru, Dunedin and Naseby.[8]

By this time the Ballarat Hibernian Society had amalgamated with the Irish Australian Catholic Benefit Society and the Albury Catholic Benefit Society. Prolonged wrangling over the name resulted in a compromise, agreed to in April 1871, and the Hibernian Australasian Catholic Benefit Society was born. All existing New Zealand branches received fresh dispensations from the executive directory, the new society's ruling body. The papers for St Patrick's, Greymouth, Branch No. 17, were issued on 16 May 1872.[9]

It was not surprising that Hibernianism crossed the Tasman Sea, given the close links between Victoria and the West Coast. Many of the members of the first branch, including Kennedy and Sheedy, had spent time in Australia before moving on to New Zealand. The Ballarat Hibernian Society was well known to the West Coast Irish, as shown by Byrne's original invitation. Nor was the rapid success of his evangelising effort entirely unexpected. Misfortune came suddenly on the diggings, often in the form of a crippling injury or sickness. With no social security or even organised charity, what frequently followed was a wretched death and a pauper's funeral. This helps to explain the attraction of an organisation which provided relief to members in case of sickness or accident, and paid for funeral expenses through an insurance scheme.

European settlers brought the friendly society movement with them to the Antipodes. Official statistics show that nine branches of various bodies had sprung up in New Zealand in the 1840s, fourteen in the 1850s, and eighty-one in the 1860s. This growth was encouraged by the state, which passed legislation to foster and control them in 1854, 1867 and 1877. The last Act provided for the appointment of a Registrar, and for all societies to make annual returns of their membership, benefits and contributions, and also a five-yearly statement of their assets.[10]

The proliferation of friendly societies – Oddfellows, Druids, Foresters and the like – meant that West Coast residents were rather spoiled for choice. Why then did the Irish Catholics start a new one? The society is said to have begun in Australia after an insult was offered to Irishmen during their celebration of St Patrick's Day. While Bishop James Goold of Melbourne was firmly opposed to anything that smacked of secrecy, he gave his blessing to the formation of a separate organisation for Catholics, thereby keeping them away from societies which might endanger their religious beliefs. On this version, Irish Catholics banded together not only for their own benefit, but also as a response to the hostility shown to their faith and fatherland.[11]

Can a similar story be told of Hibernian beginnings in New Zealand? At first glance it would seem so. During the two years prior to the foundation meeting at the Brian Boru Hotel, the colony had been troubled by the local repercussions of Fenianism, a revolutionary movement which had climaxed in Ireland with an abortive rebellion in 1867. The Fenians aimed at separation from England and the establishment of an Irish republic. Despite the alarm and anger that this excited at the farthest edge of Britain's empire, sympathy for the defeated rebels moved West Coast Irishmen to action in early 1868. After three Fenians – the 'Manchester Martyrs' – were executed in England for killing a policeman in a bungled rescue attempt, meetings, collections and marches took place in several towns. In Charleston and Hokitika, mock funerals were conducted and a memorial cross was planted in the Hokitika cemetery, where prayers were said by an Irish-born priest, Father William Larkin, and an estimated 3000 sympathisers.

Soon after these events, news arrived from Sydney of an attempted assassination of Queen Victoria's son, Prince Edward, by an alleged Fenian, Henry James O'Farrell. The explosion of anti-Irish sentiment roused in the Australian colonies also fuelled hysterical fears of rebellion and mayhem on the West Coast. Hundreds of special constables were enrolled and a detachment of the Royal 18th Regiment was sent to the region by the central government. Meanwhile, Father Larkin and six others were arrested and detained at the Hokitika gaol. Although Larkin claimed not to have 'one drop of Fenian blood in his veins', he was subsequently convicted and imprisoned for one month.[12]

Colonial Fenianism was largely illusory. Nonetheless, the colony could not escape the spread of Fenian contagion. During the years 1866-67, Fenian revolutionary organisations attempted an uprising in Ireland, bombings in England and the invasion of Canada.[13] It was easy for the local authorities to fear the worst. Yet some colonists interpreted Governor Bowen's actions as an attempt to justify the retention of British troops in the country for service against Maori. The *Otago Daily Times* also dismissed rumours of Fenianism as 'tall talk', but the affair placed an onus on New Zealand Irish Catholics to distance themselves from anything that remotely resembled it.

A similar pressure was coming from their spiritual mentors. The birth of Hibernianism coincided with the arrival of two Irish bishops, Thomas Croke and Patrick Moran, to take control of the Auckland and Dunedin Catholic dioceses. Both men sincerely believed that preserving the Irish national identity overseas would stiffen Catholic spines and help prevent leakage from the faith; the excesses of Fenianism, however, were to be avoided. Anti-clerical, secret, oath-bound, violent and provocative, doomed to failure, the movement was damned in episcopal eyes.[14] Richard Davis has claimed that the bishops hoped to use the new Society as a rallying point for local Catholics and a substitute for Fenianism. It may be that protecting Father Larkin reawakened latent Hibernian instincts dating back to the mid-seventeenth century. An organisation of lay Catholics prepared to risk public wrath in order to stand by their beliefs had a natural appeal for the bishops.[15]

While the fight over the Fenian commemorative marches showed the limits beyond which expatriate politics would not be tolerated, it does not follow that Irish Catholics were forced to found their own benefit society. There is insufficient evidence to show that these newcomers were made unwelcome in places such as the West Coast. Indeed, their persistence in joining and remaining in other friendly societies was a continual source of frustration for the Hibernian leaders. Rather than stressing Irish patriotism as a reason for joining, they distanced the Society from Irish political enthusiasms.

Despite this, Hibernian members found that they were obliged to meet the rhythm of Irish politics. Given the identification between Irish and Catholic, there was a constant need to explain, defend and justify Irish political events. Uncomfortable immigrants, keen to assimilate but also to retain their national and religious identity, Hibernians found that attempting to fulfill the Society's innocuous-sounding obligation to cherish the memory of Ireland often drew a hostile response from their fellow-colonists. As their colonial residence lengthened, were they to forget Ireland or to continue fighting for her?

Episcopal approval was earned principally by the fact that the Society was not Fenian, a point emphasised by its leaders at every opportunity. Frederick Bunny, who greatly assisted the spread of Hibernianism in the south, later told an Invercargill audience of the resistance he had encountered:

> When the movement was first mooted in Dunedin he found it very uphill work owing to a prejudice that had sprung up against it. Despite every persuasion, people would persistently maintain that it was a party society, ushered into life for the mere purpose of serving a political end, and they sternly set their backs against it... as calculated to do more harm than good.[16]

Bunny rejected this charge. Were not men of all nationalities admitted as members, as long as they were practical Catholics and in a sound state of health? The rules had been scrutinised by lawyers and the Registrars of both Australia and New Zealand and no fault had been found with them. Similar complaints were heard in Auckland and Christchurch. William Kane, the future long-serving district secretary, joined the Auckland branch only after the St Patrick's Day procession showed him that its brand of Irishness was inoffensive. From the late 1860s, Auckland's Irish celebrated the festival with a huge picnic in the Domain: the local Hibernian branch (founded in 1873) soon added a march through the city streets, a sports meeting and an evening ball to the day's entertainment. Public marches, with banners and regalia proudly displayed, became a colourful feature of colonial life.[17]

The Hibernian displays were matched by those of the Loyal Orange Order, another Irish society which found fertile ground in Britain's colonies. It is not hard to understand why non-Irish settlers regarded the rival organisations as equally divisive. Both employed symbolism and colours that were provocative. However, fears of conflict between Orange and Green in the colony were largely exaggerated, although occasional clashes did occur. On Boxing Day in 1879, for example, a Protestant Alliance picnic party in Christchurch was set upon by Catholics armed with picks, staves and other weapons. Ten Orangemen were badly hurt. At Timaru on the same day around 500 Catholics gathered to attack Orangemen in a procession of friendly societies. Many of the rioters were later jailed and their actions immortalised in Thomas Bracken's satirical poem 'The Saige O Timaru'. On both occasions the Irish Catholic aggressors claimed that they had been deliberately provoked by the public parade of symbols signifying Orange victories over them in the past.[18]

The immigration that swelled Hibernian ranks through the 1870s also fed the Orange Order. Some 20,000 Irish arrived in this decade, almost doubling the number of Irish-born in the country.[19] Many Protestant males turned to the organisation most familiar to them for help in adjusting to their new environment. The first lodge appeared in Auckland in 1858 and from there the movement spread throughout the country. Eighteen lodges existed by 1876, and separate Grand Lodges were established for both islands ten years later.[20] Just as the Hibernians began to make their presence known, they found the Orangemen doing the same. (In 1874 more than seven hundred people attended Auckland celebrations to mark the anniversary of the Battle of the Boyne.)[21]

Each organisation claimed that the other's stated aims masked more malevolent purposes, and believed that its rival was getting more than its proper share of influence in the community. At the Christchurch Boyne Day gathering in 1873, the Reverend James Buller warned that 'the battle for religious freedom and liberty would have one day to be fought in New Zealand, as Catholicism was endeavouring by all the means in its power to obtain an increased footing in the colony.'[22] Catholics believed that the Orangemen aimed at political ascendancy and at their own reduction to the status of second-class citizens. Whatever the truth of this, the Orange Order strongly opposed both state grants to Catholic schools and Irish Home Rule. (There were moments of co-operation, as in 1885 when they celebrated St Patrick's Day together in Christchurch.)[23]

When not distracted by Orangeism, Hibernian leaders found that distancing the Society from Irish troubles was an exercise that had to be repeated constantly. The threat of Fenianism was succeeded during the 1880s by the Irish Land War, a violent struggle between landlords and tenants led by the Irish Land League. While the onset of agrarian depression in Ireland evoked widespread sympathy, colonial reaction to the activities of the Irish peasantry against their perceived oppressors was less favourable. Moreover, the brutal murders of British government officials at Dublin's Phoenix Park in 1882, like the 'boycotting' and shooting of landlords and their agents, shocked an uncomprehending colonial audience which drew its Irish news from hostile cable sources. The Hibernian Society was deeply involved in the huge meetings held in Wellington and Dunedin to express support for the suffering Irish, and it helped to set up branches of the Land League in several centres. However, the escalation of violence in Ireland soon alienated moderate New Zealand opinion. Many of the Liberal politicians who had cheered for the Land League promptly dropped all things Irish.[24]

II

In 1883 the visit of the brothers John and William Redmond, Irish nationalist members of the British Parliament, was an opportunity to educate New Zealanders on the realities of Irish life. The hostility of their reception indicated how difficult this task would be. Public halls were denied to them, while the press was largely critical. The English-born Catholic Bishop of Auckland, J.E. Luck, also held aloof, insisting that a true colonial should avoid 'mixing oneself up in an adopted country in the feuds and strifes of the land of one's birth, especially when the land of one's adoption is at the very antipodes of the field of action'.[25] Though merely a policy of non-involvement, Luck's stand was taken as a declaration of war by his Irish flock and he had to suffer the indignity of a slanging match in the local press. Fortunately for the visitors, news soon arrived absolving the Irish Parliamentary Party from blame for the Phoenix Park murders.

The Redmonds were also careful to cut the cloth of Irish national ambition to a colonial measure. The Irish Parliamentary Party, led by Charles Stewart Parnell, sought merely a limited self-government – Home Rule – which would ensure the unity of the British empire rather than its dismemberment. As such, it soon won the sympathy of most New Zealanders as the means to reconcile Irish national ambition and imperial security. Despite this, some Hibernians worried that the excesses of the Land War had made many potential recruits fear being identified with Irish violence. In late 1887, the *New Zealand Tablet* carried a vigorous debate on the issue. An anonymous 'Member' argued that while the Society's Hibernian identity might put off those who were not Irish by birth or descent, 'it ought to be a powerful motive to those who are such to join it'. He abhorred the 'no politics' rule and pointed out its inconsistency with the wording of the initiation ceremony:

> The exclusion of politics and the cherishing of the memory of Erin are not in harmony, and one ought to give way. There are many, the writer among the number, who would much prefer to retain the politics, as a society bearing the title of Hibernian is unworthy of its name, if, during the crisis that Ireland is now passing through it does not rise to the occasion and in some way manifest that their people in New Zealand are in sympathy and active co-operation with O'Brien and Dillon to resist that vilest of Coercion Acts.[26]

Advocates of a deeper involvement in Irish political battles were cheered in late 1885 by the news of William Ewart Gladstone's surprise conversion to the cause of Irish Home Rule. Overnight the Irish cause became again respectable in Liberal circles. The British Premier's unsuccessful Home Rule Bill in 1886 was described by the *Evening Post* as 'one of the greatest national reforms which ever statesman essayed'.[27]

This transformation in colonial attitudes is well charted by comparing the 1883 tour by the Redmond brothers with that undertaken six years later by their colleagues John Dillon, John Deasy and Sir Thomas Esmonde. The Irish delegates were rapturously received, with even Bishop Luck making an appearance on Dillon's platform. Some newspapers were still hostile, but most applauded, while New Zealand audiences showed their approval in an unmistakable form. The delegates raised £6,000 through some thirty-seven meetings, a result which surprised Dillon given the country's relatively thin Irish population.[28]

The formation in early 1886 of a separate New Zealand Hibernian District came in time to embrace the new Irish political orthodoxy.[29] Members in the major centres competed with each other to receive the Irish delegates in as splendid a manner as possible. In April 1890, for example, the *New Zealand Tablet* praised the reception organised by the Christchurch branch, which 'showed that their distinctive admonition to ever cherish the memory of Ireland is for them no empty formula'.[30] The pattern was set for the next twenty-five years, as the various branches of the Society chaperoned visiting Irish politicians, collected money for the cause, passed supportive resolutions and worried about the growing Ulster resistance to the Home Rule measure so fervently desired.

In late 1890 came the destruction of Charles Stewart Parnell's influence on the Irish Parliamentary Party following the revelations of the O'Shea divorce case. There ensued a decade of internecine squabbling in Irish nationalist ranks, which plunged their supporters overseas into despair. The scandal of disunity was almost as great an embarrassment to colonial Irish Catholics as Parnell's disgrace. Many withdrew in confusion, led by their bishops who jointly declared that 'it is not expedient to extend our support to the representatives of either of the rival parties'.[31] Bishop Moran refused to sanction the spread of the Irish

National Federation 'till our friends at Home drop their dissensions which made us all here lower our heads and blush for shame'.[32] The INF was an anti-Parnellite organisation whose cause was espoused in 1891 by yet another visiting Irish MP, J.R. Cox. He was coolly received by the Australian and New Zealand bishops, who were belatedly attempting to insulate the colonies from the divisive effects of Irish politics. Parnell's death in October 1891, followed by the defeat of Gladstone's second Home Rule Bill two years later, temporarily removed the Irish issue from the political forefront.[33]

During his brief visit, Cox founded an INF branch in Auckland, whose membership was largely Hibernian in composition. Michael Joseph Sheahan, land agent and longtime district treasurer, took up the cause eagerly. In mid-1894 he established branches at Denniston, Westport, Charleston and Addison's Flat.[34] The Wellington branch was also run by Hibernians J.J. Devine (lawyer) and Michael Bohan (coachmaker). On Parnell's death, it sent a cable to John Dillon calling for 'union over the grave'. Some years later the Wellington Hibernians handed over the profits of the St Patrick's Day celebrations to their INF counterparts to be sent to Dublin for the relief of the evicted tenants.[35]

Clerical efforts to control the contagion of Irish political strife were boosted with the appointment of Father Henry William Cleary as editor of the *New Zealand Tablet* in early 1898. A strong supporter of Hibernianism since his arrival in Australia a decade earlier, Cleary had made his name by writing a lengthy exposé of *The Orange Society*.[36] His expertise on the Order's politico-religious activities was immediately put to the test. In March 1898, New Zealand's Governor, Lord Ranfurly (an Ulsterman and ex-Orange Grand Master) made a speech in Dunedin praising the Orangemen. Cleary responded by giving him a verbal roasting in the *New Zealand Tablet*, while M.J. Sheahan (Hibernian district secretary) persuaded John Dillon to have a question asked in the House of Commons.[37] Over the next twelve years Cleary would write numerous articles in defence of his native land, some of which were published separately in 1909, under the title *An Impeached Nation*.[38]

Cleary's approach was not altogether apologetic. A new assertiveness on matters Irish was demonstrated by his drive to commemorate the centenary of the 1798 Irish Rebellion. A grandson of one of the rebels, he had grown up in Wexford and was well versed in the tragic and bloody events of that year. By contrast, other prominent Irishmen felt that the anniversary was best left unsung. Dunedin Hibernians were reluctant to initiate the organisation of celebrations, while even Cardinal Moran was at first opposed to marking the event in Sydney. Cleary, however, had in mind no mere waving of 'the bloody shirt'. He successfully encouraged the participation of several Irish Protestant clergymen. In Auckland, Bishop Lenihan, another whose grandfather had fought and died on the rebel side, celebrated a Requiem Mass for the repose of the souls of the '98 men.[39]

As editor of the sole Catholic paper in New Zealand, Cleary was well placed to influence his readers' perception of, and response to, the Irish issue. In December 1898, he explained his editorial policy to John Dillon: 'I have not permitted the insertion of any letters, news or correspondence that could create divisions here on the question of Irish politics'. Cleary urged a similar sense of discretion on the leaders at home, who were bitterly divided over Parnell's fall and the failure of Home Rule. He promised to support any movement that would 'put an end to a disunion which has been the despair of our people in these colonies for many years past' by writing leading articles and organising fundraising appeals.[40]

When it finally arrived in 1900, the healing of Irish political divisions posed fresh problems. The earliest expression of nationalist unity, under new leader John Redmond, was an attack on the war in South Africa. It was a turn of events that fully exercised Cleary's talents as an apologist. His own opposition to the Boer War had to be explained to a New Zealand public whose enthusiasm for the imperial adventure rose once colonial contingents had departed for South Africa ('under the hollow pretence of fighting for liberty!' a Wellington Hibernian commented sourly).[41] Rather than impugning imperial integrity, Cleary dwelt on the alternatives to armed conflict that had been ignored and could still be accepted. M.J. Sheahan confided to John Dillon in February 1901: 'Our people here to a man almost are with the Boers, but are compelled to keep their opinions, as several have suffered locally for giving vent to them'.[42]

The *New Zealand Tablet's* criticism of the war effort was balanced by Bishop Grimes of Christchurch, who praised a contingent of troops departing for South Africa as latter-day 'crusaders'. When Queen Victoria allowed Irish troops to wear the shamrock on St Patrick's Day in recognition of their courageous service against the Boers, enthusiastic meetings of 'loyal Irishmen' were held in Auckland and Dunedin. William Ferguson Massey, Ulsterman, ex-Orange Grand Master and future Prime Minister, attended the former and praised the 'splendid bravery' of the Irish, which he predicted would encourage unity in Ireland itself. Another future Prime Minister, Joseph Ward, an Australian-born Irish Catholic, organised a message of thanks to the Queen from those gathered in Dunedin.[43] By contrast, Father Treacy told a patriotic gathering in Hanmer Springs how 'England's successes on the battlefield were purchased with the lifeblood of Ireland's best sons'.[44]

Cleary's task was complicated by the mixed messages sent out by the Irish Catholic body on the issue of loyalty to the British empire. Political events in Ireland had long raised fears of a threat to the unity of the empire. Some suspected a papal plot to ruin Protestantism; many more were afraid of the implications of Irish separatism for Britain's ability to defend its colonies. In response, prominent Catholics praised the 'Anglo-Celtic empire' and stressed the contribution that Ireland had made to its creation. As Prime Minister from 1906-12, Sir Joseph

Ward was the perfect lay spokesman for his church; he turned the identification of Catholicism with imperialism into an art form. For Ward, Irish Home Rule was a stage in the growth of the British empire, which would eventually include separate parliaments for England, Scotland and Wales, topped off by a great imperial assembly to be graced by Dominion leaders like himself.[45]

Cleary's successor as editor at the *New Zealand Tablet*, J.A. Scott (1910-16), continued to portray the Catholic Church as a pillar of loyalty to King and empire. However, the loyal posturing of the Catholic social élite barely concealed a deep scorn and hostility lurking among the lower stratum of the Catholic community towards these displays of 'jingoism'. The subsequent rise of revolutionary Irish nationalism – in the guise of Sinn Féin – would give the discontented Catholic proletariat a cause to rally around and a means of expressing its anger at the British government's treatment of Ireland.

The loyalty issue was a live one for the Hibernian Society. While branches had been divided over whether to join in the celebrations of Queen Victoria's Jubilee in 1887, when news came of her death in 1901 the district executive adjourned its meeting as a mark of respect.[46] The new King, Edward VII, was praised at the 1904 triennial movable meeting as a monarch 'the sole purpose of whose heart was to do justice to Ireland'.[47] The refusal of the Irish Parliamentary Party to take any part in successive coronation ceremonies drew criticism around the empire. (It argued that attendance would be interpreted as acceptance of the Union between Britain and Ireland.) In mid-1911, after initial hesitation, Hibernians in Wellington and Dunedin decided to participate in the Coronation Day processions with the other friendly societies, while also pushing ahead with preparations to welcome the visiting Irish delegates.[48]

The Hibernian Society also kept faith with Home Rule. In both 1903 and 1909 the Biennial Movable Meetings in Sydney and Hobart passed votes of confidence in John Redmond and declared that 'we will continue to assist the [Irish Parliamentary] Party in every way possible'.[49] From 1905 this support was expressed in tangible form with each branch aiming to collect a voluntary payment of 1/- from its members towards the Irish Parliamentary Fund.[50] A close watch was kept on Irish developments. Delegates assembled at Timaru in 1904 sent their congratulations to George Wyndham (Irish Chief Secretary) on the passage of the Land Purchase Act 'to settle a question which involves the very existence of the residue of the Irish race in Ireland'.[51] The next triennial movable meeting offered thanks to the visiting Irish MPs. Joseph Devlin and J.T. Donovan, for their efforts 'to dispel many if not all of the slanders against Ireland and its people'.[52]

Cleary was also as good as his word when the reunified Irish Party resumed its fundraising visits to the colonies. The columns of the *New Zealand Tablet* frequently carried appeals on behalf of Irish causes. Cleary orchestrated the New Zealand tour of delegations in 1906-07 and 1911, both prompted by the need for colonial contributions to defray electoral expenses. The delegates were not disappointed in the generosity of their New Zealand sympathisers: Devlin and Donovan collected more than £5000 in their 1906-07 tour, while William Redmond, Richard Hazleton and Donovan (once again) carried off more than twice this amount in 1911.[53]

The 1911 delegates silenced the few remaining critics of Home Rule. They presented their arguments in an impeccably moderate and reasonable manner to which New Zealanders readily responded. Popular demand ensured that an original schedule of twelve meetings was expanded to a total of seventy-two over three exhausting weeks.[54] The Irish politicians were welcomed as heralds of an approaching triumph, and not as the spokesmen for a violent, unpopular cause as in 1883. Ironically, it was the increasingly extreme opposition of Ulster Unionists, led by Edward Carson, that would take Ireland to the brink of civil war over the next three years and discredit the anti-Home Rule cause in colonial eyes. The violence of their rhetoric and repeated threats of armed resistance served to highlight the moderation of the nationalists.

At the Society's triennial movable meeting in April 1913, Father James Coffey expressed the hope that when Home Rule reached the Statute Book 'a new and brighter era will dawn upon Ireland'. J.B. Stead expressed his pleasure, as an Englishman, in seconding the motion.[55] The confidence that Ireland's long struggle was won at last can be seen in the naming of the new Hibernian branch at Hokitika after Robert Emmet. A Protestant nationalist executed in 1803 after leading an abortive rebellion, Emmet had concluded his speech from the dock with the famous words: 'When my country takes her place among the nations of the earth, then and not till then, let my epitaph be written'.[56] Christchurch Hibernians, meeting in June to celebrate the passing of the Home Rule Bill, greeted F.J. Doolan's recitation of Emmet's speech from the dock with a storm of applause. Negotiations were begun with shipping companies to charter a special steamer to enable members to attend the opening of the new Irish parliament.[57]

Would the cup of victory be dashed from Hibernian lips at the last moment? A stream of nervous cables were sent to London by Hibernian and Celtic Societies at critical stages during the progress of the Home Rule Bill. In March 1914 news of amendments to the measure prompted a meeting of Auckland Hibernians to send Asquith a resolution protesting at the 'mutilation' of Home Rule, and regretting that 'concessions offered to the forces of anarchy and disorder are tending to the dismemberment of Ireland'.[58] The district executive cabled Redmond in April 1914: 'Hibernians with you in the final struggle. Hope you will never allow one rood of Ireland to be a stranger to Irish rule'.[59] Some Hibernians even privately discussed despatching men and money should they be required to ensure the success of Home Rule. In June, Tom O'Sullivan placed advertisements in the Auckland press mentioning 'numerous applications in response to his appeals for recruits for the Irish National Volunteers to proceed to Ireland'.[60]

The outbreak of general hostilities in Europe in August 1914 averted the looming Irish crisis by causing a closing of ranks against the foreign enemy. Unity became the order of the day. The Home Rule Bill duly received the royal assent in September, but was suspended for the duration of the war. District President Dan Flynn cabled John Redmond: 'New Zealand Hibernians rejoice at the consummation of Ireland's national aspirations'.[61] The rival Irish armies, Ulster and National Volunteers, went off to share the same trenches in Flanders. A sigh of relief from politicians, lay and cleric, was almost audible throughout the empire. The Prime Minister, William Massey, captured the mood at a patriotic meeting in Wellington on 12 August:

> I am proud of being of Irish birth… a fortnight ago the two great sections of the Irish people were looking at each other along the barrels of their rifles, but today they are standing side by side and shoulder to shoulder ready to fight for their country and their Empire. (Cheers.)[62]

New Zealand Irish Catholics were among the first to send their sons to fight Britain's war. Belgium and France were viewed as Catholic nations brutally attacked by Protestant Germany. John Redmond's offer of Irish troops for the war effort was greeted with delight by New Zealand Catholics. Money collected to further the Home Rule cause was now devoted to assist the Irish leader in defending the empire. While the great celebrations planned to welcome the arrival of Home Rule were postponed indefinitely, the passage of the Bill allowed Irish Catholics to add their collective voice to the praise of Empire.

III

The enthusiasm with which Irish Catholics in New Zealand greeted the outbreak of war owed a great deal to their hope that the Irish question might finally be resolved at the front. The removal of the last remaining issue dividing Ireland and England was the theme of most Catholic patriotic addresses. The high percentage of members who volunteered for service from Catholic colleges, Celtic clubs and Hibernian Society branches throughout the country drew much self-congratulatory comment at school prize-givings, fundraising functions and in the columns of the *New Zealand Tablet*. A return of volunteers produced in late 1917 confirmed that the Catholic community had done its duty.[63]

New Zealand Hibernians went willingly to war. At the outbreak of hostilities, Thorndon's branch secretary immediately volunteered to join the expeditionary force, while the St Mary's (Hokitika) Hibernians reported that three members were 'leaving us to fight for the safety of the Empire'.[64] When J.T. Carr, the future district secretary, went off to the front in mid-1915, he was the tenth member of the Dunedin branch to join up. In November, St Patricks (Wellington) set up a roll of honour in their lodge room to remind members of fallen comrades. Six months later Ashburton Hibernians 'claimed credit – and rightly so – for every eligible member for service with the New Zealand Reinforcements having responded to the call'.[65]

There was an equal amount of activity on the home front. The Hibernians supported the Field Service Fund, established to provide tents and other supplies for Catholic troops and chaplains. Branches poured their energies into raising funds for the war effort. Wellington Hibernian women sold green badges printed with the words 'It's a long way to Tipperary' in aid of the Belgian Relief Fund, while the Wounded Soldiers' Fund, the Polish Relief Fund and the Red Cross Fund also benefited from their efforts.

Despite the joy at high Catholic numbers in the military forces, one can detect a more defensive tone in the *New Zealand Tablet* over the issue of Irish nationalist recruiting. The Irish Party had spoken out against conscription being applied to Ireland, while Redmond refused the offer of a place in the British Cabinet. The Catholic weekly fed its readers a steady diet of imported articles on Irish heroism and gallantry, defending the nationalist war effort with a mixture of pride and sensitivity. It blamed the cable agent for sending a stream of anti-Irish reports, whose alleged object was the blackening of Ireland's name.[66] In mid-1915, Christchurch Hibernians congratulated the paper for its protest against the anti-Irishness of the Christchurch *Press* and its defence of 'Ireland's incomparable leader and statesman, John Redmond'.[67] The *Press* had offended many Catholics by suggesting that German submarines were being harboured in lonely inlets on the south-west coast of Ireland. A Timaru Hibernian reminded *New Zealand Tablet* readers that 'half a million sons of Ireland were fighting the Empire's battles today.[68]

In May 1915, the entry of the Ulster Unionist leaders into the British Cabinet exposed the Home Rule victory as a pyrrhic one. It was final proof that the original deserters of constitutionalism in Ireland had prevailed. A year later, the Easter Rising in Dublin completed the reversal of roles of loyalist and disloyalist. The clerical championing of Home Rule had made of it a Catholic cause, to be opposed and supported as such. While few observers would swallow the Orange Order's view that it was all part of a deep plot hatched in Rome against the Protestant Empire, this interpretation was to prove more persuasive when applied to the new Irish orthodoxy, Sinn Féin.

After Easter 1916, Irish politics once more brought a sword to divide Catholics from their fellow-New Zealanders. Over six bloody days, some 2000 Irish rebels waged an unequal war with 20,000 British troops in the streets of Ireland's capital. The Easter Rising came to many as confirmation of suspected Irish Catholic disloyalty. The 'gallant allies in Europe' upon whom the insurgents relied for aid were none other than the Central Powers, Germany and Austro-Hungary. During May and June 1916, the New Zealand press fed its readers a tale of sedition and violence in Ireland.[69]

The *New Zealand Tablet* also denounced the 'Made-In-Germany Rebellion', blaming the Kaiser and Roger Casement ('an out-and-out traitor') in equal part for the entire sorry affair. It took a Redmondite view of the Sinn Féin rebels, as did Irish critics in the United States and Australia. (Archbishop Carr of Melbourne dismissed it as 'an outbreak of madness'.) All agreed, however, on the culpability of the British government for Carsonite excesses.[70]

The Catholic community followed the *New Zealand Tablet* line. A protest meeting was held in Dunedin ('fully representative of Irish opinion') at which J.J. Marlow, a leading Hibernian, dwelt on the need to register as quickly as possible an expression of their 'abhorrence and detestation' of the Rising. There was a call for all Irishmen to enlist 'as a practical means of showing our condemnation of the rebellion'. Father James Coffey, another stalwart of the Society, then took centre stage, stating that they would be true to neither Ireland nor the Empire if they did not condemn the Sinn Féiners as 'dupes' who would discredit Ireland. They had to show that the hearts of Irishmen throughout the empire were sound. It was agreed to send this message to both Asquith and Redmond. In a subsequent sermon Coffey referred to the Dublin insurrection as a riot, and denounced Sinn Féin as syndicalist and anti-Catholic, though adding that the British government's weakness towards Carson was also to blame.[71]

Reaction in Auckland was equally severe. News of the insurrection reached the Hibernian delegates to the annual district meeting as they returned from an outing to Lake Takapuna. They read the report in the *Auckland Star* in shocked silence. 'The faces of those present were a study, each one betraying intense emotion', recalled the *New Zealand Tablet* correspondent. They agreed that their first business on resumption should be to cable their sympathy to John Redmond: 'New Zealand Hibernians at annual meeting assembled learned with abhorrence and regret of the disturbances in Dublin and desire to express deep sympathy and entire confidence in your party and followers'.[72]

Apologists soon tried to shift the focus back to acceptable forms of Irish violence by insisting that the real Irish patriots were to be found on the Western Front. However, the execution of the Irish rebel leaders and the wholesale arrests and deportations which took place in the aftermath of the Rising soon ended the unanimity among New Zealand commentators. St Patrick's (Wellington) was one of several Hibernian branches which sent a resolution deploring the executions and appealing to Prime Minister Asquith for leniency to be extended.[73] P.J. O'Regan reminded Wellington Hibernians of the pre-war immunity afforded to Carson and his colleagues. As the Irish Party now seemed willing to bargain away Ireland's territorial integrity, staunch Redmondite supporters became disillusioned. In mid-August, the Hibernian executive sent off a further cable, this time emphatically protesting against the treatment of Ireland by the British government and demanding the commencement of Home Rule at once.[74]

This change of attitude was partly prompted by press criticism of all things Irish. The sneers of Ireland's enemies demanded an equal assertion of Irish rectitude and attacks on the Easter rebels drew a defence of them, fuelled by the reports of a sea change in Irish opinion. The *New Zealand Tablet* followed Irish Catholic journals in stressing the piety and pure lives of the rebel leaders, and the manner of their death was described in term of martyrdom. Father O'Farrell urged his flock not to be ashamed of the men who had participated in the Rising: 'They were talented men and some of the best that Ireland could produce'. Most were good Catholics, whose 'noble and edifying deaths' had resulted in the conversion of some British officers who witnessed it.[75]

How to express support for Irish nationalism without dwelling on the less pleasant details of the insurrection? The relief of the suffering in post-Rising Dublin gave frustrated sympathisers a cause around which to rally. In September 1916, the Hibernian National Directory had appealed for assistance on behalf of the Dublin victims: 'Distress once more, and in the capital of Ireland, will stir to the depths every son and daughter of Erin, and in a special manner every Hibernian'.[76] A fund was set up to assist 'thousands of our kith and kin on the verge of starvation'. If every Hibernian contributed at least 1/- when paying the next quarter's dues, the Society's 60,000 members would raise £3,000. The *New Zealand Tablet* quoted Psalm 136 in the course of an impassioned full-page appeal: 'If I forget thee, let my right hand forget her cunning; let my tongue cleave to the roof of my mouth, if I do not remember thee'.[77] The Napier branch decided to circularise each member to ask for his co-operation, while in Palmerston North it was agreed to strike a levy.[78] Bishop Verdon endorsed the fund in emotional terms: 'To you, too, of the Greater Ireland, Irish by blood if not by birth, we appeal'.[79]

A critical figure in shaping the New Zealand Catholic perception of Irish events was the new editor of the *New Zealand Tablet*, Dr James Kelly, an Irish priest for whom the failure of Home Rule had exposed constitutionalism as 'a sham and a fraud' and the idea of conciliating the enemies of Ireland and Catholicism as a 'heresy'.[80] From his arrival in the editor's chair, in late March 1917, he fed his readers an insider's account of the rise of Sinn Féin. To Kelly's joy, the post-Rising years witnessed a swing in Irish opinion which culminated in Sinn Féin's landslide electoral victory in December 1918. The successful Irish members then formed their own assembly (Dáil Éireann) and proceeded to ignore the apparatus of British government. After this native parliament was suppressed in September 1919, the drift towards violence proved unstoppable. During the Anglo-Irish War (1919-21) the rival forces – the troops and police of the Crown versus the Irish Republican Army – both adopted terrorist tactics, while blaming each other for the resultant chaos and loss of life.[81]

Irish nationalism in the guise of Home Rule had given New Zealand Catholics a platform from which to express their loyalty to empire, but it returned to haunt them once Sinn Féin separatism replaced constitutionalism as the political orthodoxy in Ireland. The pursuit of self-determination under the ex-rebel leader turned Irish President, Eamon de Valera, appeared to be part of an attempt by the Irish to tear the British empire apart. Moreover, the support for Sinn Féin voiced by men like Archbishop Redwood and Dr Kelly seemed to confirm suspicions of Catholic guilt among those who did not normally regard the Pope as the source of all evil.

As the troops were welcomed home, honour boards were unveiled in most Hibernian branch meeting rooms. But while the Society joined in processions around the country to mark the signing of the Versailles Peace Treaty in July 1919, many members felt unable to participate fully in the celebrations. The 1919 annual report stated ruefully: 'Our brothers fought and died for the freedom of small nations. We hope that they did not die in vain. We hope that all small nations suffering from the evils inseparable from alien government shall be freed'.[82] St Patrick's Day was marked by huge gatherings, most of which passed resolutions calling for the granting of Irish self-determination.

The sectarian conflict which scarred Australia and New Zealand in these years was particularly virulent in Victoria. The Hibernian National Directory had long supported Daniel Mannix, Melbourne's outspoken Catholic archbishop, describing him in May 1918 as 'the greatest prelate Australia has yet seen'.[83] When Mannix hosted an Irish Race Convention in November 1919, Paul Hoskins, Michael Sheahan and F.J. O'Meara were among the many New Zealand Hibernians attending. Hoskins was given a send-off by the Wellington branches, at which P.J. O'Regan 'denounced the false god of Imperialism as applied to Ireland'.[84] Sheahan represented the district executive, while P.J. Nerheny was also nominated for Auckland, but could not accept. After the convention, all branches turned to the task of collecting contributions for the self-determination fund agreed to there. Kelly was importunate in demanding as large a return as possible.

Under fire from his ecclesiastical superiors for his provocative editorials on the Irish issue, Dr Kelly was cheered by the motion of appreciation passed in January 1920 by St Mary's (Christchurch) branch which lauded his 'splendid services to the cause of religion and nationality'.[85] Leading Hibernians took a prominent part in supporting the testimonial presented to him shortly afterwards. Instead of forgetting Ireland as some had advised them to, many New Zealand Catholics preferred to follow Dr Kelly into a passionate commitment to Sinn Féin.[86] Greymouth and Oamaru Hibernians responded to his call to establish a prize fund to encourage the study of Irish history. The district executive inaugurated a Thomas Moore Musical Committee 'for the purpose of inculcating a love for the study of Irish music and literature amongst the young', while Wellington members chose this moment to form an Irish War Pipe band.[87]

The dramatic unfolding of Irish events encouraged this deep involvement.

In November 1920, the Society hosted Archbishop Redwood on his return from Europe. He spoke of his meeting with the Irish President, Eamon de Valera, in the United States, and of how the leader had impressed him; and also of the protest he had led against the British navy's arrest of Archbishop Mannix when en route to Ireland.[88] Following the death of Terence MacSwiney, Lord Mayor of Cork, after a prolonged hunger strike in Brixton Prison, the district executive and several branches sent his widow a letter of sympathy, while Requiem Masses were held in the larger centres.[89]

Feelings hardened as the tempo of Irish conflict increased. Ambushes and assassinations were countered by raids and arrests, all of which cost about 2000 lives before a truce was called in mid-1921. Three months earlier Wanganui Hibernians met to condemn 'the frightfulness of the army of occupation in Ireland and [to] demand that the British Government withdraw its armed forces and honour its own pledges to soldiers who died for the freedom of small nations'.[90]

This theme was taken up by the Society at its triennial movable meeting in Christchurch in April 1921, when a resolution was passed in favour of the right of the Irish people 'to control their own affairs'. The moderation of the resolution's wording was masked by the use of quotations from Herbert Asquith, Arthur Henderson and Lord Robert Cecil condemning British policy in Ireland. Dr Kelly described this as 'one of the finest resolutions in favour of Irish self-determination yet passed in New Zealand by any society'. He was unaware that its proposer, M.J. Sheahan, had been deputed by Bishop Cleary to prevent the meeting from making a much stronger endorsement of an Irish Republic. Sheahan cabled to his bishop in triumph: 'Situation saved – vitriolic resolution out-manoeuvred'. Kelly admitted to 'a more personal motive for gratitude', as the delegates had also voted their appreciation of his work as editor of the *New Zealand Tablet*.[91]

After five months of stalling and tortuous negotiation, the Anglo-Irish Treaty was signed in London on 6 December 1921. It was greeted with joy and relief in New Zealand. A meeting of Wellington sympathisers heard P.J. O'Regan praise the agreement, which had been accepted 'by the appointed representatives of the Irish people'.[92] The terms represented a compromise on both sides: an oath of allegiance to the King, no reversal of the partition of North and South, naval facilities to be granted, Ireland to be a new Dominion of the British empire. There was a note of surprise in the *New Zealand Tablet*'s acknowledgment that the Treaty had been welcomed 'by practically all sections of the community'.[93] The Hibernian Society joined in the celebrations. A typical reaction came from members of St Patrick's branch (Christchurch) who declared that 'all should return thanks to Almighty God for the victory now gained'.[94]

In March 1922, the coadjutor Bishop of Auckland, James Liston, made a public speech which appeared to question the worth of the Treaty, and to advocate a renewal of armed conflict to secure the full freedom still denied to Ireland.

The press storm that followed forced the Reform Government to order Liston's prosecution on a charge of sedition, at which the Catholic community mobilised in his defence. While Auckland Hibernians were at first taken aback, among the two hundred letters and telegrams of support and sympathy received by the Bishop during his two months of anxiety, there were several from local branches and from prominent individual members. The St Benedict's branch, of which Liston was a member, expressed its 'warmest appreciation and unbounded and unalterable confidence' in him, while Michael Sheahan wrote a private letter to Prime Minister Massey in an unsuccessful effort to have the proceedings halted. An all-Protestant jury eventually found Liston not guilty, after a two-day trial in the Supreme Court. In September, the district executive rejoiced: 'We feel sure that all Hibernians were delighted at the acquittal of Bishop Liston'.[95]

Liston had offended most by his apparent refusal to accept the Treaty as a final solution to the Irish question. As most New Zealanders had earlier come to embrace Home Rule, so they now supported the nascent Irish Free State. The subsequent outbreak of civil war in Ireland both confused and embarrassed those who had cheered for Sinn Féin; from June 1922 to May 1923 came news of fratricidal strife to rival the worst excesses of the Anglo-Irish war. Both Catholic organs, the *Month* and the *New Zealand Tablet*, denounced the Republican diehards and lauded the Free State forces. When news arrived of the death of Michael Collins, the *Month* described his killers as rebels 'in the truest sense of the word'. Eamon de Valera was denounced as the leader of a gang of 'robbers and assassins'.[96] Visits from Irish delegates were no longer encouraged. When two of them appeared on the horizon in 1925, Bishop Brodie was unsympathetic, remarking dryly, 'I leave the affairs of Ireland to the Irish in Ireland'.[97]

The Hibernian Society followed Brodie's lead. From this time Irish political issues disappear from sight in the surviving records. The continued partition of the country, a cause that might have stirred renewed passions, was largely ignored, save for occasional references. In late 1926, for example, Father O'Regan exhorted the women of St Matthew's branch (Christchurch) 'to foster and love Irish traditions, to rejoice with Ireland's people in their joys, to sorrow with them in their sorrows, and hope to see an united Ireland'.[98]

IV

The new Irish Free State proved to be a loyal, if reluctant, Dominion within the emerging British Commonwealth. On St Patrick's Day 1928, its flag (the gift of Michael Sheahan) fluttered alongside the Union Jack from the pavilion at the Auckland Domain. However, Eamon de Valera's return to power in Ireland in early 1932 meant a change of agenda. The Fianna Fáil leader set about dismantling the Anglo-Irish Treaty, removing the oath of allegiance to the British

Crown, and withholding land annuities. A six-year 'economic war' ensued between Britain and Ireland. When World War Two commenced, the twenty-six-county state of Eire declared its neutrality, a stand which many New Zealanders found difficult to understand.

During World War Two, the *Hibernian Budget* (a quarterly distributed from 1934-51) regularly carried articles defending Irish patriotism and loyalty during the war. In November 1940 it boasted that of the nine Irishmen promoted by the Air Ministry, seven had come from Eire.[99] Six months later, it reproduced a protest by Glasgow's Hibernian District President at 'mischievous propaganda circulated against Eire' in the British press, at a time 'when so many young Irishmen and sons of Irishmen are laying down their lives on land and sea in order that Britain might live'. Despite these efforts at counter-propaganda, Irish neutrality won few friends, especially given British Prime Minister Winston Churchill's scathing comments in May 1945: 'We left the de Valera Government to frolic with the German and later with the Japanese representatives to their heart's content'.[100]

The effect of this caustic criticism was felt in mid-1948 when de Valera paid Australia and New Zealand a visit after his defeat at the polls. The call for a welcoming message by New Zealand Hibernians provoked sharp debate. When A.J. Mickleson proposed sending a telegram of good wishes from the annual district meeting, an unexpected note of dissent was sounded by P.P. Meffin of Timaru:

> This Society of ours is essentially a Catholic Society and a New Zealand Society and I feel it is unnecessary labouring the point in presenting such a telegram to Mr de Valera. So far as he is concerned, the average New Zealander is quite unconcerned about him. Many of us here are in our first, second and third generation of Irish descent and we have a soft spot for Ireland, but we have a soft spot for the country we were born in – New Zealand. I do not think we should associate ourselves with any country outside New Zealand and I object strongly to the motion.[101]

In the event, only two members voted against the motion and a telegram was duly sent: 'A hundred thousand welcomes from the New Zealand Hibernian Society sitting in conference at Dunedin. With fond recollection we ever cherish the memory of Ireland'. Earlier moves in favour of a more localised identity had been directed against the term 'Australasian' in the Society's title. St Patrick's branch (South Dunedin) called for this to be removed in 1931, but the National Directory rejected the idea.[102] Two years later, Dunedin's other branch, St Joseph's, lodged a notice of motion to rename their organisation the 'New Zealand Catholic Benefit Society'. This was ruled out of order at the 1934 annual district meeting as neither the National Directory nor the hierarchy were prepared to countenance the change.[103]

From the 1930s there were regular calls for New Zealand symbols to be included in the Society's regalia, emblems, and formulas. In 1935, St Patrick's

(Palmerston North) wanted the Budget's cover design (two kiwis) to be incorporated in future regalia and badges. It also requested that a reference to New Zealand be made in the initiation text: 'Considering the number of members in this country it is surprising that nothing has been done in this connection before. The title "Australasian" is not too pleasing to any "fair dinkum" New Zealander.'[104] At the tenth triennial convention held at Hobart in May 1941, a move was made to have New Zealand prominently represented in the insignia and the ritual of the Society. The same meeting discussed and rejected a motion aimed at deleting the word 'Hibernian' from the name of the Society.[105]

While these issues were given desultory attention over the next few decades, the Irish dimension was primarily a source of entertainment and a distinct flavour on social occasions. When historian Richard Davis came to investigate the Society's remaining Irish links in 1968, he found almost nothing to report:

> Very little interest is taken in Irish nationalism and younger members find the wearing of the regalia frankly embarrassing. Suggestions are sometimes made that the name Hibernian should be dropped. Branches, moreover, are never called after Irish nationalist figures.[106]

The centennial celebrations of New Zealand Hibernianism took place a year later in Greymouth. While the booklet published to mark the occasion teemed with references to the Society's early days, the proceedings themselves passed without mention of Ireland or Irish issues. In his message to the gathering, Bishop Ashby of Christchurch revived the idea of a change of name, suggesting they might become 'the Catholic Men's Society of New Zealand'.[107] No objections to this potential retreat from history were recorded in the minutes. One hundred years after the Hibernian Society's birth it was clearly no longer important to be Irish.

Notes

Introduction

1 Patricia Nelson Limerick, 'Has Minority History Transformed the Historical Discourse?', *Perspectives*, 35 (1997), p. 36.

Chapter 1

1 Emile Durkheim, *The Elementary Forms of the Religious Life*, trans. J. W. Swain, New York, 1961, p. 24.
2 For literature on the Irish diaspora, see Donald Harman Akenson, *The Irish Diaspora: A Primer*, Belfast and Toronto, 1993; P.J. Drudy, ed., *The Irish in America: Emigration, Assimilation and Impact*, Cambridge, 1985; David Fitzpatrick, *Irish Emigration, 1801-1921*, Dundalk, 1984; Richard Kearney, ed., *Migrations: The Irish at Home and Abroad*, Dublin, 1990; Kerby Miller, *Emigrants and Exiles. Ireland and the Irish Exodus in North America*, New York, 1985. An older, but still useful work is W.F. Adams, *Ireland and Irish Emigration to the New World from 1815 to the Famine*, New Haven, 1932. For a valuable compilation of recent scholarship on the Irish diaspora, see the multi-volume *The Irish World Wide* series edited by Patrick O'Sullivan: Volume 1, *Patterns of Migration*; Volume 2, *The Irish in the New Communities*; Volume 3, *The Creative Migrant*; Volume 4, *Irish Women and Irish Migration*; Volume 5, *Religion and Identity*; Volume 6, *The Meaning of the Famine*, London, 1992-97.
3 Examples include John A. O'Brien, *The Vanishing Irish: The Enigma of the Modern World*, London, 1954; Carl Wittke, *The Irish in America*, New York, 1956; George Potter, *To the Golden Door. The Story of the Irish in Ireland and America*, Boston, 1960; William V. Shannon, *The American Irish*, New York, 1963; Laurence J. McCaffrey, *The Irish Diaspora in America*, Bloomington, 1976. Some scholars in the field of Irish migration history continue to support this view. Kerby Miller's *Emigrants and Exiles*, which appeared in 1985, is the *ne plus ultra* of books in the victim-tradition of Irish-America historiography. An extended study of immigrant letters led him to the conclusion that emigration posed 'severe social, cultural and even psychological problems' for Irish Catholics. According to Miller, the 'fatalism', 'dependence', and 'passivity' which characterised traditional Irish-Catholic culture forced upon immigrants a view of emigration as exile, and conditioned their response to life in North America. Miller's views on the culture of exile have been endorsed recently in Matthew Frye Jacobson, *Special Sorrows: The Diasporic Imagination of Irish, Polish, and Jewish Immigrants in the United States,* Cambridge, 1995. For a critique of Miller's approach, see my *Being Had: Historians, Evidence, and the Irish in North America*, Toronto, 1985.

In his essay 'Revising the Diaspora', Alan O'Day observes that other historians, including Patrick O'Farrell, Cecil Houston and William Smyth, have made extensive use of immigrants' letters without reaching Miller's conclusions. See Alan O'Day, 'Revising the Diaspora', in D. George Boyce and Alan O'Day, eds, *The Making of Modern Irish History: Revisionism and the Revisionist Controversy*, London, 1996, ch. 10. O'Day's reference is to Cecil J. Houston and William J. Smyth, *Irish Emigration and Canadian Settlement: Patterns, Links and Letters*, Toronto, 1990, pp. 20-31. Roy Foster's remarks on this subject in 'Marginal Men and Micks on the Make', *Paddy and Mr. Punch. Connections in Irish and English History*, London, 1993, pp. 288-89, are also worth consulting.

4   I consider the importance of such an international perspective in the following works, which deal with Irish communities in different parts of the diaspora: *Being Had: Historians, Evidence and the Irish in North America*, Toronto, 1985; *Small Differences: Irish Catholics and Irish Protestants, 1815-1922: An International Perspective*, Montreal and Kingston, 1988; *Half the World from Home. Perspectives on the Irish in New Zealand, 1860-1950*, Wellington, 1990; *Occasional Papers on the Irish in South Africa*, Grahamstown, 1991; 'The Historiography of English-Speaking Canada and the Concept of Diaspora: A Skeptical Appreciation', *Canadian Historical Review*, 76 (1995), pp. 377-409; *If the Irish Ran the World: Montserrat, 1630-1730*, Montreal and Kingston, 1997.

5   Statistics on Irish out-migration are incomplete, but see the available data in the standard sources, N.H. Carrier and J.R. Jeffrey, *External Migration: A Study of the Available Statistics, 1815-1950, being No. 6 In the General Register Office's 'Studies on Medical Population Subjects'*, London, 1953; and *Commission of Emigration and other Population Problems, 1948-1954*, Dublin, 1954. Where possible, original emigration statistics should be consulted in the relevant House of Commons Parliamentary Papers.

Census data on the ethnicity and religious affiliation of populations varies in quantity and quality among the various English-speaking countries of the Irish diaspora. For Australia, the *Census for the Commonwealth of Australia, 1911* was the first full census for the population and included cross-tabulations on place of birth and religious affiliation. These data are broken down in my *Small Differences*, ch. 3. For the earliest detailed breakdown of population according to religious affiliation in New Zealand, see *Results of a Census on the Dominion of New Zealand, 1921*. The available data are summarised and explained in Akenson, *Half the World From Home*, ch. 3. Data on immigrants to South Africa are rather meagre. In 1891 and 1926 the authorities attempted to collect information on the ethnicity of the population, but the effort was unsuccessful. Nonetheless, an estimate of ethnicity can be calculated based on the existing data. See the *Results of the Census of the Colony of the Cape of Good Hope, 1891*; *Results of the Census, 1926*, and my commentary in *Occasional Papers on the Irish in South Africa*, ch. 3. Statistics for the later period are more complete; see F.G. Brownell, *British Immigration to South Africa, 1946-1970*, Pretoria, 1985.

The study of the Irish in the United States remains seriously impaired by the fact that the 1969-70 census was the first to ask questions concerning the ethnicity of respondents. Even then, the collection of the data was bungled and no firm conclusions could be reached. Further attempts in 1980 and 1990 were mishandled and the ethnicity question remained unproductive due to the authorities permitting individuals to list several ethnicities. Moreover, the United States census authorities have never collected information on the religious affiliation of specific individuals, and the historical relationship between religion and Irish ethnicity cannot be determined using official census data. Instead, studies of the Irish in North America must refer to data collected as part of a random survey carried out by the Graduate Center of the City University of New York in 1989-90. The study enquired into the religion, ethnicity and race of the members of 113,000 American households, a very large sample indeed. See Barry Kosmin et al., *Research Report: the National Survey of Religious Identification, 1989-90*, New York, 1991. For comparable data collected in smaller surveys, see George Gallup, Jr, and Jim Castelli, *The People's Religion: American Faith in the '90s*, New York, 1989. See also the relevant article by Michael Hout and Joshua R. Goldstein, 'How 4. 5 Million Irish Immigrants became 40 Million Irish Americans: Demographic and Subjective Aspects of the Ethnic Composition of White Americans', *American Sociological Review*, 59 (1994), pp. 64-82.

Finally, for the most substantial data on the ethnicity and religious affiliation of a nineteenth-century population, see the results of the 1870-71 Dominion of Canada Census reproduced in aggregate form in *Census of Canada, 1931*. The data for the 1861 and 1871 censuses have been retabulated from the original census manuscripts by Gordon Darroch and Michael Ornstein of York University, Ontario. Together they have constructed a data base that – on matters of ethnicity, religion, occupation, and social class – is the most sophisticated research design in North American ethnic historical studies, and should serve as a model for the construction of ethnic profiles in other countries. See A.G. Darroch and M.D. Ornstein, 'Ethnicity and Occupational Structure in Canada in 1871: the Vertical Mosaic in Historical Perspective', *Canadian Historical Review*, 61 (1980), pp. 305-33; A.G. Darroch and M.D. Ornstein, 'Ethnicity and Class, Transitions over a Decade; Ontario, 1861-1971', *Historical Papers*, Canadian Historical Association, 1984, pp. 111-137; A.G. Darroch, 'Half-Empty or Half-Full? Images and Interpretations in the Historical Analysis of the Catholic Irish in Nineteenth-Century Canada', *Canadian Ethnic Studies*, 25 (1993), pp. 1-8.

6   There are encouraging signs that this idea is being replaced in scholarship by a more ecumenical approach to Irish history and migration. See, for example, L.M. Cullen and Francois Furet, eds, *Ireland and France: Towards a Comparative Rural History*, Paris, 1981. In a study of Irish migrant labour, Jim McLaughlin favours such a comparative approach which avoids the pitfalls of 'national exceptionalism'. Jim MacLaughlin, 'Ireland: An "emigrant nursery" in the world economy', *International Migration*, 31 (1993), pp. 149-70. Timothy Guinnane challenges explicitly the notion of Irish exceptionalism in *The Vanishing Irish: Households, Migration, and the Rural Economy in Ireland, 1850-1914*, Princeton, 1997, ch. 1. See also Ulkich Kockel, 'Irish Migration to Mainland Germany', in Russell King, ed., *Ireland, Europe and the Single Market*, Dublin, 1993, pp. 128-36.

7   Collections include Dirk Hoerder, ed., *American Labor and Immigration History, 1877-1920s: Recent European Research*, Urbana, 1983; George E. Pozzetta, *American Immigration and Ethnicity. Volume 2: Emigration and Immigration. The Old World Confronts the New*, New York, 1991; Rudolph J. Vecoli and Suzanne M. Sinke, eds, *A Century of European Migration, 1830-1930*, Urbana, 1991; Dirk Hoerder and Horst Rossler, eds, *Distant Magnets: Expectations and Realities in the Immigrant Experience, 1840-1930*, New York, 1993. For the earlier period, see the recent collection of essays edited by Nicholas Canny, *Europeans on the Move: Studies on European Migration, 1500-1800*, Oxford, 1994. The chapters on English, Scottish,

Irish, Dutch, German and French migrations are accompanied by more specialised bibliographies.

H. Arnold Barton examines the history of Scandinavian-American migration studies and the current state of scholarship in 'Where Have the Scandinavian Americanists Been?', *Journal of American Ethnic History*, 15 (1995), pp. 46-55. See also Odd S. Lovoll, ed., *Scandinavians and Other Immigrants in Urban America: The Proceedings of a Research Conference, October 26-27, 1984*, Northfield, 1985; Harald Runblom and Dag Blanck, eds, *Scandinavia Overseas: Patterns of Cultural Transformation in North America and Australia*, Uppsala, 1986; Hans Norman and Harald Runblom, *Transatlantic Connections: Nordic Migration to the New World after 1800*, Oslo, 1988; Robert C. Ostergren, *A Community Transplanted: The Trans-Atlantic Experience of a Swedish Immigrant Settlement in the Upper Middle West*, Madison, 1988; Odd S. Lovoll, ed., *Nordics in America: The Future of their Past*, Northfield, 1993; J.E. Rasmussen, *New Land New Lives: Scandinavian Immigrants to the Pacific Northwest*, Northfield, 1993. There is an extensive literature on Italian migration, including some valuable local and regional studies. See, for example, the excellent article by Russell King and Brian Reynolds, 'Casalattico, Dublin and the Fish and Chip Connection: A Classic Example of Chain Migration', *Studi Emigrazione*, 31 (1994), pp. 398-426. See also Donna R. Gabaccia, *Militants and Migrants: Rural Sicilians Become American Workers*, New Brunswick, 1988; Franc Sturino, *Forging the Chain: A Case Study of Italian Migration to North America, 1880-1930*, Toronto, 1990; Samuel Baily, 'The Village Outward Approach to the Study of Social Networks: A Case Study of the Agnonesi Diaspora Abroad, 1885-1989', *Studi Emigrazione* 29 (1992), pp. 43-67. For trends in migration scholarship, see J. Salt, 'Contemporary Trends in International Migration Study', *International Migration* 15 (1987), pp. 241-51; Silvia Pedraza-Bailey, 'Immigration Research: A Conceptual Map', *Social Science History* 14 (1990), pp. 43-67; Ewa Morawska, 'The Sociology and Historiography of Immigration', in Virginia Yans-McLaughlin, ed., *Immigration Reconsidered: History, Sociology, Politics*, New York, 1991.

8   President Robinson provided this estimate in her inaugural address on 3 December 1990. *Canadian Journal of Irish Studies*, 17 (1991), p. 109.

9   For the history of the Irish in southern Africa, see the pioneering work of Donal P. McCracken, 'The Irish in Colonial South Africa: An Overview', *Southern African-Irish Studies*, vol. 1, Durban-Westville, 1991, and the essays edited by McCracken as part of the Southern-African-Irish Studies series, *Southern-African-Irish Studies*, 1 (1991); *The Irish in Southern Africa, 1795-1910*, vol. 2 (1992); and *Ireland and South Africa in Modern Times*, vol. 3 (1996). The remaining historical literature is rather thin, but see R.H. Henderson, *An Ulsterman in Africa*, Cape Town, 1944; Kathleen M. Cox, *Immigration into South Africa, 1940-67: A Bibliography*, Cape Town, 1970; E. Morse Jones, *Roll of the British Settlers in South Africa, Part I: Up to 1826*, Cape Town, 1971; Graham B. Dickason, *Irish Settlers to the Cape: A History of the Clanwilliam 1820 Settlers from Cork*, Cape Town, 1973; Pamela M. Barnes, 'Irish Immigration to South Africa: A Historical Introduction', *The Irish at Home and Abroad*, 4 (1997), pp. 165-67.

The literature on the Irish elsewhere in Africa, and throughout the West Indies and the Spanish Empire is scarce. The following works indicate the opportunity for research on this aspect of the Irish diaspora: Robert MacAdam, 'Is the Irish Language Spoken in Africa?', *Ulster Journal of Archaeology*, 7 (1859), pp. 195-200; Joseph I.

Williams, *Whence the "Black Irish" of Jamaica?*, New York, 1932; John C. Messenger, 'The Influence of the Irish in Montserrat', *Caribbean Quarterly*, 13 (1967), pp. 3-26; Stephen Clissold, *Bernardo O'Higgins and the Independence of Chile*, London, 1968; Hilary Beckles, *White Servitude and Black Slavery in Barbados, 1627-1715*, Knoxville, 1989; J. Lorimer, *English and Irish Settlement on the River Amazon, 1550-1646*, London, 1989; Hilary Beckles, 'A "Riotous and unruly lot": Irish Indentured Servants and Freemen in the English West Indies, 1644-1713', *William and Mary Quarterly*, 47 (1990), pp. 503-22; R. Burrett, 'The Eyre Brothers: Arthur and Herbert', *Heritage of Zimbabwe*, 9 (1990), pp. 37-46; Grainne Henry, *The Irish Military Community in Spanish Flanders, 1586-1621*, Dublin, 1992; Donald Harman Akenson, *If the Irish Ran the World: Montserrat, 1630-1730*, Montreal and Kingston, 1997; Jose C. Moya, *Cousins and Strangers: Spanish Immigrants in Buenos Aires, 1850-1930*, Berkeley, 1998.

The intersection of the African and Irish diasporas in North America produced the infamous New York City draft riots in 1863. See Adrian Cook, *The Armies of the Streets: The New York City Draft Riots of 1863*, Lexington, 1974; Iver Bernstein, *The New York City Draft Riots*, New York, 1990. For relations between the Irish and African-Americans in Philadelphia, see Dennis Clark, *The Irish Relations: Trials of an Immigrant Tradition*, Rutherford, 1982.

For an entry into the literature on the Irish ethnic group in England, see Roger Swift, *The Irish in Britain, 1815-1914: Perspectives and Sources*, London, 1990, and his review essay, 'The Historiography of the Irish in Nineteenth-Century Britain', in P. O'Sullivan, ed., *The Irish World Wide. Volume 2, The Irish in the New Communities*. For earlier literature, see Maureen Hartigan, *The History of the Irish in Britain: A Bibliography*, London, 1986. For specific studies of Irish migrant communities in Bristol, York, Glasgow, Liverpool, Edinburgh and Stockport, see the excellent collection of essays edited by Roger Swift and Sheridan Gilley, *The Irish in the Victorian City*, London, 1985, and their equally valuable companion volume, *The Irish in Britain, 1815-1939*, London, 1989. An extensive survey of the themes and literature concerning the Irish in Britain is Graham Davis, *The Irish in Britain, 1815-1914*, Dublin, 1991.

In addition to essays in the collections by Swift and Gilley, there are numerous local and thematic studies on the Irish in Britain. For a sample of the available literature, see the following: Lynn Hollen Lees, 'Patterns of Lower-Class Life: Irish Slum Communities in Nineteenth-Century London', in Stephan Thernstrom and Richard Sennett, eds, *Nineteenth-Century Cities*, New Haven, 1969; L.P. Curtis, *Apes and Angels: The Irishman in Victorian Caricature*, Newton Abbot, 1971; John Haslett and W.J. Lowe, 'Household Structure and Overcrowding Among the Lancashire Irish, 1851-1871', *Histoire Sociale/Social History*, 10 (1977), pp. 45-58; Lynn Hollen Lees, *Exiles of Erin: Irish Migrants in Victorian London*, Ithaca, 1979; Sean Glynn, 'Irish Immigration to Britain, 1911-1951: Patterns and Policy', *Irish Economic and Social History*, 8 (1981), pp. 50-69; M.A.G. O'Tuathaigh, 'The Irish in Nineteenth-Century Britain: Problems of Integration', *Transactions of the Royal Historical Society*, 31 (1981), pp. 149-73, reprinted in Swift and Gilley, *The Irish in the Victorian City*; Frances Finnegan, *Poverty and Prejudice: A Study of Irish Immigrants in York, 1840-1875*, Cork, 1982; Colin Holmes, 'The Impact of Immigration on British Society, 1870-1980', in Theo Barker and Michael Drake, eds, *Population and Society in Britain, 1850-1980*, New York, 1982; Michael P.

Smith-Hornsby and Angela Dale, 'The Assimilation of Irish Immigrants in England', *British Journal of Sociology*, 39 (1988), pp. 519-44; T.M. Devine, ed., *Irish Immigrants and Scottish Society in the Nineteenth and Twentieth Centuries*, Edinburgh, 1991; Steven Fielding, *Class and Ethnicity: Irish Catholics in England, 1880-1939*, Buckingham, 1993; Donald MacRaild, 'Irish Culture in an English Context', *Labour History Review*, 58 (1993), pp. 44-48; Ruth-Ann M. Harris, *The Nearest Place that Wasn't Ireland: Early Nineteenth-Century Irish Labor Migration*, Ames, 1994; Donald MacRaild, 'Irish Immigration and the "Condition of England" Question: the Roots of an Historiographical Tradition', *Immigrants and Minorities*, 14 (1995), pp. 67-85; M.A. Busteed and R.L Hodgson, 'Irish Migrant Responses to Urban Life in Early Nineteenth-Century Manchester', *Geographical Journal*, 162 (1996), pp. 139-53; Kathleen Paul, 'A Case of Mistaken Identity: the Irish in Postwar Britain', *International Labor and Working-Class History*, 49 (1996), pp. 116-42. More recent concern about the mental and physical health of the Irish migrant community has produced several important studies: James Raftery, David R. Jones and Michael Rosato, 'The Mortality Rate of First and Second Generation Irish Immigrants in the United Kingdom', *Social Science and Medicine*, 31 (1990), pp. 577-84; Helena M. Carison, M. and Erik L. Nilson, 'Ireland: Gender, Psychological Health and Attitudes Toward Emigration', *Psychological Reports*, 76 (1995), pp. 179-86; P.J. Bracken, L. Greenslade, B. Griffin and M. Smyth, 'Mental Health and Ethnicity: an Irish Dimension', *British Journal of Psychiatry*, 172 (1998), pp. 103-195.

10 An indication of the rich possibilities of commercial histories, if well done, is Patrick Lynch and John Vaizey, *Guinness's Brewery in the Irish Economy, 1759-1876*, Cambridge, 1960, pp. 89-90, 132. See also, T. Gourvish and R.G. Wilson, *The British Brewing Industry, 1830-1930*, New York, 1994, and Andy Bielenberg, *Cork's Industrial Revolution, 1780-1880*, Cork, 1991, pp. 50-60.

11 Franklin A. Walker, *Catholic Education and Politics in Upper Canada*, Toronto, 1955; J. Donald Wilson, 'The Ryerson Years in Upper Canada', in J. Donald Wilson, Robert M. Stamp and Louis-Philippe, eds, *Canadian Education: A History*, Scarborough, 1970; Donald Harman Akenson, *The Irish Education Experiment. The National System of Education in the Nineteenth Century*, London, 1973; R.D. Gidney, 'Making Nineteenth-Century School Systems: The Upper Canadian Experience and its Relevance to English Historiography', *History of Education*, 9 (1980), pp. 101-16; Donald Harman Akenson, *The Irish in Ontario: A Study in Rural History*, Montreal and Kingston, 1984.

12 The influence of the (Irish) Catholic church on systems of education throughout the empire has been studied only incidentally, as part of national or local histories, or of studies in education, but see the following: my *Half the World from Home*, ch. 6; Geoffrey Sherington, 'Australian Immigration, Ethnicity and Education', *History of Education Review* [Australia], 20 (1991), pp. 61-72; Margaret Pawsey, 'The introduction of payment by results into Victoria's schools', *History of Education Review* [Australia], 23 (1994), pp. 1-17; David L. Salvaterra, *American Catholicism and the Intellectual Life, 1880-1950*, New York, 1988; Janet A. Nolan, 'Irish-American Teachers and the Struggle over American Urban Public Education, 1890-1920: A Preliminary Look', *Records of the American Catholic Historical Society of Philadelphia*, 103 (1992), pp. 13-22.

13 An important exception is the pioneering work of the late Kathleen Hughes, *The*

Church in Early Irish Society, London, 1966. See also a collection of her essays in Hughes, *Church and Society in Ireland, A.D. 400-1200*, London, 1987. For an entry into the Patrician literature, see T.F. O'Rahilly, *Early Irish History and Mythology*, Dublin, 1964. An older but classic work is James Heron, *The Celtic Church in Ireland: the Story of Ireland and Irish Christianity from before the time of St Patrick to the Reformation*, London, 1898.

14 Donald Harman Akenson, *Surpassing Wonder. The Invention of the Bible and the Talmuds*, New York and London, 1998.

15 For example, James S. Donnelly, Jr, 'The Construction of the Memory of the Famine in Ireland and the Irish Diaspora, 1850-1900', *Eire-Ireland*, 31 (1996), pp. 26-61; Allen Feldman, '"Gaelic Gotham": Decontextualising the Diaspora', *Eire-Ireland*, 31 (1996), pp. 189-201. The Irish diaspora has also become the focus of general surveys; see the entry on Ireland in Gerard Chaliand, *The Penguin Atlas of the Diasporas*, New York, 1995. More importantly, the *New History of Ireland* devotes substantial sections to the history of the Irish abroad. For the nineteenth and twentieth centuries, see the entries by David Fitzpatrick, David Noel Doyle and Patrick O'Farrell in W.E. Vaughan, ed., *The New History of Ireland: Volume V, Ireland Under the Union, 1801-1870* and *Volume VI, Ireland Under the Union, 1870-1921*, Oxford, 1989. A comprehensive bibliography is included in Volume VI, 'Bibliography: History of the Irish Abroad', pp. 845-51. The multi-volume collection of essays on aspects of the Irish diaspora in *The Irish World Wide* series, edited by Patrick O'Sullivan, confirms the increasing depth and breadth of Irish migration research. In addition, L.M. Cullen addresses an earlier and often neglected period of Irish migration in his chapter, 'The Irish Diaspora of the Seventeenth and Eighteenth-Centuries', in Nicholas Canny, ed., *Europeans on the Move. Studies on European Migration, 1500-1800*, Oxford, 1994. For a survey of the current state of scholarship on the Irish diaspora, see the essay by Alan O'Day, 'Revising the Diaspora', in D. George Boyce and Alan O'Day, eds, *The Making of Modern Irish History. Revisionism and the Revisionist Controversy*, London and New York, 1996, pp. 188-215. Two of the more important works of larger imagination deal with the Antipodes: James Belich, *Making Peoples. A History of the New Zealanders from Polynesian Settlement to the End of the Nineteenth-Century*, London, 1996, and David Fitzpatrick, *Oceans of Consolation – Personal Accounts of Irish Migration to Australia*, Ithaca and London, 1994.

16 A valuable collection of essays appears in Volume 4 of *The Irish World Wide* series edited by Patrick O'Sullivan, *Irish Women and Irish Migration*. For additional reading on the history of women and Irish migration, see the following: Robert E. Kennedy Jr, *The Irish: Emigration, Marriage and Fertility*, Berkeley, 1973; Carol Groneman, 'Working Class Immigrant Women in Mid-Nineteenth Century New York: the Irish Women's Experience', *Journal of Urban History*, 4 (1978), pp. 255-74; Hasia Diner, *Erin's Daughters in America: Irish Immigrant Women in the Nineteenth-Century*, Baltimore, 1983; Pauline Jackson, 'Women in Nineteenth-Century Irish Emigration', *International Migration Review*, 18 (1984), pp. 1004-1020: David Fitzpatrick, '"A Share of the Honeycomb": Education, Emigration and Irishwomen', *Continuity and Change*, 1 (1986), pp. 217-34; Janet Nolan, *Ourselves Alone: Women's Emigration from Ireland 1880-1920*, Lexington, 1989; Ide O'Carroll, *Models for Movers. Irish Women's Emigration to America*, Dublin, 1990; Malcolm Campbell, 'Irish Women in Nineteenth-Century Australia: A More Hidden Ireland?', in Phillip Bull, Chris

McConville and Noel McLachlan, eds, *Irish Australian Studies*, 6, Melbourne, 1991; Donna Gabbaccia, 'Immigrant Women. Nowhere at Home?', *Journal of American Ethnic History*, 10 (1991), pp. 61-87; Ann Rossiter, 'Bringing the Margins into the Centre: A Review of Aspects of Irish Women's Emigration', in Sean Hutton and Paul Stewart, eds, *Ireland's Histories*, London, 1991; Sheelagh Conway, *The Faraway Hills are Green: Voices of Irish Women in Canada*, Toronto, 1992; Lara Marks, '"The Luckless Waifs and Strays of Humanity": Irish and Jewish Immigrant Unwed Mothers in London, 1870-1939', *Twentieth Century British History*, 3 (1992), pp. 113-37; Grace Neville, 'She Never Then After That Forgot Him: Irishwomen and Emigration to the United States in Irish Folklore', *Mid-America*, 74 (1992), pp. 271-89; Sydney Stahl Weinberg, 'The Treatment of Women in Immigration History: A Call for Change', *Journal of American Ethnic History*, 11 (1992), pp. 25-46; Laurie K. Mercier, '"We are Women Irish": Gender, Class, Religion and Ethnic Identity in Anaconda, Montana', *Montana*, 44 (1994), pp. 28-41; Suellen Hoy, 'The Journey Out: The Recruitment and Emigration of Irish Religious Women to the United States, 1812-1914', *Journal of Women's History*, 6 (1995), pp. 64-98; Joan Grant, ed., *Women, Migration and Empire*, 1996. Literature on contemporary women migrants from Ireland includes Jenny Beale, *Women in Ireland. Voices of Change*, London, 1986; Mary Lennon, Masie McAdam and Joanne O'Brien, *Across the Water: Irish Women's Lives in Britain*, London, 1988; Joy Rudd, 'Invisible Exports: The Emigration of Irish Women this Century', *Women's Studies International Forum*, 11 (1988), pp. 307-11; Kate Kelly and Triona Nic Giolla Choille, *Emigration Matters for Women*, Dublin, 1990; Breda Gray, 'Irish Women in London: National or Hybrid Diasporic Identities?', *NWSA Journal*, 8 (1996), pp. 85-109.

17 *Commission on Emigration and other Population Problems, 1948–1954*, Dublin, 1954.

18 Charles Price, who virtually established serious ethnic history in Australia, points out that there are two sorts of ethnic identification: subjective and objective. The objective aspects include place of birth, religious affiliation and first language. The subjective aspects are more intriguing, and include how people feel about their cultural heritage and how they identify themselves. Charles Price, 'Ethnic Composition of the Australian Population', in Price, ed., *Australian Immigration. A Bibliography and Digest*, no. 4, Canberra, 1981. See also Christopher McAll, *Class, Ethnicity and Social Inequality*, Montreal and Kingston, 1990; A.P. Cohen, 'Culture as Identity: An Anthropologist's View', *New Literary History*, 24 (1993), pp. 195-209. For discussions of ethnicity in the United States, see K.N. Conzen et al., 'The Invention of Ethnicity: A Perspective from the U.S.A.', *Journal of American Ethnic History*, 12 (1992), pp. 3-41; Rudolph Vecoli, 'An Inter-Ethnic Perspective on American Immigration History', *Mid-America*, 75 (1993); Elliott R. Barkan, 'Race, Religion, and Nationality in American Society: A Model of Ethnicity – From Contact to Assimilation', *Journal of American Ethnic History*, 14 (1995), pp. 38-101.

19 See Ronald Robinson, 'Non-European Foundation of European Imperialism: Sketch for a Theory of Collaboration', in Roger Owen and Bob Sutcliffe, eds, *Studies in the Theory of Imperialism*, London, 1972, pp. 117-42. The relationship of the Irish to empires is beginning to be explored by historians. See Scott B. Cook, 'The Irish Raj: Social Origins and Careers of Irishmen in the Indian Civil Service, 1855-1914', *Journal of Social History*, 20 (1987), pp. 506-29; Hiram Morgan, 'An Unwelcome Heritage: Ireland's Role in British Empire-Building', *History of European Ideas*, 19

(1994), pp. 619-25; Ann Daniel, 'Undermining British Australia: Irish lawyers and the Transformation of English Law in Australia', *Studies*, 84 (1995), pp. 61-70; Keith Jeffery, ed., 'An Irish Empire?', *Aspects of Ireland and the British Empire*, Manchester, 1996. The role of Irish soldiers in the British army is explored throughout the collection by Thomas Bartlett and Keith Jeffery, eds, *A Military History of Ireland*, 1996. Also see H.J. Hanham, 'Religion and Nationality in the Mid-Victorian Army', in M.R. Foot, ed, *War and Society: Historical Essays in Honour and Memory of J.R. Western, 1928-1971*, London, 1973; Peter Karsten, 'Irish Soldiers in the British Army, 1792-1922: Suborned or Subordinate?', *Journal of Social History*, 17 (1983), pp. 31-64; A.J. Cook, 'Irish in the British Army in South Africa, 1795-1910', in Donal P. McCracken, ed., *The Irish in Southern Africa, 1795-1910*, Southern African-Irish Studies Volume 2, 1992; Terence Denman, *Ireland's Unknown Soldiers: The 16th (Irish) Division in the Great War, 1914-1918*, Dublin, 1992. Irish soldiers have also filled the ranks of foreign armies. For example, see Alfred Hasbrouck, *Foreign Legionaries in the Liberation of Spanish South America*, New York, 1969; James Belich, *The New Zealand Wars and the Victorian Interpretation of Racial Conflict*, Auckland, 1986; Donal McCracken, *The Irish Pro-Boers, 1877-1902*, Johannesburg, 1989; Grainne Henry, *The Irish Military Community in Spanish Flanders, 1586-1621*, Dublin, 1992; Myles Dungan, *Distant Drums: Irish Soldiers in Foreign Armies*, Belfast, 1993; John Gallaher, *Napoleon's Irish Legion*, Carbondale, 1993. Ireland's military history journal, *The Irish Sword*, is a treasury of information on Irish involvement in both the British army and many foreign armies. For a discussion of the origin of policing systems throughout the empire, and the adoption of the Royal Irish Constabulary as a model for colonial police forces, see David M. Anderson and David Killingray, eds, *Policing the Empire: Government, Authority and Control, 1830-1940*, Manchester, 1991. Richard Hawkins is sceptical about the adoption of an Irish model to colonial police systems; see ch. 2 in Anderson and Killingray: 'The "Irish Model" and the Empire: A Case for Reassessment'. Other contributors to the volume, however, confirm links between the Royal Irish Constabulary and policing in the colonies.

20 In an important article, Brian Stoddart argues that the consolidation of the British empire was achieved in large part through the import of 'cultural power', the set of ideas, beliefs and conventions concerning social behaviour that was carried throughout the empire by civil servants, military officers, traders, settlers and educators. He points to the English language as a primary example. Also crucial was the introduction of British sports and games into the colonies, and his article sets a framework for an analysis of the elaboration of cultural power through sport. Brian Stoddart, 'Sport, Cultural Imperialism, and Colonial Response in the British Empire', *Comparative Studies in Society and History*, 30 (1988), pp. 649-73.

21 For an entry into the literature on the Irish in North America, see Seamus Metress, *The Irish American Experience: A Guide to the Literature*, Washington, D.C., 1981 and subsequent editions; R.A. Burchell, 'The Historiography of the American Irish', *Immigrants and Minorities*, (1982), pp. 281-305; David Noel Doyle, 'The Regional Bibliography of Irish America, 1800-1930: A Review and Addendum', *Irish Historical Studies*, 23 (1983), pp. 24-283; Donald Harman Akenson, 'An Agnostic View of the Historiography of the Irish-Americans', *Labour/Le Travail*, 14, (1984), pp. 123-59; Michael F. Funchion, 'Irish-America: An Essay on the Literature Since 1978', *The Immigration History Newsletter*, 17 (1985), pp. 1-8; Kenneth W. Keller, 'The Origins

of Ulster Scots Emigration to America: A Survey of Recent Research', *American Presbyterians*, 70, (1992), pp. 71-80; David Noel Doyle, 'Small Differences? The Study of the Irish in the United States and Britain', *Irish Historical Studies*, 29 (1994), pp. 114-19; Graham Davis, 'Models of Migration: The Historiography of the Irish Pioneers in South Texas', *Southwestern Historical Quarterly*, XCIX (1996), pp. 327-45.

The history of the Irish in America has been well served by regional and community studies: Dennis Clark, *The Irish in Philadelphia: Ten Generations of Urban Experience*, Philadelphia, 1973, and *Erin's Heirs: Irish Bonds of Community*, Lexington, 1991; Patrick J. Blessing, *West Among Strangers: Irish Migration to California, 1850-1880*, Los Angeles, 1977; R.A. Burchell, *The San Francisco Irish 1848-1880*, Manchester, 1979; Timothy Meagher, ed., *From Paddy to Studs: Irish-American Communities in the Turn of the Century Era, 1880-1920*, Westport, 1986; L.J. McCaffrey et al., *The Irish in Chicago*, Urbana, 1987; B.C. Mitchell, *The Paddy Camps: The Irish of Lowell 1821-1861*, Urbana, 1988; Grady McWhinney, *Cracker Culture: Celtic Ways in the Old South*, Tuscaloosa, 1988; P.J. Drudy, ed., *Irish Studies 4: The Irish in America: Emigration, Assimilation and Impact*, op. cit.; Patrick J. Blessing, 'Paddy: The Image and Reality of Irish Immigrants in the American Community: A Review Essay', *Journal of American Ethnic History*, 9 (1989), pp. 112-19; David M. Emmons, *The Butte Irish: Class and Ethnicity in an American Mining Town, 1875-1925*, Urbana, 1989; Rory Fitzpatrick, *God's Frontiersmen: The Scots-Irish Epic*, London, 1989; David Noel Doyle, 'The Irish as Urban Pioneers in the United States', *Journal of American Ethnic History*, 10 (1990/1991), pp. 36-59; Michael A. Gordon, *The Orange Riots: Irish Political Violence in New York City, 1870 and 1871*, New York, 1993; Malcolm Campbell, 'The Other Immigrants: Comparing the Irish in Australia and the United States', *Journal of American Ethnic History*, 14 (1995), pp. 3-22; Thomas H. O'Connor, *The Boston Irish: A Political History*, Boston, 1995; Ronald H. Bayor and Timothy J. Meagher, *The New York Irish*, Baltimore, 1996; H. Tyler Blethen and Curtis W. Wood, Jr, eds, *Ulster and North America: Transatlantic Perspectives on the Scotch-Irish*, Tuscaloosa and London, 1997.

The history of the Irish in America is actually the history of the Irish in North America, and the high quality of literature on the Irish migrant group in Canada is frequently overlooked by historians of the Irish in the United States. As a corrective, see the following: Bruce S. Elliott, *Irish Migrants in the Canadas: A New Approach*, Montreal and Kingston and Belfast, 1988; Robert O'Driscoll and Lorna Reynolds, eds, *The Untold Story: The Irish in Canada*, 2 vols, Toronto, 1988; Thomas Power, ed., *The Irish in Atlantic Canada 1780-1900*, Fredericton, 1988; David Wilson, *The Irish in Canada*, Ottawa, 1989; Margaret B. Fitzgerald and Joseph A. King, *The Uncounted Irish in Canada and the United States*, Toronto, 1990; Cecil J. Houston and William J. Smyth, *Irish Emigration and Canadian Settlement: Patterns, Links, and Letters*, Toronto, 1990; Gerald L. Pocius, *A Place to Belong: Community Order and Everyday Space in Calvert, Newfoundland*, Montreal and Kingston, 1991; Catherine Anne Wilson, *A New Lease on Life: Landlords, Tenants and Immigrants in Ireland and Canada*, Montreal and Kingston, 1994.

There is a rich literature in fiction on the Irish experience in America. See Finley Peter Dunne, *Mr. Dooley in the Hearts of His Countrymen*, Boston, 1899; Finley Peter Dunne, *Mr. Dooley's Philosophy*, New York, 1900; James T. Farrell, *Studs*

Lonigan: A Trilogy (Young Lonigan, The Young Manhood of Studs Lonigan, Judgement Day), New York, 1978; Edwin O'Connor, *The Last Hurrah*, Boston, 1956. The literature is reviewed with commentary and a comprehensive bibliography in Charles Fanning, *The Irish Voice in America: Irish-American Fiction from the 1760s to the 1980s*, Lexington, 1990. Literature on the Irish experience in Canada is not nearly as extensive, but see Brian Moore, *The Luck of Ginger Coffey*, Boston, 1960, and Jane Urquhart, *Away*, Toronto, 1993. For a unique perspective on the Irish in New Zealand, Dan Davin's works of historical fiction are required reading. See Dan Davin, *Selected Stories*, Wellington and London, 1981.

22 For the most part, the influence of the Irish Catholic and Protestant churches on the British empire has been explored only incidentally, through studies of specific congregations, missions and key figures in ecclesiastical history. Most, but not all, of the literature focuses on the Roman Catholic church. The following literature confirms the significance of Irish religious influence in every corner of the diaspora and invites research in this understudied area of scholarship. Rev. John Colgan, 'Irish missionaries in South Africa', *Studies*, December (1931), pp. 611-26; Aubrey Gwynn, 'The First Irish Priests in the New World', *Studies*, 21 (1932), pp. 213-28; Henry Koren, *The Spiritans: A History of the Congregation of the Holy Ghost*, Pittsburgh, 1958; W.E. Brown, *The Catholic Church in South Africa*, London, 1960; W.J. Lowe, 'The Lancashire Irish and the Catholic Church, 1846-71: The Social Dimension', *Irish Historical Studies*, 20 (1976), pp. 129-55; Antoine Demets, *The Catholic Church in Montserrat, West Indies, 1756-1980*, Plymouth, 1980; Cecil J. Houston and William J. Smyth, *The Sash Canada Wore: A Historical Geography of the Orange Order in Canada*, Toronto, 1980; Patrick Carey, *An Immigrant Bishop: John England's Adaptation of Irish Catholicism to American Republicanism*, Yonkers, 1982; Edmund Hogan, 'African Conversion to Roman Catholicism', *African Ecclesiastical Review*, 24 (1982), pp. 71-80; Sheridan Gilley, 'The Roman Catholic Church and the Nineteenth-Century Irish Diaspora', *Journal of Ecclesiastical History*, 35 (1984), pp. 188-207; Norman W. Taggart, *The Irish in World Methodism, 1760-1900*, London, 1986; Paul O'Leary, 'Irish Immigration and the Catholic Welsh District, 1840-50', in G.H. Jenkins and J.B. Smith, eds, *Politics and Society in Wales, 1840-1922: Essays in Honour of Ieuan Gwynedd Jones*, Cardiff, 1988; Hugh McLeod, 'Popular Catholicism in Irish New York, c. 1900', in W.J. Shiels and Diana Woods, eds, *The Churches, Ireland and the Irish*, London, 1989; Edmund M. Hogan, *The Irish Missionary Movement: A Historical Survey, 1830-1980*, Dublin and Washington D.C., 1990); Elaine McFarland, *Protestants First: Orangeism in Nineteenth Century Scotland*, Edinburgh, 1990; Louis McRedmond, *To the Greater Glory: A History of the Irish Jesuits*, Dublin, 1991; William Sloan, 'Religious Affiliation and the Immigrant Experience: Catholic Irish and Protestant Highlanders in Glasgow, 1830-1850', in T.M. Devire, ed., *Irish Immigrants and Scottish Society in the Nineteenth and Twentieth Centuries*, Edinburgh, 1991; J.B. Brain, 'The Irish Influence on the Roman Catholic Church in South Africa', in Donal P. McCracken, ed., *The Irish in Southern Africa, 1795-1910, Southern African-Irish Studies*, volume 2, 1992; M.M. Goedhals, 'The Road to Disestablishment: Irish Anglicans in Nineteenth-Century South Africa', in Donal P. McCracken, ed., *The Irish in Southern Africa, 1795-1910*; Leo J. Hynes, *The Catholic Irish in New Brunswick 1783-1900: A History of their Prominent Role in the Shaping of the Province and the Structuring of the Roman Catholic Church*, Moncton, 1992; Brian P. Clarke, *Piety and Nationalism. Lay Voluntary Associations and the Creation of an Irish-Catholic Community in Toronto,*

1850-1895, Montreal and Kingston, 1993; Terrence Murphy and Gerald Stortz, ed., *Creed and Culture. The Place of English Speaking Catholics in Canadian Society, 1750-1930*, Montreal and Kingston, 1993; Patricia T. Rooke, 'Baptists and Proselytisers: Non-denominational Education in the British Caribbean after Emancipation', *History of Education*, 23 (1994), pp. 257-73; Joseph Akinyele Omoyajowo, ed., *Makers of the Church in Nigeria*, Lagos, 1995; James White McAuley, 'Under an Orange Banner: Reflections on the Northern Protestant Experiences of Emigration', in Patrick O'Sullivan, ed., *The Irish World Wide*, volume 5, *Religion and Identity*; Michael J. McNally, 'Diocesan Clerical Life in Florida', *Records of the American Catholic Historical Society of Philadelphia*, 106 (1995), pp. 50-62.

Although the influence of the Irish Catholic church worldwide has been underestimated, the emerging history of Irish Catholicism in Australia provides a growing exception to this rule, much of the work being a continuing footnote to the pioneering work of Patrick O'Farrell. See, especially, the following: Michael Gilchrist, *Daniel Mannix, Priest and Patriot*, Victoria, 1982, and a critique of the Mannix literature in R.M. Sweetman, 'Daniel Mannix and His Biographers', *Australian Studies*, 1 (1988), pp. 61-71; Helen Hoizer, 'The Sisters of Mercy in Auckland of the 1850s and 1860s', *Auckland-Waikato Historical Journal*, 44 (1984), pp. 30-35 and 45 (1984), pp. 22-28; Patrick O'Farrell, *The Catholic Church and Community in Australia: A History*, Kensington, 1985; A.E. Cahill, 'Cardinal Moran's Politics', *Journal of Religious History*, 15 (1989), pp. 525-31; Marie Therese Foale, *The Josephite Story*, Sydney, 1989; M.S. McGrath, *These Women? Women Religious in the History of Australia: Sisters of Mercy, Parramatta 1888-1988*, Sydney, 1989; Ruth Schumann, 'The Catholic Priesthood of South Australia,1844-1915', *Journal of Religious History*, 16 (1990), pp. 51-73; Jane Tolerton, *Convent Girls*, Auckland, 1994; Lyndon Fraser, '"The Ties that Bind": Irish Catholic Testamentary Evidence from Christchurch, 1876-1915', *New Zealand Journal of History*, 29 (1995), pp. 67-82; Janice Tranter, 'The Irish Dimension of an Australian Religious Sisterhood: the Sisters of St Joseph', in Patrick O'Sullivan, ed., *The Irish World Wide*, volume 5, *Religion and Identity*; Patrick O'Farrell, 'The Irish in Australia and New Zealand, 1870-1990', in W.E. Vaughan, ed., *A New History of Ireland. Volume VI, Ireland Under the Union, 1870-1921*, Oxford, 1996; Rory Sweetman, *Bishop in the Dock: the Sedition Trial of James Liston*, Auckland, 1997. For a contrast, a throwback to the old idea (albeit wrapped in post-modernspeak) that the Protestants were not really Irish, see Mary J. Hickman, *Religion, Class and Identity. The State, the Catholic Church and the Education of the Irish in Britain*, Aldershot, 1995.

23 Two classic books which served as a model for this virtually racialist distinction between the Ulster Scots and the Irish Catholics in North America are Charles A. Hanna, *The Scotch-Irish, or, The Scot in North Britain, North Ireland, and North America*, New York, 1902, and Henry Ford Jones, *The Scotch-Irish in America*, Princeton, 1915. For a revival of this opinion, see R. Hanna, *Land of the Free: Ulster and the American Revolution*, Lurgan, 1992. The related assumption that Irish migrant communities are culturally homogeneous continues to distort current scholarship. See James White McAuley's critique in 'Under an Orange Banner', pp. 43-44 and *passim*. Also see the thoughtful essay by Kenneth W. Keller, 'What is Distinctive about the Scotch-Irish?', in Robert D. Mitchell, ed., *Appalachian Frontiers*, Lexington, 1991.

24 Donald MacRaild, *Culture, Conflict and Migration: The Irish in Victorian Cumbria*, Liverpool, 1998.

Chapter 2

1. *Journal of Religious History*, 9 (1976), p. 217.
2. Subtitled *A History of Catholics in New Zealand*, Auckland, 1997.
3. Auckland, 1996.
4. MA thesis, University of Canterbury, 1976.
5. Patrick O'Farrell, *Vanished Kingdoms: Irish in Australia and New Zealand: A Personal Excursion*, Kensington, 1990, pp. 153-55.
6. This is a matter discussed in Ibid., ch. 7.
7. Patrick O'Farrell, 'Defining Place and Home: Are the Irish Prisoners of Place?', in David Fitzpatrick, ed., *Home or Away? Immigrants in Colonial Australia. Visible Immigrants: Three*, Canberra 1992, pp. 1-18. See also Patrick O'Farrell, 'Landscapes of the Irish Immigrant Mind', in John Hardy, ed., *Stories of Australian Migration*, Kensington, 1988, pp. 33-46.
8. Auckland, 1989.
9. Patrick O'Farrell, 'How Irish was New Zealand?', in S. Briggs, P. Hyland, and N. Sammells, *Reviewing Ireland. Essays and Interviews from Irish Studies Review*, Bath, 1998, pp. 100-04.
10. All Curnow's poems quoted here are from *A Book of New Zealand Verse, 1923-50*, Christchurch, 1951.
11. Peter Whitehead, 'Introduction', in Eileen Duggan, *Selected Poems*, Wellington, 1994, p. 17.
12. Ibid., p. 32.
13. Ibid., p. 18.
14. *A Book of New Zealand Verse*, p. 110.
15. Quoted in Bill Coffey, *The Brackens*, South Melbourne, 1990, p. 99.
16. Quoted in J. Eisen and K.J. Smith, eds, *Strangers in Paradise*, Auckland, 1991, p. 189.
17. O'Farrell, *Vanished Kingdoms*, pp. xvii-xix. The argument in the text, which follows, is neatly illustrated by Ruth Park, the classic novelist of Irish-Australian inner city Sydney with *The Harp in the South* (1948). The first volume of her autobiography *A Fence Around the Cuckoo*, Ringwood, 1992, makes it very clear that her New Zealand childhood, in the King Country, was Catholic but not Irish in any other than a minor background way. Her world was a typically New Zealand one. Even the books of Sister Pauline O'Regan, *Aunts & Windmills*, Wellington, 1991, and *There's Hope For a Tree*, Auckland, 1995, are strongly 'colonial' in flavour. A visit to Ireland in 1979 brought no sense of identification (although a wonderful human experience) but rather puzzlement, a feeling of 'pain and paradox' on encountering the North, and an acknowledgement that anti-Irish racism and bigotry had once existed in New Zealand 'although I cannot claim to have been inhibited by it'. Its reality, however, is amply demonstrated in Rory Sweetman's *Bishop in Dock: The Sedition Trial of James Liston*, Auckland 1997.

Chapter 3

1. Joseph Carnahan, *A Brief History of the Orange Institution in the North Island of New Zealand from 1842 till the Present Time*, Auckland, 1886, p. 28.
2. Arthur Gray, *An Ulster Plantation: The Story of the Katikati Settlement*, 2nd edn., Wellington, 1950.

3   These estimates are extracted from Trevor Parkhill, 'Sources for the Study of Emigration from Ulster to New Zealand (1840-1900)', *British Review of New Zealand Studies*, (1991), pp. 8-9.
4   Donald Harman Akenson, *Half the World from Home: Perspectives on the Irish in New Zealand, 1860-1950*, Wellington, 1990, p. 158.
5   Ibid., p. 55; James White McAuley, 'Under an Orange Banner: Reflections on the Northern Protestant Experiences of Emigration', in Patrick O'Sullivan, ed., *The Irish World Wide: History, Heritage, Identity, Vol. 5, Religion and Identity*, London and New York, 1996.
6   See A.T.Q. Stewart, *The Narrow Ground: The Roots of Conflict in Ulster, 1609-1969*, London, 1977; Philip Robinson, *The Plantation of Ulster*, Dublin, 1984; Raymond Gillespie, *Colonial Ulster: The Settlement of East Ulster, 1600-1641*, Cork, 1985; Kerby A. Miller, *Emigrants and Exiles: Ireland and the Irish Exodus to North America*, New York and Oxford, 1985, pp. 19-20, 22. See also W.E. Vaughan and A.J. Fitzpatrick, eds, *Irish Historical Statistics: Population*, Dublin, 1978, p. 53. On the Protestants of Ireland's southern provinces, see J.C. Beckett, *The Anglo-Irish Tradition*, London, 1975; Terence DeVere White, *The Anglo-Irish*, London, 1972; Martin Maguire, 'A Socio-Economic Analysis of the Dublin Protestant Working Class, 1870-1926', *Irish Economic and Social History*, 20 (1993), pp. 35-59; Martin Maguire, 'The Organisation and Activism of Dublin's Protestant Working Class, 1883-1935', *Irish Historical Studies*, 29 (1994), pp. 65-87; Jacqueline Hill, 'The Protestant Response to Repeal: The Case of the Dublin Working Class', in F.S.L. Lyons and R.A.J. Hawkins, eds, *Ireland Under the Union: Varieties of Tension, Essays in Honour of T.W. Moody*, Oxford, 1980, pp. 35-68; Ian d'Alton, 'Keeping Faith: An Evocation of the Cork Protestant Character, 1820-1920', in Patrick O'Flanagan and Cornelius G. Buttimer, eds, *Cork: History and Society, Interdisciplinary Esssays on the History of an Irish County, Cork, 1993*, pp. 759-92; Ian d'Alton, 'A Contrast in Crises: Southern Irish Protestantism, 1820-1843 and 1885-1910', in A.C. Hepburn, ed., *Minorities in History*, New York, 1979.
7   Vaughan and Fitzpatrick, pp. 49, 53.
8   See for example, the contemporary evidence in Angelique Day and Patrick McWilliams, eds, *Ordnance Survey Memoirs of Ireland*, Belfast, 1991, Vol. 20, p. 55, and Vol. 9, p. 87 ('Scotch'), Vol. 9, p. 82 ('Irish'), Vol. 2, pp. 23, 113 ('Protestants').
9   G.C. Bolton, 'The Anglo-Irish and the Historians', in Oliver McDonagh and W.F. Mandle, eds, *Irish Culture and Nationalism, 1750-1950*, New York, 1983, pp. 239-45.
10 Paschal Grousset, *Ireland's Disease: The English in Ireland*, 1887, Belfast, 1986, pp. 271-72.
11 Ibid., p. 273.
12 Miller, Emigrants and Exiles, p. 39.
13 William Makepeace Thackeray, *The Irish Sketch Book, and Contributions to the 'Foreign Quarterly Review', 1842-4*, London, 1844, p. 303.
14 Day and McWilliams, Vol. 5, p. 129.
15 Ibid., p. 72.
16 Ibid., p. 109.
17 Ibid., pp. 100-101.
18 Ibid., p. 116.
19 Day and McWilliams, Vol. 2, p. 63.

20 Ibid., p. 11.
21 Ibid., p. 23.
22 Ibid., p. 113.
23 Ibid., p. 63.
24 Ibid., p. 23.
25 Day and McWilliams, Vol. 21, p. 89.
26 Ibid., p. 89.
27 Ibid., p. 89.
28 Alan O'Day, 'Revising the Diaspora', in D.G. Boyce and Alan O'Day, eds, *The Making of Modern Irish History: Revisionism and the Revisionist Controversy*, London and New York, 1996, p. 191.
29 Rory Sweetman, 'The Irish in Nineteenth Century New Zealand', in Antonia Jones, ed., *Under the Southern Cross: Papers Presented at the Third Australasian Congress on Genealogy and Heraldry*, Hamilton, 1983, p. 268. One of the most obvious literary displays of old New Zealand's prejudices against the Catholic Irish is found in Helen Wilson, Moonshine, 2nd edn, Hamilton, 1956. See also Alitia Lynch, '"Drunken, Dissipated and Immoral": Perceptions of Irish Immigrants to New Zealand, 1868-1918', MA Thesis, University of Auckland, 1997, pp. 72-77.
30 Donald Harman Akenson, *The Irish Diaspora: A Primer*, Toronto, 1993, p. 64.
31 Richard Davis, *Irish Issues in New Zealand Politics, 1868-1922*, Dunedin, 1974, p. 36.
32 *Cyclopaedia of New Zealand, Vol. 2: Auckland Provincial District*, Christchurch, 1902, p. 433. The interpretation advanced in this paragraph owes much to Lynch, pp. 72-77.
33 *New Zealand Parliamentary Debates* (NZPD), 1870, 9, p. 271.
34 *Appendices to the Journals of the House of Representatives (AJHR)*, 1865, D3, no. 10, p. 13.
35 *NZPD*, 1872, 12, pp. 572-3.
36 *AJHR*, 1875, D1, no. 26, p.1 3.
37 Davis, *Irish Issues*, pp. 38-41. Note the use here of the term 'double-distilled', an allusion to Irish whiskey.
38 *AJHR*, 1876, D3, no. 44, p. 30.
39 *New Zealand Herald* (NZH), 10 July 1874, p. 5.
40 Davis, *Irish Issues*, pp. 34-5.
41 Ibid., pp. 32-6; Akenson, *Half the World From Home*, pp. 127-30.
42 *Journals of the Auckland Provincial Council* (JAPC), 1873-4, 29, A23, pp. 5-10.
43 Akenson, *Half the World From Home*, fn. 19, p. 238.
44 *AJHR*, 1873, D1A, no. 13.
45 *AJHR*, 1873, D1A, no. 17; see also Davis, *Irish Issues*, pp. 34-5.
46 See Lesley Dugdale, *Captain W.C. Daldy, 1816-1903*, Auckland, 1989, pp. 158-71; *JAPC*, 1864, 17, A6, p. 1; 1864-5, 18, A3, pp. 3-6; 1865-6, 19, A12, pp. 3, 5, 12-16, 22, 26; 1864-5, 18, A3, pp. 4-5.
47 *AJHR*, 1865, D3, no.10, p. 13; Nona Morris, *Early Days in Franklin*, Auckland, 1965, pp. 135, 137.
48 Anthony Buckley, 'We're Trying to Find Our Identity: Uses of History among Ulster Protestants', in E. Tonkin, M. McDonald and M. Chapman, eds, *History and Ethnicity*, London, 1989, pp. 191-2; *AJHR*, 1872, D1, no. 20; *AJHR*, 1873, D2, no. 31; *Dictionary of New Zealand Biography* (DNZB), Vol. 2, pp. 137-8.
49 *AJHR*, 1873, D2D, no. 31. As early as May 1873, in a recruiting notice circulating

Ulster Orange Lodges, Stewart describes Farnall as 'a personal friend, who is officially connected with the New Zealand Government'. *AJHR*, 1874, D3, no.2, sub-enclosure to enclosure no.7, p. 6. For the background to Farnall's involvement in the Katikati affair, see Davis, *Irish Issues*, p. 31.
50 *AJHR*, 1873, D2, no. 8, pp. 4-7; no. 20, pp. 18-19.
51 Ibid., pp. 6-7; no. 20, pp. 19-20.
52 Christine Clement, 'Ships of the Waikato Immigration Scheme, 1864-65', *New Zealand Genealogist*, 20, no. 199, pp. 796-8; *AJHR*, 1864-5, D3, no. 10; *JAPC*, 1864-5, A3, p. 72; *AJHR*, 1877, D2, no. 31, pp. 50-1. Davis, *Irish Issues*, pp. 37-42. See also Akenson, *Half the World From Home*, pp. 142-3.
53 Davis, *Irish Issues*, pp. 37-43.
54 Ibid., pp. 42-3.
55 Akenson, *Half the World From Home*, p. 42.
56 Lynch, p. 71.
57 Malcolm Campbell, *The Kingdom of the Ryans: The Irish in Southwest New South Wales, 1816-1890*, Sydney, 1995, p .78.
58 Russell Stone, *James Dilworth*, Auckland, 1995, p. 4.
59 Pukekohe Public Cemetery headstone nos. 1789 and 2303.
60 Maguire Letter, Public Record Office of Northern Ireland (PRONI), no. D1420/123, p. 1. On nineteenth-century Ulster terminology, see Day and McWilliams, Vol. 9, p. 82.
61 Murray Gray and Winifred Macdonald, eds, 'The Journal of William Gray, 1875', *Auckland-Waikato Historical Journal*, no .47, September 1985, p. 27.
62 Roberta Nicholls, 'Martin, John, 1822-1892', *Dictionary of New Zealand Biography (DNZB)*, Wellington, 1993, Vol. 2, pp. 312-313.
63 Akenson, *Half the World From Home*, p. 156.
64 John Mulgan, *Home: A New Zealander's Adventure*, p. 4; Alan Mulgan, 'Two Worlds: A Chapter of Autobiography', *Landfall*, Vol. 2, no. 3, September 1948, pp. 181-90.
65 Mulgan, 'Two Worlds', pp. 183, 184.
66 Ibid., p. 5.
67 Ibid., pp. 6-7.
68 Akenson, *Half the World From Home*, pp. 84-5, 158.
69 James Belich, *Making Peoples: A History of the New Zealanders, From Polynesian Settlement to the End of the Nineteenth Century*, Auckland, 1996, p. 297.
70 Ibid., p. 287; Akenson, *Half the World From Home*, pp. 193-4, 196. For a critique of the debate between pluralism and environmental determinism in New Zealand, see Keith Pickens, 'The Writing of New Zealand History: A Kuhnian Perspective', *Historical Studies*, 17 (1977), pp. 384-98.
71 Geoffrey Charles Buckley, *Of Toffs and Toilers: From Cornwall to New Zealand: Fragments of the Past*, Auckland, 1983.
72 Akenson, *Half the World From Home*, p. 193.
73 Ibid., p. 158.
74 Akenson, *The Irish Diaspora*, p. 253; Charlotte Erickson, *Invisible Immigrants: The Adaptation of English and Scottish Immigrants in Nineteenth Century America*, Miami, 1972.
75 Akenson, *Half the World From Home*, p. 158.
76 Ibid., p. 85.
77 K.A. Hamilton, *They Came From Tully Wiggin: The Hamilton Story*, Whitianga, 1991, p. 1.

78 Kathryn D. Mooney, *The Kilgour Family, of Huia, West Auckland*, Napier, 1997, pp. 1-2.
79 Moira Neal, 'The Tartan and the Green', *Something of Interest: Proceedings of the 1994 Conference Held by the New Zealand Society of Genealogists at the University of Waikato, Hamilton, 6-8 May 1994*, Hamilton, 1994, p. 230.
80 Anna Rogers, *A Lucky Landing: the Story of the Irish in New Zealand*, Auckland, 1996, p. 66.
81 Peter Lineham, 'The Nature and Meaning Of Protestantism in New Zealand Culture', *Turnbull Library Record*, Vol. 26, no. 1, p. 60.
82 Lineham, p. 60.
83 Alasdair Galbraith, 'New Zealand's "Invisible" Irish: Irish Protestants in the North Island of New Zealand, 1840-1900', MA thesis, University of Auckland, 1998, pp. 30-32.
84 Lineham, p. 63.
85 Akenson, *The Irish Diaspora*, p. 148.
86 Carnahan, p. 29.
87 Alison Drummond, ed., *The Thames Journals of Vicesimus Lush, 1868-1882*, Christchurch, 1975, p. 213. Note that of the four Irish clergymen Lush cites, Edward Mulgan was the father of Katikati settler Alan Mulgan, mentioned earlier in this chapter, and Richard Augustus Hall, an Orangeman from Dungannon, County Tyrone, was the founding figure of the small Ulster community at the Bay of Islands Special Settlement at Kawakawa in 1866. See Galbraith, pp. 126-9.
88 Stone, p. 224.
89 Drummond, p. 53.
90 Ibid., p. 184.
91 Ibid., p. 141.
92 Galbraith, pp. 30-31.
93 Peter Matheson, 'The Settler Church', in Dennis McEldowney, ed., *Presbyterians in Aotearoa, 1840-1990*, Wellington, 1990.
94 Ibid., p. 21.
95 Ibid., p. 30.
96 Ibid., p. 34.
97 Ibid., p. 34.
98 Ibid., p. 28.
99 Auckland Presbytery Induction Records, 1855-1976, Auckland Institute and Museum, Ms 1149, see for example nos. 47, 56, 87, 94, 107, 181.
100 Lineham, pp. 63, 73.
101 Belich, *Making Peoples*, p. 297.

Chapter 4

1 R.A.A. Sherrin and J.H. Wallace, *Early History of New Zealand*, Thompson W. Leys, ed., Auckland, 1890, p. 159. This essay forms part of the British and Irish immigration project conducted by the Historical Branch of the Ministry for Culture and Heritage.
2 R. Alexander, *The Royal New Zealand Fencibles 1847-1852*, Waiuku, 1997.
3 *New Zealander*, 18 January 1860, 1 February 1860, 4 February 1860, 17 March 1860, 24 March 1860 and 9 May 1860.
4 John McDonald and Eric Richards, 'The Great Emigration of 1841: Recruitment for

New South Wales in British Emigration Fields', *Population Studies*, 51 (1997), p. 347.
5   Ibid., p. 348.
6   W.H. Scotter, 'The moderate success of the assisted immigration scheme', in W.J. Gardner, ed., *A History of Canterbury: Volume II*, Christchurch, 1971, p. 217.
7   Stevan Eldred-Grigg, , Dunedin, 1982, p. 20.
8   See Lyndon Fraser, *To Tara via Holyhead: Irish Catholic Immigrants in Nineteenth-Century Christchurch*, Auckland, 1997.
9   Ibid., Table 1.5, p. 43.
10 See R.H. Silcock, 'Immigration into Canterbury under the Provincial Government', MA thesis, University of Canterbury, 1963.
11 K.A. Pickens, 'Canterbury 1851-1881: Demography and Mobility: A Comparative Study', PhD thesis, Washington University, St Louis, 1976. See also K.A. Pickens, 'The Origins of the Population of Nineteenth-Century Canterbury', *New Zealand Geographer*, 33 (1977), pp. 60-75.
12 Walter Nugent, *Crossings: The Great Transatlantic Migrations, 1870-1914*, Bloomingdale, 1992, pp. 50-51.
13 See, for example, Erik Olssen, *A History of Otago*, Dunedin, 1984, p. 75.
14 Premier to Agent-General, 4 November 1872, *AJHR*, D1, 1873, p. 12, and Premier to Agent-General, 27 November 1872, *AJHR*, D1, 1873, p. 20.
15 David Fitzpatrick, 'Emigration, 1871-1921', in W.E. Vaughan, ed., *New History of Ireland: Vol. V: Ireland Under the Union, I, 1801-70*, Oxford, pp. 612-13.
16 Ibid., p. 613.
17 Ibid., p. 613.
18 David Fitzpatrick, 'Irish Emigration in the Later Nineteenth Century', *Irish Historical Studies*, 22 (1980), p. 133.
19 Ibid., p. 134.
20 David Fitzpatrick, *Oceans of Consolation: Personal Accounts of Irish Migration to Australia*, Melbourne, 1995, p. 644.
21 Seán G. Brosnahan, *The Kerrytown Brosnahans*, Timaru, 1992, p. 34.
22 Fraser, *To Tara via Holyhead*, p. 44.
23 The following section is based on an analysis of the religious affiliation of the person officiating at the funeral service.

Chapter 5

1   See Donald Harman Akenson, *Half the World from Home: Perspectives on the Irish in New Zealand, 1860-1950*, Wellington, 1990, and Lyndon Fraser, *To Tara via Holyhead: Irish Catholic Immigrants in Nineteenth-Century Christchurch*, Auckland, 1997. This essay forms part of the British and Irish immigration project conducted by the Historical Branch of the Ministry for Culture and Heritage.
2   See Terry Hearn, Biographies of Gabriel Read, Horatio Hartley, and William Fox, in *The Dictionary of New Zealand Biography, Volume One, 1769-1869*, Wellington, 1990, pp. 358-59, 178-79, and 138.
3   See J. Forrest, 'Population and Settlement on the Otago Goldfields, 1861-1870', *New Zealand Geographer*, 17 (1961), pp. 64-86.
4   British Parliamentary Papers, 1863.
5   John McDonald and Eric Richards, 'Workers for Australia: a profile of British and Irish migrants assisted to New South Wales in 1841', unpublished research paper.

6   David Fitzpatrick, 'Emigration 1801-1870', in W.E. Vaughan, ed., *New History of Ireland: Vol. V: Ireland Under the Union, I, 1801-70*, Oxford, 1989, pp. 573, 603. See also Patrick O'Farrell, *The Irish in Australia*, Kensington, 1986, p. 65.
7   O'Farrell, pp. 86, 96.
8   See David Fitzpatrick, 'Irish Immigration, 1840-1914', in James Jupp, ed., *The Australian People. An Encyclopaedia of their Nation, its People and their Origins*, North Ryde, 1988, pp. 560-65.
9   This population was created using registers of deaths, probate records, electoral rolls, marriage registers, obituaries, bankruptcy records, passenger lists, cemetery and burial registers, and directories. The information entered into the registers of deaths was used as the basis. These registers have distinct limitations. The data recorded were not invariably reliable, particularly where the individuals concerned had not married, or the couples had been childless. For those whose days ended in hospital, 'lunatic asylums' or charitable institutions, ages were often estimated or rounded, as was the length of residence in New Zealand. Obituaries similarly contained inaccuracies or information inconsistent with that entered into the registers of deaths. Wherever possible, the information contained in the registers of deaths was checked against other registers and records. It was possible, for example, to check for many of these men and women details relating to age and to year and place of marriage and age at marriage. Inaccuracies remain, but it is unlikely that these significantly affect the analyses offered.

Chapter 6

1   See James S. Donnelly, Jr, 'The Irish Agricultural Depression of 1859-64', *Irish Economic and Social History*, 3 (1976), pp. 33-54.
2   For Callinan's property holdings, see *General Valuation of Rateable Property in Ireland, Union of Ballyvaghan*, Dublin, 1855, p. 49. Although precise details have been lost, oral evidence suggests that Michael Callinan married twice in the district. His second marriage to Mary Noonan of Lismacteige took place in 1834 and produced eight surviving children. Descendant information, Brian Nolan.
3   Descendant information, Brian Nolan and Barrie Lynn Callinan.
4   The couple's first child, Michael, was born in Kyneton on 13 October 1871, but died the following day. Descendant information, Brian Nolan.
5   Ibid.; *Grey River Argus*, 1 May 1933.
6   A notable exception is Patrick O'Farrell, *Vanished Kingdoms: Irish in Australia and New Zealand: A Personal Excursion*, Kensington, 1990. See also Neil Patrick Vaney, 'The Dual Tradition: Irish Catholics and French Priests in New Zealand – the West Coast Experience, 1865-1910', MA thesis, University of Canterbury, 1976.
7   Malcolm Campbell, *The Kingdom of the Ryans: The Irish in Southwest New South Wales, 1816-1890*, Sydney, 1997.
8   This chapter uses the term 'West Coast' to denote the entire region which stretches northwards from Awarua to Kahurangi Point and incorporates both 'Westland' and 'Nelson South-West Goldfield'. See the discussion of nomenclature in Philip Ross May, *The West Coast Gold Rushes*, Christchurch, 1962, pp. 14-16.
9   This movement of people formed one aspect of the 'Perennial Interchange' described by Rollo Arnold, 'The Dynamics and Quality of Trans-Tasman Migration, 1885-1910', *Australian Economic History Review*, 26 (1986), pp. 1-20. On the West Coast's

connections with Australia, see especially May, *The West Coast Gold Rushes*, ch. 17.
10 The sample in this study comprised a total of 1951 individuals, of whom 1346 were male and 605 female. In the first instance, data was extracted from death registers at the following localities: Ross, Okarito, Jackson's Bay, Waimea, Kumara, Hokitika, Greymouth, Cobden, Ahaura, Reefton, Lyell, Brunnerton, Charleston and Buller. These records were then linked systematically with probate files, shipping lists and church registers. Additional information was obtained from genealogies and other fragmented archival sources such as newspaper obituaries and cemetery transcripts. On record linkage, see especially Andrejs Plakans, *Kinship in the Past: An Anthropology of European Family Life, 1500-1900*, New York, 1984, pp. 51-75. For an outstanding example of this method in practice, see Charlotte Macdonald, *A Woman of Good Character: Single Women as Immigrant Settlers in Nineteenth-Century New Zealand*, Wellington, 1990.
11 A substantial body of scholarship in international migration studies emphasises the importance of personal networks in explaining the origins, composition and dynamics of migrant flows. For a useful introduction to the literature, see Monica Boyd, 'Family and Personal Networks in International Migration: Recent Developments and New Agendas', *International Migration Review*, 23 (1989), pp. 638-70; Stephen Castles and Mark Miller, *The Age of Migration: International Population Movements in the Modern World*, London, 1998.
12 Miles Fairburn, *The Ideal Society and Its Enemies: The Foundations of Modern New Zealand Society, 1850-1900*, Auckland, 1989, p. 165.
13 Ibid., pp. 164-67.
14 Ibid., p. 191-92. By contrast, he claims, the combined weight of penal settlement, chain gang, and assignment system may have provided the earliest waves of Australian migrants with 'an organisation in embryo'.
15 These findings match those reported in micro-studies of other groups by Raewyn Dalziel, Maureen Molloy, Charles Sedgwick, James Ng and Andrew Trlin, further underlining the importance of informal social networks in shaping migration outcomes. See Raewyn Dalziel, 'Emigration and Kinship: Migrants to New Plymouth, 1840-1843', *New Zealand Journal of History*, 25 (1991), pp. 112-28; Maureen Molloy, 'Kinship, Authority, and Transitions to Adulthood: the Highland Scots at Waipu, New Zealand, 1854-1914', *Journal of Social History*, 22 (1989), pp. 487-506; Charles P. Sedgwick, 'The Politics of Survival: A Social History of the Chinese in New Zealand', PhD thesis, University of Canterbury, 1982; James Ng, *Windows on a Chinese Past* (Volumes 1 & 2), Dunedin, 1993 & 1995; Andrew Trlin, *Now Respected, Once Despised: Yugoslavs in New Zealand*, Palmerston North, 1979.
16 On Irish migration to Australia, see especially Patrick O'Farrell, *The Irish in Australia*, Sydney, rev. ed., 1993 and David Fitzpatrick, *Oceans of Consolation: Personal Accounts of Irish Migration to Australia*, Melbourne, 1995. An excellent introductory survey is found in Donald Harman Akenson, *The Irish Diaspora: A Primer*, Toronto, 1993, ch. 4.
17 John Macdonald and Ralph Shlomowitz, 'Passenger Fares on Sailing Vessels to Australia in the Nineteenth Century', *Explorations in Economic History*, 28 (1991), pp. 192-207.
18 David Fitzpatrick, *Irish Emigration 1801-1921*, Dublin, 1985, p. 22.
19 David Fitzpatrick, 'Irish Emigration in the Later Nineteenth Century', *Irish Historical Studies*, 22 (1980), p. 131.

20 On Irish women's government-assisted migration see Robin Haines, '"The priest made a bother about it": the travails of "that unhappy sisterhood" bound for colonial Australia', in Trevor McClaughlin, ed., *Irish Women in Colonial Australia*, St Leonards, 1998, pp. 43-63. The subject is more fully developed in Robin Haines, *Emigration and the Labouring Poor: Australian Recruitment in Britain and Ireland, 1831-61*, New York, 1997. Useful case studies include Pauline Rule, 'Honora and Her Sisters: Success and Sorrow among Irish Immigrant Women in Colonial Victoria', in Rebecca Pelan, ed., *Irish-Australian Studies: Papers Delivered at the Seventh Irish-Australian Conference*, Sydney, 1994, pp. 151-60, and Eric Richards and Ann Herraman, '"If she was hard up she would sooner be hard up in a strange land than she would be known": Irish women in Colonial South Australia', in McClaughlin, ed., pp. 82-104.
21 O'Farrell, *The Irish in Australia*, pp. 70-71.
22 Ibid., pp. 69-85; Patrick O'Farrell, 'The Irish In Australia and New Zealand, 1791-1870', in W.E. Vaughan, ed., *A New History of Ireland: Vol. V: Ireland Under the Union, I, 1801-70*, Oxford, 1989, pp. 670-71.
23 Akenson, *The Irish Diaspora*, p. 96; R.F. Foster, *Modern Ireland, 1600-1972*, London, 1988, pp. 323-24.
24 Fitzpatrick, *Oceans of Consolation*, p. 7.
25 Ibid., pp. 7-9; Akenson, *The Irish Diaspora*, pp. 98-108.
26 Census figures are extracted from Fitzpatrick, *Oceans of Consolation*, fn. 9, p. 6.
27 Akenson, *The Irish Diaspora*, Table 23, p. 102; O'Farrell, *The Irish in Australia*, pp. 66-7.
28 Descendant information, John F. Tourelle.
29 *The Cyclopedia of New Zealand, Vol. 5*, Christchurch, 1906, pp. 258, 549, and 571.
30 Descendant information, Ron Patterson.
31 *Census of New Zealand*, 1867-1906. The Australian Census figures for 1901 are extracted from Fitzpatrick, *Oceans of Consolation*, fn. 10, p. 6.
32 Census data from the counties and small goldfields boroughs for the years 1878-1906 reveal this distinctive pattern. The same observation has been made by McCaskill, 'The Historical Geography of Westland', p. 6/20.
33 Jack Greene employs the term 'charter group' to denote the disproportionate influence exerted by the earliest arrivals in new societies, 'who took possession of the land, devised ways to manipulate local resource materials for their own survival and profit, reordered the physical and social landscape, and worked out the political, legal, and other cultural arrangements appropriate to their situation'. See Jack P. Greene, 'Pluribus or Unum? White Ethnicity in the Formation of Colonial American Culture', *History Now. Te Pae Tawhito o Te Wa*, 4 (1998), p. 4.
34 Murray McCaskill, 'The Goldrush Population of Westland', *New Zealand Geographer*, 12 (1956), 31-50.
35 Cummins to Forrest, 29 July 1874, Marist Archives, Wellington.
36 See, for example, Diocesan Return for the Parish of Ahaura, 1 July 1892, Christchurch Diocesan Archives (CDA); Carew to Grimes, 9 April 1895, CDA.
37 The Canterbury percentages are taken from Keith Pickens, 'Canterbury 1851-1881: Demography and Mobility. A Comparative Study', PhD thesis, Washington University, St Louis, 1976, Table 1:21, p. 192. While Pickens's research was confined to emigrant males, his figures closely match my own unpublished data taken from the death certificates of all Irish-born migrants whose deaths were recorded in

Christchurch between the years 1876 and 1900. For the Australian proportions from 1911 cited here, see Fitzpatrick, *Oceans of Consolation*, fn. 24, p. 14.
38 See Kerby Miller, *Emigrants and Exiles: Ireland and the Irish Exodus to North America*, New York, 1985, pp. 350, 376-78 and W.E. Vaughan and A.E. Fitzpatrick, eds, *Irish Historical Statistics: Population, 1821-1971*, Dublin, 1978, *passim*. Irish Anglicans belonged to the Church of Ireland, which was the established state church from 1537 to 1870. For a succinct analysis of Irish religious life during the period covered by this essay, see S.J. Connolly, *Religion and Society in Nineteenth-Century Ireland*, Dublin, 1985.
39 The phrase is taken from a letter by Henry Selfe Selfe to John Hall, 19 November 1862, Hall Papers, quoted in Richard Greenaway, 'Henry Selfe Selfe and the Origins and Development of Canterbury', MA thesis, University of Canterbury, 1972, pp. 197-98.
40 Miller, pp. 369-80.
41 Of the 548 women in this sample, 257 were married overseas and 39 in New Zealand locations other than the West Coast.
42 Weldon's biography is sketched by Anne Hutchison in *Dictionary of New Zealand Biography, Volume 1, 1769-1869*, Wellington, 1992, p. 581. On Goodwin, see Kathleen W. Orr, in *A People's History: Illustrated Biographies from the Dictionary of the New Zealand Biography, Volume 1, 1769-1869*, Wellington, 1992, pp. 88-90.
43 Chris McConville, 'The Victorian Irish: Emigrants and Families, 1851-91', in Patricia Grimshaw, Chris McConville and Ellen McEwen, eds, *Families in Colonial Australia*, Sydney, 1985, p. 5.
44 This sense of estrangement is neatly captured in David Fitzpatrick's analysis of the background to a sequence of thirteen letters written by members of the Dunne family in Queensland and County Meath. Christopher Dunne, the son of a substantial tenant farmer, had broken with parental control and the closely regulated property match by eloping to Dublin with a labourer's daughter, Bridget Timmins, before either of them had come of age. The couple were married in the city five years later despite 'a dramatic protest on the church steps from Christy's mother' and their impropriety entailed separation from the Dunne household as well as free passages to Brisbane on the *Golden City* in 1864. See Fitzpatrick, *Oceans of Consolation*, pp. 296-333; Miller, *Emigrants and Exiles*, 402-9.
45 The median age for West Coast Irish males at the time of their arrival in New Zealand during the nineteenth century was 28.5 years, compared with 25.9 years for Irish women.
46 A similar pattern existed in San Francisco. See R.A. Burchell, *The San Francisco Irish, 1848-1880*, Manchester, 1979, pp. 49-51.
47 See David Fitzpatrick, 'The Disappearance of the Irish Agricultural Labourer, 1841-1918', *Irish Economic and Social History*, 7 (1980), pp. 60-82; W.E. Vaughan, *Landlords and Tenants in Mid-Victorian Ireland*, New York, 1994, p. 7.
48 Lyndon Fraser, *To Tara via Holyhead: Irish Catholic Immigrants in Nineteenth-Century Christchurch*, Auckland, 1997, Table 1.5, p. 43.
49 See May, *The West Coast Gold Rushes*, p. 285.
50 See Fraser, *To Tara via Holyhead*, pp. 32-49.
51 See O'Farrell, *The Irish in Australia*, esp. pp. 85-88.
52 Raewyn Dalziel, *The Origins of New Zealand Diplomacy: The Agent-General in London, 1870-1905*, Wellington, 1975, ch. 3.

53 The same point is made in an Australian context by Robin Haines, *Emigration and the Labouring Poor*, p. 20.
54 Im 10/4, National Archives, Wellington (NA).
55 Similar patterns of sponsorship are evident in mid-nineteenth-century Victoria. See David Fitzpatrick, 'Emigration, 1801-70', in W.E. Vaughan, ed., *A New History of Ireland*, pp. 602-3.
56 See, for example, J.A. Bonar to Minister for Immigration, 22 January 1876, Im 3/1, NA. The proportion of single women nominated in Westland closely match the percentages recorded in Victoria. See Fitzpatrick, in W.E. Vaughan, ed., *A New History of Ireland*, Table 9, p. 616.
57 The phrase is from Fitzpatrick, *Oceans of Consolation*, p. 12.
58 Mary Neylon to Under Secretary, 6 February 1873, Im 3/1, NA.
59 Henry Ellis to Under Secretary, 23 October 1874, Im 3/1, NA. See also James Wylde to Under Secretary, 24 October 1874, and Henry Ellis to Under Secretary, 19 September 1874, Im 3/1, NA.
60 See Im 10/4, NA.
61 Edward Duffy to Immigration Officer, 26 September 1871, Im 1/1, NA.
62 James Wylde to Under Secretary, 24 November 1873, Im 3/1, NA.
63 Charles Elliot to Under Secretary, 1 December 1875, Im 3/1, NA.
64 Ellen Connell to Immigration Officer (Nelson), 23 December 1875, Im 3/1, NA.
65 See also, Sub-immigration Officer (Westport) to Immigration Officer (Nelson) 13 January and 14 January 1876, Im 3/1, NA.
66 This analysis is based on a total of 265 probate files held at National Archives, Christchurch. Of these documents, 214 were left by male testators (80.8%), while the remaining 51 belonged to women (19.2%). The marital status of will-makers were as follows: 105 married men (39.6%), 88 unmarried men (33.2%), 22 widowers (8.3%), 12 married women (4.5%), 4 single women (1.5%), and 34 widows (12.8%).
67 Twenty-one widows named Irish executors in their wills (61.85%) and another nine entrusted their immediate kinsfolk alone (26.5%). Similarly, almost three-fifths of widowers chose to appoint compatriots (59.1%), with about one-quarter relying solely on kinship ties (27.3%)
68 Will of Bridget Houlahan, HK 329/1888, National Archives, Christchurch (henceforth NA-CH).
69 Will of James Jones, HK 1015/1902, NA-CH.
70 Sixty-six testators transferred the residuary interest in their estates to their spouses absolutely (62.9%), while another 15 bequeathed most of their property to their wives (14.3%). Twenty-two wills created life-interests in an estate (21.0%) and two documents completely excluded the claims of widows (1.9%).
71 Lyndon Fraser, '"The Ties That Bind": Irish Catholic Testamentary Evidence from Christchurch, 1876–1915', *New Zealand Journal of History*, 29 (1995), pp. 71-73. About one-quarter of all West Coast Irish Catholic testators excluded their wives as executors (28.0%), but nearly two-thirds (65.3%) entrusted spouses with an absolute residuary interest in their estates (N=75). The corresponding percentages for Christchurch were 42.1% and 37.2% respectively.
72 A further 25 probates contained bequests to churches, charities or parish priests (28.4%). Only one non-Catholic will contained any disposition of this nature. John Tyrrell, a Dublin-born Anglican printer, bequeathed £5 per annum to an Irish orphanage, £70 to local churches, and a sum of £600 in trust 'for the establishment

of a Home to be erected in Westport for the succor relief and comfort of the aged and needy of all or any denomination or creed'. See Will of John Tyrrell, WP 7/92, NA-CH.
73 Will of James Quillinan, RN 140/1902 and HK 1014/1902, NA-CH.
74 Will of Thomas O'Rourke, HK 1015/1902, NA-CH.
75 Will of Richard Purdon Bayley, GM 77/1883 and HK 219/1883, NA-CH.
76 This sample comprises 119 intestacy cases from the period 1865-1910 held at National Archives, Christchurch. Ninety-seven files involved the estates of males (81.5%), while 22 belonged to women (18.5%). The marital status of intestates were as follows: 46 married men (38.7%), 44 unmarried men (37.0%), 7 widowers (5.9%), 7 married women (5.9%), 2 single women (1.7%), and 13 widows (10.9%).
77 John Clerehan, intestate, GM 237/1896 and HK 617/1896, NA-CH.
78 Patrick Donovan, intestate, WP 3/1892, NA-CH.
79 Alexander Mitchell to James Mitchell, 1 August 1847, CH A474/1865, NA-CH.
80 Alexander Mitchell to Jane Mitchell, 1 September 1850, CH A474/1865, NA-CH.
81 Ibid., NA-CH; Alexander Mitchell to James Mitchell, 24 January 1850, CH A474/1865, NA-CH.
82 Richard Megaffin to his parents, 3 September 1857, CH A474/1865, NA-CH.
83 Michael Flanagan to Reverend Richard Flanagan, 18 February 1865, courtesy of Donald Murphy. I am indebted to Angela McCarthy for assistance in locating these letters.
84 Ibid., 18 February 1865.
85 Bridget Kirk to Michael Flanagan, 10 May 1870, courtesy of Donald Murphy.
86 Ibid., 10 May 1870; Bridget Kirk to Michael Flanagan, 5 December 1871, courtesy of Donald Murphy.
87 For a different interpretation of this correspondence, see David Fitzpatrick, '"An Ocean of Consolation": Letters and Irish Immigration to Australia', in Eric Richards, Richard Reid and David Fitzpatrick, *Visible Immigrants: Neglected Sources for the History of Australian Immigration*, Canberra, 1989, p. 71.
88 Reverend Richard Flanagan to Michael and Patrick Flanagan, 12 May 1870, courtesy of Donald Murphy.
89 Fitzpatrick in Richards et al., p. 71.
90 May, *The West Coast Gold Rushes*, p. 480.
91 See Campbell, *The Kingdom of the Ryans*, esp. pp. 75-9.

Chapter 7

1 Alice Gilmore (Auckland) to her parents (Down), 1876. This letter was kindly supplied by Alice Gemming. All letters in the Gilmore sequence not referenced to the Public Record Office of Northern Ireland (PRONI) were kindly supplied by Alice Gemming.
2 John Gilmore (Tauranga) to his parents (Down), 16 September 1876, PRONI T1611/2. All extracts that follow from collections held at PRONI are reproduced by permission of the Deputy Keeper of the Records, PRONI.
3 John Gilmore (Tauranga) to his parents (Down), 3 April 1877.
4 Andrew Gilmore (Tauranga) to his parents (Down), 1878.
5 *New Zealand Herald*, 23 May 1934, p. 12.
6 Patrick O'Farrell, *Letters from Irish Australia, 1825-1929*, Sydney, 1984, p. 3.

7 David Fitzpatrick, *Oceans of Consolation: Personal Accounts of Irish Migration to Australia*, Cork, 1995, p. 35.
8 Kerby Miller, *Emigrants and Exiles: Ireland and the Irish Exodus to North America*, New York, 1985, p. 512.
9 O'Farrell, *Letters from Irish Australia*, p. 6.
10 Frances Porter and Charlotte Macdonald, eds., *'My Hand Will Write What My Heart Dictates': The Unsettled Lives of Women in Nineteenth-Century New Zealand as Revealed to Sisters, Family, and Friends*, Auckland, 1996, p. 3.
11 Miles Fairburn, *The Ideal Society and its Enemies: The Foundations of Modern New Zealand Society, 1850-1900*, Auckland, 1989, p. 195.
12 These letters include 37 letters composed by 20 female correspondents and 9 letters written by 7 male correspondents.
13 The two major studies of Irish female emigration to America are Hasia R. Diner, *Erin's Daughters in America: Irish Immigrant Women in the Nineteenth Century*, Baltimore, 1983, and Janet A. Nolan, *Ourselves Alone: Women's Emigration from Ireland, 1885-1920*, Lexington, 1989. For discussion of the Irish female experience in Australia see Trevor McClaughlin, ed., *Irish Women in Colonial Australia*, St. Leonards, 1998.
14 Kerby A. Miller, David N. Doyle, and Patricia Kelleher, '"For love and liberty": Irish women, migration and domesticity in Ireland and America, 1815-1920' in Patrick O'Sullivan, ed., *Irish Women and Irish Migration*, London, 1995, p. 53.
15 Agnes Lambert (Auckland) to her sister Susan Jenkins (Antrim), 16 January 1877, courtesy of Beverley Baird.
16 Isabella McNeice (Belfast) to her sister Agnes Lambert (Auckland), 13 August 1877, courtesy of Garry Lambert.
17 Transcript of a letter from Martha Jane Wilson (Canada) to her brother Thomas Reid (Armagh), 15 December 1862, PRONI T2466/1, p. 17.
18 Brigid Dawson (Wanganui) to her sister Ellen Quinn (Armagh), 1924, courtesy of Joan Leonard.
19 Mary Anne Reid (Armagh) to her daughter Margaret Kilpatrick (Auckland), 5 February 1863. All letters in the Kilpatrick sequence not referenced to PRONI were kindly supplied by Alan Kilpatrick.
20 Elizabeth McCleland (Londonderry) to her daughter Ann McCleland (Wellington), 1 October 1840, PRONI, T3034/1.
21 Miller, *Emigrants and Exiles*, p. 482.
22 Bessie Macready (Canterbury) to her cousins (Down) 27 March 1878, PRONI D1757/2/4/1.
23 Margaret Kilpatrick (Auckland) to her brother Thomas Reid (Armagh), 25 November 1862, PRONI D3014/3/3/1.
24 See O'Farrell, *Letters from Irish Australia*, p. 5 and David Fitzpatrick, '"That beloved country, that no place else resembles": Connotations of Irishness in Irish-Australasian Letters, 1841-1915', *Irish Historical Studies*, 27, (1991), p. 333. Despite Alice Gilmore's initial perceptions, she established a life-long friendship with her shipmate Bridget Burke, a Catholic migrant from Galway, who also settled in Te Puke.
25 James McIlrath (Australia) to his parents (Down), 15 March 1861, courtesy of Jenny Langford.
26 Catherine Sullivan (Manawatu) to her brother-in-law Tom Sullivan (Limerick), 7 March 1905, courtesy of Catherine Habes.

180 · A Distant Shore

27 Bessie Macready (Christchurch) to her cousins M. and Jane (Down), 14 July 1881, PRONI D1757/2/4/3.
28 Samuel Gilmer (Wellington) to his brother William Gilmer (Monaghan), 29 June 1886, courtesy of Juann Ryan.
29 Ellen Piezzi (Goldsborough) to her brother-in-law Victer Piezzi (California), undated, courtesy of Teresa O'Connor.
30 Ellen Piezzi (West Coast) to her brother-in-law Victer Piezzi (California), undated.
31 Margaret Kilpatrick (Auckland) to her sister-in-law Jane Kilpatrick (Armagh), 7 August 1903, PRONI D3014/3/4/2.
32 Agnes Lambert, 16 January 1877.
33 Ellen Piezzi (Goldsborough) to her sister-in-law Mrs Victer Piezzi (California), 12 August 1878.
34 Maurice Keane (Waterford) to his sister Mary Keane (Wellington), 2 June 1886, courtesy of Gary Walsh.
35 Andrew Gilmore, 1878.
36 Porter and Macdonald, '*My Hand Will Write*', p. 9.
37 Catherine Colgan (Antrim) to her daughter Rose Gamble (Otago), 3 November 1901, courtesy of Richard Herbert.
38 Margaret Kilpatrick (Auckland) to her brother Thomas Reid (Armagh), 22 November 1903, PRONI D3014/3/3/2.
39 Ellen Piezzi (Goldsborough) to her sister-in-law Mrs Victer Piezzi (California), 6 June 1879.
40 Ellen Piezzi (Goldsborough) to her brother-in-law Victer Piezzi (California), 3 June 1879.
41 Catherine Colgan (Antrim) to her daughter Rose Gamble (Otago), 6 February 1899.
42 Bessie Macready to her cousins M and Jane, 14 July 1881.
43 Maurice Keane (Waterford) to his sister Mary Keane (Wellington), 24 February 1886.
44 William Lysaght (Limerick) to his brother Edward Lysaght (Auckland), 19 December 1869, courtesy of Reg Brown.
45 Mary Anne Gilpin (Armagh) to her sister Lizzie Ayson (Balclutha), 5 January 1904, courtesy of Lorna Neame.
46 Maurice Keane, 24 February 1886.
47 John Keane (Waterford) to his sister Mary Keane (Wellington), 8 March 1886.
48 Elizabeth McCleland, 1 October 1840.
49 Elizabeth McCleland (Londonderry) to her daughter Ann McCleland (Wellington), 6 September 1841, PRONI, T3034/2.
50 Elizabeth McCleland, 1 October 1840.
51 Margaret Kilpatrick, 25 November 1862.
52 Agnes Lambert, 16 January 1877.
53 Margaret Kilpatrick, 25 November 1862.
54 Bessie Macready, 27 March 1878.
55 Bessie Macready to her cousins M. and Jane, 14 July 1881.
56 Bessie Macready (Canterbury) to her cousin William (Down), 14 July 1881, PRONI D1757/2/4/2.
57 Margaret Kilpatrick, 25 November 1862.
58 Elizabeth Walker (Armagh) to her friend Margaret Kilpatrick (Auckland), 14 July 1864.
59 Margaret Kilpatrick (Auckland) to her brother Thomas Reid (Armagh), 14 July 1905.

60 Catherine Colgan (Antrim) to her daughter Rose Gamble (Otago), 22 September 1894.
61 Ellen Piezzi (Goldsborough) to her brother-in-law Victer Piezzi (California), 8 October 1881.
62 Bessie Macready to her cousins M. and Jane, 14 July 1881.
63 Agnes Lambert (Auckland) to her sister Susan Jenkin (Antrim), 30 August 1890.
64 Sarah Reid (Armagh) to her sister-in-law Margaret Kilpatrick (Auckland), 29 September 1916.
65 Elizabeth Walker, 14 July 1864.
66 Ellen Piezzi, 3 June 1879.
67 Margaret Kilpatrick, 14 July 1905.
68 Mary Kilpatrick (Armagh) to David and Margaret Kilpatrick (Auckland), 26 August 1875.
69 Kate Keane (London) to her sister Mary Keane (Wellington), 18 October 1902.
70 Kate Keane (London) to her sister Mary Keane (Wellington), 12 May 1903.
71 Mary Shanahan (Kerry) to her niece Winifred Furlong (Auckland), 21 September 1892. The Shanahan letters were kindly supplied by Virginia McClennan.
72 Mary Shanahan (Kerry) to her niece Winifred Furlong (Auckland), 16 June 1892.
73 Ibid.
74 Mary Shanahan, 21 September 1892.
75 Lizzie Strong (Tipperary) to her cousin Daniel Strong (Auckland), 12 December 1898, courtesy of Ginny Dow.
76 Catherine Colgan, 6 February 1899.
77 Elizabeth McCleland, 6 September 1841.
78 Agnes Lambert, 30 August 1890.
79 Agnes Lambert (Wanganui) to her niece Alice McMeekin (Antrim), 1925.
80 Cecilia Coghlan (Mayo) to her daughter-in-law Ellen Anne Edwards (Wellington), 24 June 1890, courtesy of John Coghlan.
81 Elizabeth McCleland, 6 September 1841.
82 Donald Harman Akenson, 'Reading the Texts of Rural Immigrants: Letters from the Irish in Australia, New Zealand, and North America', in Donald Harman Akenson, ed., *Canadian Papers in Rural History Volume VII*, Ontario, 1990, pp. 395-6.

Chapter 8

1 *Shoneen* is an Irish term with similar connotations to 'Uncle Tom' in African-American history.
2 Malcolm Campbell contrasts Irish-American nationalism with the 'timid tone and limited influence' of the nationalist cause in Australia where '[it] was to be embraced only warily'. See Malcolm Campbell, 'Irish Nationalism and Immigrant Assimilation: Comparing the United States and Australia', *Australasian Journal of American Studies*, 16 (1996), passim. In my view, this description also applies to the Irish in New Zealand.
3 On the Roman Catholic clergy and New Zealand politics, see P.S. O'Connor, 'Sectarian Conflict in New Zealand, 1911-1920', and R.P. Davis, 'The New Zealand Labour Party's "Irish Campaign", 1916-1921', in *Political Science*, 19, nos. 1 & 2 (1967), pp. 3-16, 13-23; Rory Sweetman, 'New Zealand Catholicism, War, Politics and the Irish Issue, 1912-1922', PhD thesis, University of Cambridge, 1991, p. 4.

My essay investigates the electoral swing to Labour at the Catholic 'grassroots' level.
4   Catholic clergy also played a leading role on these platforms. Their stamp of approval was essential in the context of a clerically dominated church community.
5   Michael Davitt, for example, told a Lawrence audience that '[w]hat New Zealand had... was what the advocates of Home Rule wanted for Ireland, and this they must obtain if there was to be peace between Ireland and Great Britain'. *Otago Witness*, 14 November 1895.
6   See T. Desmond Williams, *Secret Societies in Ireland*, Dublin, 1973.
7   See Seán G Brosnahan, '"The Battle of the Borough and the Saige O'Timaru": Sectarian Riot in Colonial Canterbury', *New Zealand Journal of History*, 28 (1994), pp. 41-59.
8   A surviving report from an Australian convict Fenian, Edward Kelly, suggests that a Fenian 'organisation' was in actively raising funds in New Zealand in 1868 for the release of Fenian prisoners in Western Australia. Kelly claimed one of these convicts, John Flood, visited New Zealand after his release and 'started the organisation anew, remodelling the old one'. Edward Kelly to O'Donovan Rossa, April 1876, quoted in Keith Amos, *The Fenians in Australia 1865-1880*, Kensington, 1988, p. 196.
9   Aside from Kelly's report to Rossa, I have two carte-de-visite sized photographic reproductions taken from portrait sketches of the 'Irish Invincibles' in the *Weekly Irish Times Supplement*, 3 March 1883. They were printed in Dunedin by local photographer W. R. Frost, suggesting that there was a market for 'souvenirs' of this type among local Fenian sympathisers.
10 For an account of these groups and their respective roles, see Leon O'Broin, *Revolutionary Underground: The Story of the Irish Republican Brotherhood, 1858-1924*, Dublin, 1976.
11 There is anecdotal evidence to suggest that the British government used the colonies as a dumping ground for the disreputable. Tom Troy recalls that his father, John, a Sinn Féin activist from County Limerick, was given a choice between imprisonment at home or exile in the colonies in 1915. Descendant information, Tom Troy.
12 O'Broin, p. 2.
13 Ibid., p. 7.
14 R.F. Foster, *Modern Ireland 1600-1972*, London, 1988, p. 471.
15 *New Zealand Tablet*, 4 May 1916.
16 J.J. Marlow, chairman of the Dunedin meeting, received general applause for the stating that '[T]he lowest strata only were concerned in it, and it was their proud privilege to know that the bulk and the flower of their people were doing their duty at the front involved'. *Otago Witness*, 3 May 1916. Father Coffey denounced Sinn Féin as anti-clerical and anti-Catholic from the cathedral pulpit. *New Zealand Tablet*, 4 May 1916.
17 Dublin crowds jeered the defeated rebels in April. Within a few months they were venerated as martyrs. See O'Broin, 1976, p. 174.
18 Sweetman, 'New Zealand Catholicism', p. 102.
19 Francis Sheehy-Skeffington was arrested while trying to prevent looting and shot by an officer whom he had previously seen shooting an unarmed boy. Foster, p. 484.
20 *New Zealand Tablet*, 7 September 1916.
21 Ibid., 2 November 1916.
22 The New Zealand Labour Party was formed in Wellington in July 1916. See Paul

Baker, *King and Country Call: New Zealanders, Conscription and the Great War*, Auckland, 1988, pp. 153-54. There was also strong support *for* conscription within Labour circles, especially in Dunedin. See Barry Gustafson, *Labour's Path to Political Independence*, Auckland, 1980.
23 No account survives of the inaugural meeting. The date is derived from an entry in the diary of Dunedin Catholic Thomas Hussey. Hussey Papers, AG 545, Hocken Library.
24 *Green Ray*, January 1917.
25 This claim suggests an IRB circle had been established in Dunedin. The personnel certainly existed for an organisation of this type, but the secret nature of the Brotherhood means we have no documentary evidence to confirm its existence. The actions of MIS members in propagandising for Irish causes through the *Green Ray* and in assisting Irish objectors to avoid conscription is certainly consistent with an IRB programme.
26 Armstrong was the son of a Wexford Anglican, J.P. Armstrong, who settled in Dunedin after sojourns in North America and Victoria.
27 See Bernard Cadogan, 'Lace Curtain Catholics: the Catholic Bourgeoisie of the Diocese of Dunedin, 1900-1920', B.A. (Hons) research essay, Otago University, 1984.
28 Kerry-born John Timothy Sullivan emigrated to Napier in 1870. He moved to Otago in the early 1890s and worked the Customs Department and then the Government Life Insurance Office. See *New Zealand Tablet*, 5 December 1934.
29 *Green Ray*, September 1917.
30 Ibid., September 1917.
31 See Patrick O'Farrell, *The Irish in Australia*, Kensington, 1993, ch. 6.
32 *Green Ray*, April 1917.
33 Ibid., February 1917.
34 *New Zealand Tablet*, 1 August 1918.
35 Descendant infromation, Peter Tohill.
36 *Green Ray*, March 1917. On the Dungannon Clubs, see Foster, p. 474.
37 *Green Ray*, June 1917.
38 Bulmer Hobson, founder of the Belfast Dungannon Clubs, stated that their aim was 'really to create an intense conviction and a passionate faith among a necessarily small number of people'. These persons 'supplied the driving force to organise the country, in so far as it ever was organised'. Bulmer Hobson, *Ireland Yesterday and Tomorrow*, Tralee, 1968, p. 22. The *Green Ray* matches Hobson's own mode of operation as an inveterate publisher of propaganda organs. Oral testimony suggests that John Tohill attempted to form an 'organisation' in New Zealand. Descendant information, Peter Tohill.
39 H.S. Moores, 'The Rise of the Protestant Political Association: Sectarianism in New Zealand during World War One', MA thesis, University of Auckland, 1966, p. 63.
40 Descendant information, Hugh and Peter Tohill.
41 Moores, p. 63.
42 Descendant information, Catherine Craig.
43 *Police Gazette*, 1918-1920.
44 Descendant information, Pat Cody.
45 *Police Gazette*, 1917-1918.
46 See *Green Ray*, September 1917, and *Police Gazette*, 1918.
47 *Police Gazette*, 1920.

48 Archibald Baxter, *We Will Not Cease*, Christchurch, 1968.
49 *Green Ray*, September 1917.
50 Amos, p. 84.
51 Ibid., p. 194.
52 Ibid., pp. 196-99, 268; O'Broin, p. 19.
53 Amos, p. 219.
54 Ibid., Amos, ch. 7.
55 Baker estimates that somewhere between 3900 and 8500 men evaded military service or who failed to register at all. Of these, between 2800 and 6400 were never found by the authorities. Baker, p. 208.
56 Ibid., pp. 178-201.
57 *Green Ray*, January 1918.
58 P.S. O'Connor, 'Storm Over the Clergy – New Zealand 1917', *Journal of Religious History*, 4 (1966), pp. 129-48.
59 Doreen Lange, *Cricklewood*, Invercargill, 1982, p. 45. The West Coast was probably the best place for an objector to go. Its working-class Irish communities were notoriously sympathetic to military evaders. They were also among the *Green Ray*'s most loyal readership.
60 Moores, 1966. Gerald Griffin was the son of Dave Griffin, the MIS President in Wellington. The Griffins and John Troy were Cork-born migrants with Sinn Féin backgrounds. Troy and Dave Griffin had known each other in Ireland and quickly established themselves as leading lights in the Irish Republican movement in New Zealand. Dave Griffin's son, Gerald, founded the Irish Republican Association in Wellington in 1924 to carry on the propaganda war on behalf of Irish Republicanism in the colony. He was also a founding member of the New Zealand Communist Party. Troy, on the other hand, was a fervent Labour Party member, acting as local organiser in Miramar for Bob Semple and Peter Fraser. Descendant information, Richard Griffin, Des Griffin, and Thomas Troy.
61 Salmond to Police Commissioner, 11 July 1917, Opinion Book (1917), Crown Law Office, National Archives, Wellington, quoted in Sweetman, 'New Zealand Catholicism', p. 205.
62 Sweetman, 'New Zealand Catholicism', provides an authoritative account of Kelly and the *New Zealand Tablet* in this period.
63 *New Zealand Tablet*, 8 March 1918. The allusion would have been obvious to Catholic readers as the passage from Isaiah 53.12 is part of the Easter liturgy.
64 Ibid., 19 April 1917.
65 The journal was officially suppressed by a notice in the *New Zealand Gazette*, 4 July 1918.
66 The Solicitor General's instructions on the *Green Ray* are referred to in AG 168/75/3742, 26 September 1918, National Archives, Dunedin.
67 Ironically, newspaper reports of the trial quoted the text in full, thereby disseminating a 'seditious' article to thousands of readers around the country. The irony was not lost on Father Kelly. See *New Zealand Tablet*, 5 September 1918.
68 *Otago Witness*, 31 July 1918.
69 *Green Ray*, October 1917
70 See, for example Erik Olssen, *Building the New World: Work, Politics and Society in Caversham 1880s-1920s*, Dunedin, 1995, p. 220.
71 Cadogan, p. 13.

72 McCarthy was national secretary of the United Labour Party between 1912-13 and national vice-president of the Social Democrat Party from 1913 to 1914. He stood as a Labour candidate in the 1911 general election. Gustafson, p. 160.
73 James Coffey to T.K. Sidey, 28 October 1918, Sidey Papers Ms 605/21, Hocken Library. A copy of the petition form is in the Griffin Papers, ATL. Cabinet rejected the petition.
74 An advertisement for the appeal in the *Truth* on 7 September contained a passage describing the Easter rebels as 'that gallant band of heroes'. This led to the prosecution of the Wellington MIS President, Dave Griffin, and the secretary, John Troy, for making a seditious utterance. A transcript of the court case is held with the Griffin Papers, Alexander Turnbull Library.
75 *Maoriland Worker*, 30 April and 11 June 1919.
76 See, for example, Davis, *passim*.
77 *New Zealand Tablet*, 1 November 1917.
78 See the biography in *Southern People*, Dunedin, 1998.
79 *New Zealand Tablet*, 24 March 1921.
80 Hussey diaries, 31 May 1921. J.B. Callan was a prominent 'shoneen' lawyer and loyalist, who had served in the First World War.
81 Hazlett's mother, on the other hand, was an Irish Catholic and his parents had married in a Catholic ceremony. Their upbringing, however, was Protestant and Hazlett was very much part of the Dunedin Protestant establishment.
82 Hussey diaries,17 September 1921.
83 Ibid., 9 April 1922.
84 Diehard Republicans in Wellington established an Irish Republican Association in 1923. Their invitation to John Robinson to form a Dunedin branch was spurned. 'In the first place Dunedin is a very conservative town, and the question of an Irish Republican Association is not a burning one with local Irishmen. The appeal directed to national sentiment and to humanitarianism in the days of the "Black and Tans" now falls upon deaf ears'. Robinson to Griffin, 11 August 1924, Griffin Papers, 86-43, 3/11, ATL.
85 Erik Olssen, *A History of Otago*, Dunedin, 1984, p. 187.

Chapter 9

1 *New Zealand Tablet*, 2 April 1897.
2 For the Catholic Federation see Rory Sweetman, 'New Zealand Catholicism, War, Politics and the Irish Issue 1912-1922', PhD thesis, University of Cambridge, 1991, pp. 57-58. See also Rev. V.W. McEvoy, 'The Story of the Holy Name Society', *Catholic Review*, 1 (1945), pp. 110-15. The Hibernian Society exists in only Queensland and New South Wales at present.
3 See Richard. P. Davis, *Irish Issues in New Zealand Politics 1868-1922*, Dunedin, 1974, ch. 3. Donald Harman Akenson, 'Immigration and Ethnicity in New Zealand and the USA – The Irish Example', in Jock Phillips, ed., *New Worlds? The Comparative History of New Zealand and the United States*, Wellington, 1989. pp. 28-58.
4 See my forthcoming history of the Hibernian Society in New Zealand.
5 Philip Ross May, *The West Coast Gold Rushes*, Christchurch, 1962. p. 284.
6 *Grey River Argus*, 17 December 1869. For details of the founding members see *New Zealand Tablet*, 13 December 1939.

7   Davis, *Irish Issues*, p. 64. For Martin Kennedy, see *New Zealand Tablet*, 31 August 1916.
8   Davis, p. 65.
9   P.H. O'Connor, *The Hibernian Society of New South Wales 1880-1980*, Sydney, 1980. pp. 14-19.
10 Jennifer Carlyon, 'Friendly Societies 1842-1939', *New Zealand Journal of History*, 32 (1998), pp. 121-42. Erik Olssen, 'Friendly Societies in New Zealand 1840-1990', in Marcel van der Linden, ed., *Social Security Mutualism: The Comparative History of Mutual Benefit Societies*, Berne, 1996. pp. 177-206.
11 David McGill, *The Lion and the Wolfhound: The Irish Rebellion on the New Zealand Goldfields*, Wellington, 1990. But see also my review in the *New Zealand Listener*, 21 January 1991, p. 82.
12 *West Coast Times*, 27 March 1868.
13 Keith Amos, *The Fenians in Australia 1865-1880*, Kensington, 1988; Patrick Quinlivan and Paul Rose, *The Fenians in England 1865-1872*, London, 1982; H. Senior, *The Fenians and Canada*, Toronto, 1978.
14 Bishop Croke to Grahamstown Hibernians, 15 February 1871, in Grahamstown Branch minute book, Auckland Catholic Diocesan Archives. [ACDA]; Davis, *Irish Issues*, p. 65.
15 Davis, *Irish Issues*, p. 63.
16 *New Zealand Tablet*, 24 October 1874.
17 *New Zealand Tablet*, 2 April 1897.
18 See Davis, *Irish Issues*, p. 59; Seán G. Brosnahan, 'The "Battle of the Borough" and the "Saige O Timaru": Sectarian Riot in Colonial Canterbury', *New Zealand Journal of History*, 28 (1994), pp. 41-59; Thomas Bracken, *Musings in Maoriland*, Dunedin, 1890, pp. 341-44.
19 Akenson, *Half the World from Home*, p. 68.
20 J.A. Carnahan, *A Brief History of the Orange Institution in the North Island of New Zealand from 1842 to the present time*, Auckland, 1886.
21 Cited in Davis, *Irish Issues*, p. 52.
22 Ibid., p. 35.
23 *New Zealand Tablet*, 3 April 1885.
24 Davis, *Irish Issues*, pp. 101-103.
25 *New Zealand Freeman's Journal*, 23 March 1883.
26 *New Zealand Tablet*, 28 October 1887.
27 *Evening Post*, 14 June 1886, cited in Davis, *Irish Issues*, p. 106.
28 Davis, *Irish Issues*, p. 111.
29 *New Zealand Freeman's Journal*, 27 November 1885 and 26 March 1887.
30 *New Zealand Tablet*, April 1890.
31 Davis, *Irish Issues*, p. 113.
32 *New Zealand Tablet*, 7 December 1894.
33 Sweetman, 'New Zealand Catholicism', p. 21.
34 Davis, *Irish Issues*, p. 117.
35 Ibid., p. 114. *New Zealand Tablet*, 5 May 1895.
36 Melbourne, 1897. It quickly ran through twelve editions. See my essay on Cleary in the *Dictionary of New Zealand Biography, Volume 3*, pp. 100-101.
37 Sweetman, 'New Zealand Catholicism', pp. 71-72.
38 Dunedin, 1909.

39 Sweetman, 'New Zealand Catholicism', pp. 72-73.
40 Cleary to Dillon, 21 December 1898, Dillon Papers, Trinity College Dublin [TCD].
41 Patrick Twomey to Dillon, 3 April 1902, Dillon Papers, TCD.
42 Sheahan to Dillon, 6 February 1901, Dillon Papers, TCD.
43 Davis, *Irish Issues*, p. 123.
44 *New Zealand Tablet*, 1 March 1900.
45 Sweetman, 'New Zealand Catholicism', pp. 38-9, 80. See also Michael Bassett, *Sir Joseph Ward. A Political Biography*, Auckland, 1993.
46 *New Zealand Tablet*, 31 January 1901.
47 Ibid., 3 March 1904.
48 Ibid., 15 and 22 June 1911.
49 Ibid., 14 May 1903, 3 June 1909.
50 Ibid., 14 September 1905.
51 Ibid., 3 March 1904
52 Ibid., 28 March 1907.
53 Davis, *Irish Issues*, pp. 126-27.
54 Richard P. Davis, 'The Irish-Catholic Question and New Zealand Society 1868-1922', PhD thesis, University of Otago, 1968, p. 339.
55 *New Zealand Tablet*, 17 April 1913.
56 Ibid., 19 June 1913.
57 Ibid., 27 November 1913.
58 *Auckland Star*, 12 March 1914.
59 *New Zealand Tablet*, 9 April 1914.
60 Ibid., 18 June 1914.
61 Ibid., 24 September 1914.
62 Ibid., 13 August 1914.
63 Ibid., 20 September 1917.
64 Ibid., 3 September 1914.
65 Ibid., 1 July 1915, 4 November 1915 and 30 March 1916.
66 Ibid., 2 September 1915.
67 Ibid., 17 June 1915.
68 Ibid., 25 November 1915.
69 Especially the *New Zealand Herald*, published in Auckland.
70 *New Zealand Tablet*, 4 May 1916.
71 Ibid., 4 May 1916.
72 Ibid., 4 May 1916.
73 Ibid., 25 May 1916.
74 *New Zealand Herald*, 17 August, 1916; *New Zealand Tablet*, 28 September, 5 October 1916.
75 *New Zealand Tablet*, 5 October 1916.
76 Ibid., 14 September 1916.
77 Ibid., 14 September 1916.
78 Ibid., 5 and 12 October 1916.
79 Ibid., 19 October 1916.
80 Ibid., 22 November 1917 and 23 December 1920.
81 C. Townshend, *The British Campaign in Ireland 1919-1921*, Oxford, 1975.
82 *New Zealand Tablet*, 3 March 1919.
83 Ibid., 21 May 1918.

84 Ibid., 30 October 1919.
85 Ibid., 8 January 1920.
86 See my forthcoming history of the Society.
87 *New Zealand Tablet*, 8 April and 29 July 1920.
88 Ibid., 4 November 1920.
89 Ibid., 18 and 25 November 1920.
90 Ibid., 31 March 1921.
91 Sheahan to Cleary, 6 April 1921, Cleary Papers, ACDA; *New Zealand Tablet*, 14 April 1921.
92 *New Zealand Times*, 12 December 1921.
93 *New Zealand Tablet*, 15 December 1921.
94 Ibid., 19 January 1922.
95 Rory Sweetman, *Bishop in the Dock. The Sedition Trial of James Liston*, Auckland, 1997; Report of the Thirty-Seventh Annual District Meeting, March 1923 (also the Half-yearly District Meeting held on 27 September 1922). p. 6.
96 *Month*, 15 September 1922. Cleary to Liston, 29 September 1922, Liston Papers, ACDA.
97 Brodie to Cleary, 18 March 1925, Cleary Papers, ACDA.
98 *New Zealand Tablet*, 27 October 1926.
99 *Hibernian Budget*, 7, 2 (November 1940).
100 T. Gray, *The Lost Years: The Emergency in Ireland 1939-45*, London. 1997. p. 236.
101 *Hibernian Budget*, 9, 4 (1948).
102 Report of the 45th Annual District Meeting, May 1931.
103 Report of the 48th Annual District Meeting, May 1934.
104 *Hibernian Budget*, 2, 2 (June 1935).
105 *Hibernian Budget*, 7, 5 (October 1941). The word 'Australasian' was omitted from the Society's title in 1995. Minutes of the Annual General Meeting, Auckland, 22 July 1995, p. 6.
106 Davis, *Irish Issues*, p. 70.
107 Minutes and Proceedings of the Centennial Annual Meeting, Greymouth, 23 May 1969. p. 4.

Index

Addison's Flat 87, 97, 136, 142
African diaspora, the 19
Ahaura 92
Akenson, Donald Harman 9-10, 31, 42, 44, 47, 48, 49, 51, 68, 75, 116, 135
Albion 98
All Hallows College, Dublin 26
American Civil War 89
Anglicans, Irish, in Ireland 38, 39, 41; in New Zealand 47, 49, 50-52, 53, 59, 60, 72-3, 92-3, 94, 95
Anglo-Irish 29, 38, 60, 74
Anglo-Irish War (1919-21) 149-52
anti-Catholicism 35, 41, 42, 50, 51, 53, 121, 128, 130, 132-3, 139-40, 143
anti-Irish sentiment 35, 42-4, 65, 88
Antrim, Co. 38, 40-41, 59, 61, 64, 68, 69, 70, 71, 72, 79, 81, 83, 84, 91, 92, 93-94, 103, 112
Ards Peninsula, Co. Down 105
Argentina 123
Armagh, Co. 45, 47, 58, 59, 61, 64, 68, 71, 79, 107, 108, 109, 114, 115
Armstrong, Frank 122
Ashby, Bishop Brian 154
Asia 43, 46
Asquith, Herbert Henry 120, 121, 148, 151
Athenic 109
Aubert, Mother Suzanne 26
Auckland 33, 36, 43, 44, 47, 50, 52, 56, 97, 105, 106, 107, 108, 113, 114, 115, 133, 136, 139, 142, 143, 145, 146, 148, 150, 152; and Irish migration, 57-61, 68, 74; Provincial Council, 44, 45, 56, 58
Auckland Star, 158
Australia, and Irish migration 10, 20, 28, 30, 32, 34, 47, 56, 58, 59, 62, 67, 68, 71, 72, 74, 75, 76-9, 80, 83, 84, 87, 88-91, 93, 94, 95, 97, 98, 101, 102, 103, 104, 105, 118, 122, 142, 153
Avalanche 58

Ballance, John 33, 49
Ballarat 86, 87, 99, 101
Ballarat Hibernian Society 136
Ballinaskeagh, Co. Down 101
Balloo, Co. Down 109
Ballycastle, Co. Antrim 69
Ballyvaughan, Co. Clare 91
Barry, J.M. 31
Baxter, Archibald 125
Bay of Plenty 42
Bayley, Richard 100
Beamish and Crawford 19
Bebington SS 105, 108, 109
Belfast, Co. Antrim 43, 44, 45, 46, 47, 48, 53, 58, 67, 71, 72, 93, 109, 123
Belich, James 53
Belgium 146
Benchley, Robert 15
'Bible-in-Schools' controversy 119
biculturalism, *see* New Zealand historiography
Birr, King's Co. 94
'Black and Tans' 130, 132
Blue Jacket 58
Bluff 76
Boer War 143
Bohan, Michael 142
Boorowa 87
Boston 17
Bourke, Patrick and Catherine, 90
Bowen, Charles, 29, 44, 137
Boxing Day riot (1879) 139
Boyle, James 40
Bracken, Thomas 32, 139
Bradley, Alexander 43
Bradley, Ben 124, 126, 127
Bradley, James 11, 124, 126, 127
Brighton 136
British Columbia 19
British Isles, *see* Great Britain
Brodie, Bishop Matthew 121, 152
Brosnahan, Seán 11, 67
Brown, John A. 132, 133
Brunnerton 87
Buller, Rev. James 139
Bunny, Frederick 138
Burawn, Co. Cork 87, 100
Burren, Co. Clare 104
Byrne, Francis H. 136

California 97, 102
Callan, Co. Kilkenny 125
Callan, J.B. 131, 133
Callinan, family, migration of 86
Callinan, John Noonan and Bridget 86-7
Campbell, Malcolm 87
Canada 19, 20, 58, 67, 71, 78, 101, 107, 137
Canterbury 29, 43, 56, 61-4, 69, 74, 91, 92, 93, 95, 96, 99, 103, 108, 110, 114
Cape Town 17
Capleston 99
Carisbrooke Castle 46
Carelton, Hugh 44
Carlow, Co. 70
Carr, J.T. 146
Caroline 46
Carrick Castle 46
Carson, Edward Henry 145, 148
Casement, Roger 148
Castlegregory, Co. Kerry 96
Castletown, Queen's Co. 58
Catholic emancipation 47
Catholics, Irish 23-4, 25-6, 48, 53, 74, 79; attitudes towards 42, 43, 50; clergy 10, 26-27; education 19-20; First World War 117-21, 124-9; in Ireland 40-41; migration of 10, 59, 60, 61-2, 69, 72-3, 91-3, 94, 95; support for Labour Party 117-18, 121, 128-9, 132, 133-4, *see also* anti-Catholicism, conscription, Easter Rising (1916), *Green Ray, New Zealand Tablet*, Sinn Féin
Cavan, Co. 58, 64, 71, 79
Cecil, Lord Robert 151
Celts/Celtic 10, 20, 46, 74
Ceylon (Sri Lanka) 59
Charleston 87, 100, 102, 136, 137, 142
charter groups 14, 91
Chile 116
Christchurch 61, 69, 110, 112, 136, 139, 140, 141, 145, 151
Church of Ireland 41, 60, 73, 92, 93, 95, *see also* Anglicans
Churchill, Sir Winston Leonard Spencer 153
Clan na Gael 118, 125
Clare, Co. 9, 61, 64, 67, 70, 72, 79, 81, 83, 84, 87, 91, 93, 96, 97, 103
Clarke, Thomas 124
Cleary, Rev. Henry William 120, 142, 143, 144, 151
Clerehan, John 100
Clones, Co. Monaghan 32
Clonoulty, Co. Tipperary 87

Clune, David 97
Cochrane, Samuel 43
Cody, family of Laurence and Patrick (Southland); Fenian pedigree, 124-6
Cody, Michael 118, 125
Coffey, Rev. James 129, 145, 148
Coghlan, Cecilia 116
Coleraine, Co. Londonderry 53
Colgan, Catherine 112, 114, 115
Collins, Dennis 100
Collins, Michael 152
'colonial', as a concept, 33-4
Commission on Emigration and Other Problems (1948-54) 21-2
Conflict 43, 47
Connaught 58, 59, 60, 61, 64, 67, 68, 69, 70, 72, 74, 79, 81, 83, 91, 103
Connecticut 23
Connell, Ellen and Johanna 98
Connolly, James 119, 120
conscription 121, 122, 123, 124-6, 127-9, *see also* Catholics, Sinn Féin
Coolesholl, Co. Wexford 89
Cork, city of 43
Cork, Co. 58, 59, 61, 64, 69, 70, 72, 81, 83, 84, 90
Cornish miners 81, 83, 84
Coromandel 136
Cox, J.R. 142
Croke, Thomas, Bishop of Auckland 138
Cromwell, Oliver 19
Croninville 100
Cross, Ian 26
Cummins, Rev. Michael 92
Cummins, Thomas Padraic 123, 126, 127, 128, 129, 130, 132
Curnow, Allen 30
Cyclopaedia of New Zealand 42, 64

Dáil Éirann 130, 133, 149
Daldy, William Crush 45
Dargaville, Joseph McMullen 36, 44
Dargaville, Northland 9
Davin, Dan 26, 35
Davis, Richard 44, 138, 154
Davitt, Michael 118
Dawson, Brigid 107, 109, 114
Dawson, Peter 107
de Valera, Eamon, 130, 133, 150, 151, 152, 153
Deasy, John 141
Dee, Patrick 99
Denniston 142

Devine, J.J. 142
Devlin, Joseph 144, 145
Devon 84
Devoy, John 125
Dilharee 124
Dillmanstown 99
Dillon, John 118, 141, 142, 143
Dilworth, James 47, 51
Dolan, B.J. 129
Donacavey, Co. Tyrone 40
Donegal, Co. 64, 67, 71, 79, 91
Donovan, J.T. 118, 144, 145
Donovan, Patrick 100-101
Doolan, F.J. 145
Dover Castle 46
Down, Co. 38, 47, 61, 64, 68, 70, 71, 72, 81, 84, 91, 92, 93-4, 103
Doyle, Murtagh and Susan 89
Dromore, Co. Tyrone 87
Dublin, city of 17, 33, 38, 45, 58, 64, 75, 117, 119, 120, 121, 123, 125, 130, 148
Dublin, Co. 58, 59, 64, 68, 69, 70, 72, 91, 93
Duffy, Edward 97
Duggan, Eileen 26, 31
Duggan, Maurice, 26
Dunedin 11, 27, 33, 43, 53, 76, 117, 118, 121, 122, 123, 136, 140, 142, 143, 144, 148, 153, *see also Green Ray*, Maoriland Irish Society, *New Zealand Tablet*
Dunedin Irish Club 121-2, 131, 132
Dunphy, Richard 99
Dunstan 75
Durkheim, Emile 13, 15
Dynes, John 47

Easter Rising (1916) 117; and New Zealand, 119-21, 123, 128, 147-9
Eastern Empire 86
Edward VII 144
Eldred-Grigg, Stevan 61
Elliot, Charles 98
emigration, *see* migration
emigration agents 42, 43, 44, 45-7, 56, 58, 74, 90, *see also* anti-Catholicism, anti-Irish sentiment, migrants
Emmet, Robert 145
Engels, Marian 21
England 31, 43, 48, 55, 58, 59, 62, 65, 66, 67, 68, 70, 71, 80, 82, 83, 88, 120, 137, 144, 146
English, as migrants 14, 43, 49, 53, 54, 56-7, 58, 59, 61, 62-4, 77, 78, 80-84, 90
English diaspora, the 19

Ennis, Co. Clare 96
Esmonde, Sir Thomas 118, 141
Ethnicity, and Irish diaspora studies 22; and 'Pakeha' history 14
Euroa 86
Europe 14, 17, 96
Evening Post 141

Fairburn, Miles 29, 88, 106
Farnall, Harry Warner 44, 45-6
Featherston, Isaac 44, 46
Fenians 118, 124-6, 137-8, 140
Fenton, James 105
Fermanagh, Co. 58, 64, 71, 79
Fermoy, Co. Cork 69
Fianna Fáil 152
Fitzgerald, James Edward 29, 44
Fitzpatrick, David 65-7, 71, 79, 94, 105
Flanagan, Michael 102-3
Flanders 146
Flynn, Dan 146
Fox, William 75
Foxford, Co. Mayo 116
Foxton 109, 111
France 130, 146
Fraser, Lyndon 59-60, 69, 75
Freud, Clement 34
friendly societies 136-7
Furlong, Winifred 115

Gabriels's Gully 75, 90
Gaelic Athletic Association 119
Gaelic League 119
Galbraith, Alasdair 10
Galway, city of 58
Galway, Co. 58, 59, 64, 68, 69, 70, 72, 79, 83, 84, 91, 103, 125
Gamble, Rose 112
Geelong 99
Germany 119, 146
Gillespies Beach 9
Gilmer, Abigail 110
Gilmore, Alice 105, 106, 108, 109, 111
Gilmore, Andrew 105, 111
Gilmore, John 105, 109
Gilpin, Mary Anne 112
Gisborne 122
Gladstone, William Ewart 48, 141, 142
Glenavy, Co. Antrim 33, 41
Globe and Mail, Toronto 18
Godley, Charlotte 50
Godley, John Robert 29
gold rushes 56, 74, 75, 77, 82, 89, *see also*

migrants, Otago, Victoria, West Coast
Goldsborough, 86 110
Goodwin, Bridget 94
Goold, Archbishop James 137
Gordon, Nat 124
Graham, James 47
Grahame, William 43, 45
Grahamstown 136
Gray, William 48
Great Britain 14, 29, 30, 36, 42, 62; migration from, 55, 56-9, 61, 65, 67, 68, 69, 70, 76, 78, 80, 83, 84, 96; regional identities, 48-9
Great Famine, the (1845-50) 9, 29, 31, 42, 64, 67, 82, 85, 89
Green Ray 122-24, 125, 127, 128, *see also* Catholics, Sinn Féin
Grey county 91
Greymouth 10, 26, 87, 89, 90, 92, 93, 97, 100, 135, 136, 150, 154
Griffin, Gerlad 126
Griffin, Patrick 136
Grimes, John Joseph, Bishop of Christchurch 143
Grousset, Paschal 39

Halley, Annie and Bridget 97
Hamilton, James 50
Hamilton, K.A. 50
Hanmer Springs 143
Hannah, Robert 33
Hartley, Horatio 75, 76
Hastings 122
Hayes, Alice 99
Hazleton, Richard 118, 145
Hazlett, Edgar 133
Headford, Co. Galway 69
Hearn, Terry 10, 39
Heddon Bush 124
Henderson, Arthur 151
Hibernians 11, 121, 122, 131; Anglo-Irish War 149-52; establishment of 135-8; First World War 146-9; Irish politics 140-46; membership 139; self-identity 152-4; women 147, 152, *see also* Irish delegations, *New Zealand Tablet*, Orange Order
Hill, Samuel 110
Hobart 144, 154
Hobson, Bulmer 119
Hokitika 86, 90, 103, 136, 137, 145
Holland, Harry 129
Home Rule 48, 119, 133, 140-47, 149-50
Hoskins, Paul 150

Houlahan, Bridget 99
Howard, Caroline 46
Howick 57
Hughes, Katherine 133

Illawarra 87
immigrants, *see* migrants
Inangahua 136
India 58, 59
Indian Empire 107
Ireland, Republic of 33, 133, 152, 153
Irish delegations 118, 122, 140-45
Irish diaspora studies; empires 22-3; ethnicity 22; female migration 21-2; sectarianism 23-4
Irish diaspora; as a concept 16-17; in world history 18-19
Irish Folklore Commission 31
Irish historiography, developments in 15-20, 24
Irish Land League 140
Irish Land War (1879-83), 47, 140
Irish National Federation 142
Irish Parliamentary Party 123, 140, 141, 144, 148
Irish Rebellion (1798) 142-3
Irish Republican Army, 130, 149
Irish Republican Brotherhood 118, 119, 123, 126, 129
Irish Self-Determination Leagues 130, 133
'Irishness' 10, 11, 25, 27, 28, 31, 33-5, 42, 108, 135, 139

Jackson, Margaret 132
James I 37
Jones, James 99
Joyce, James 31
Joyce, Thomas 136

Kane, William 135, 139
Katikati Special Settlement 28, 44-5, 46, 47, 48, 53, 66
Kawakawa Special Settlement 45, 53
Keane, John 113
Keane, Kate and Mary 115
Keane, Maurice 111, 112, 113
Kelleher, John 24
Kelly, James, Rev. 127, 128, 131-2, 149-51
Kelly, William 44
Kennedy, Martin 136
Kerry, Co. 59, 61, 64, 67, 69, 70, 72, 81, 84, 91, 99
Kerrytown, South Canterbury 27, 67

Kilfyn, Co. Kerry 115
Kilgour, William 50
Kilkenny, Co. 67, 79, 91, 103, 132
Killinchy, Canterbury 9
Kilpatrick, David 107
Kilpatrick, Mararget 107, 108, 111, 112, 113, 114, 115
Killyleagh, Co. Down 89
Kilrush, Co. Clare 87
Kilskeery, Co. Tyrone 40
King, Michael 26
King's Co. 70, 77, 91, 103
Kirk, Bridget 103
Kirk, Patrick 102-3
Kittson, Patrick 100
Kotuku 87
Kumara 87
Kyneton 86

Labour Party 11, *see also* Catholics, Sinn Féin, socialism
Lady Jocelyn 46
Lambert, Agnes 106-7, 111, 113, 114, 116
Larkin, Rev. William 137, 138
Lawlor, Patrick 26
Lean, David 28
Lehinch, Co. Tipperary 115
Leinster 58, 59, 60, 61, 67, 68, 69, 70, 72, 73, 74, 79, 81, 83, 91, 99, 103
Lenihan, Bishop George 142
Liberal Party 117
Limerick, Co. 58, 59, 61, 64, 67, 70, 72, 79, 81, 83, 84, 90, 91, 93, 96, 103
Lindis Pass 75
Lineham, Peter 50
Lismore, Mid-Canterbury 9
Liston, James, Bishop of Auckland 133, 151-2
Liverpool 17, 103, 106, 107
Loburn 27
London 44, 145
Londonderry, city of 45, 53, 58
Londonderry, Co. 38, 59, 68, 70, 71, 72, 81, 83, 84, 91, 103, 107, 116, 133
Longfield West, Co. Tyrone 40
Louth, Co. 102
Luck, Bishop J.E. 140, 141
Lurgan. Co. Down 61
Lush, Rev. Vicesimus 51, 52
Lysaght, William 112
Lyttelton 43, 89

MacBride, John 124
McCaffrey, James 99

McCarthy, Angela 10
McCarthy, Arthur 129
McCaskill, Murray 91
McCleland, Ann 105, 113, 116
McCleland, Elizabeth 105, 113, 115, 116
McCleland, Nancy 113
McConville, Chris 94
McCracken, Thomas 127
Macready, Bessie 108, 109-10, 112, 113, 114
McCullough, Dennis 119
McDonagh, Thomas 123, 124
McDonnell, Peter 99
McGirr, Margaret 88
McIlraith, James 109
McIvor, Jill 33
McManus, Rev. Matthias 99
MacRaild, Donald 23
MacSwiney, Terence 151
Maguire, Hugh 48
Makikihi 28
Mannix, Archbishop Daniel 150, 151
Maori Creek 100
Maoriland Irish Society 122, 123, 124, 126, 127, 129
Maoriland Worker 129
Martin, John 48
Martinborough 48
Mason, R.A.K 32, 35
Massey, William Ferguson 49, 143, 146, 152
Mataura 98
Mataura 124, 127
Matheson, Peter 52
Maunsell, Rev. Robert 51
Mayo, Co. 58, 68
Meath, Co. 102
Meehan, Paula 27
Meffin, M.J. 153
Megaffin, Richard 101
Melbourne 86, 98, 100, 102, 103, 109
Men, age 57; kinship ties 98-103; marital status 59, 62, 63, 64, 65; migration patterns 57-8, 59, 62, 63, 64, 65, 66, 71, 73; on Otago goldfields 75-6, 80-82, 84; on the West Coast 89, 90, 93-4, 95, 98-103, 104; work experiences 63, 66, *see also Green Ray*, Hibernians, Irish delegations, migrants, *New Zealand Tablet*, Orange Order, religious denominations, Royal New Zealand Fencibles, Sinn Féin
Methodists 59; in Ireland 38, 39
Mexico 123
Mickelson, A.J. 153

Migrants, age 59, 62, 71, 82, 84; assisted passages 61-8, 74; attitudes towards 34-5; family structure 62-3, 64, 66, 69, 81, 82-3, 84; nominated passages 61, 62, 67, 74, 79; numbers 56-7; regional variations 26, 27-8; remittances 67, 74; social networks 10, 87-8, 116; socio-economic background 60, 62, 63, 69, 73, 81-2, 83-4, *see also* men, religious denominations, West Coast, women

migrant recruitment 42-7, 74, 88; location of emigration agents 45-6; newspaper advertising 46; provision of shipping, 46-7, *see also* anti-Catholicism, anti-Irish sentiment, emigration agents

migration, as a concept 15-18; causes of 30; Christianity 20; Irish commercial relations 19; Irish national schools 19-20

Miller, Kerby 94, 106
Mitchel, John 31
Mitchell, Alexander 101-2
Monaghan, Co. 64, 71
Month 152
Mooney, Kathryn 50
Moore, Rev. Lorenzo 51
Moran, Bishop Patrick 34, 138, 144
Moran, Cardinal Patrick Francis 140
Morgan, Rev. John 51
Mornington 124
Morrison, John 43, 45
Motuihe Island 105
Mount Ida 75
Mulgan, Alan 48
Mullaghanee, Co. Monaghan 110
Mullin, Frank 132
Mullins, William 100
multiculturalism 14, 34
Munro, Jessie 26
Munster 58, 59, 60, 61, 62, 64, 67, 68, 69, 70, 72, 73, 74, 79, 81, 83, 84, 85, 91, 96, 103

Napier 122, 123, 129, 149
Naseby 136
Nationalism/nationalists 11, 117-18, *see also* Catholics, conscription, *Green Ray*, Maoriland Irish Society, *New Zealand Tablet*, Sinn Féin
Neal, Moira 50
Nelson 98, 99, 103
Nelson Creek 87
Nengh, Co. Tipperary 58, 69, 91

Nerheny, P.J. 150
Newmarket, Co. Tipperary 86
New South Wales, and Irish migration 59, 60, 62, 74, 79, 87, 89, 90, 92, 104, 125
New Zealand Herald 43-4
New Zealand historiography, and bi-culturalism 9, 13-14
New Zealand Ireland Association 33
New Zealand Land Wars 23, 30
New Zealand Tablet 120, 123, 127-9, 131, 132, 140, 141, 142, 143, 144, 146, 147, 148, 149, 151, 152
New York 103
Newry, Co. Down 45, 58
Neylon, Mary 97
Nimrod 58
Nolan, Edmund 132
Noonan, William 99
North America 14, 24, 28, 30, 78, 88, 96, 106, 107, *see also* United States, Canada
Northern Ireland 33

Oamaru 150
O'Brien, Flann 31
O'Connor, Gerald 126
O'Connor, John and Maurice 97
occupational status, of migrants 62, 63-4, 66, 69, 73, 81-2, 83-4, 94-5
O'Donnell, Jeremiah 100
O'Farrell, Henry James 137
O'Farrell, Patrick 10, 79, 105, 106
O'Leary, Michael 31
O'Leary, Monsignor Patrick 127
O'Meara, F.J. 150
Onehunga 57
Ontario 19
Opawa 89
Orange Order 9, 44, 48, 51, 52, 139-40, 143, 147
Ordnance Survey Memoirs of Ireland 40
O'Regan, P.J. 121, 148, 150, 151
O'Rorke, George Maurice 44
O'Rourke, Thomas 99
O'Sullivan, Tom 145
Otago 42, 43, 46, 62, 74, 75, 76, 77, 91, 93, 103, 111, 114, 135, *see also* gold rushes, migrants, men, women
Otago Daily Times 43, 130, 132, 137
Otahuhu 57

Palmerston North 149
Panmure 57
Parnell, Charles Stewart 140, 141, 143

Patterson Robert, 89
Patutahi 126
Pearse, Patrick 119, 120, 123, 124
Phoenix Park murders (1882) 140
Pickens, Keith 64
Piezzi, Ellen 110, 111, 112, 114, 115
plantations 37-8
Pleiades 108
Plunkett, Joseph Mary 124
Pollen, Daniel 43, 44, 46, 49
Port Chalmers 76, 90
Portadown, Co. Down 61
Presbyterians 49-50, 52-3, 59, 60, 72-3, 92-3, 95; in Ireland 38, 39, 40-41
Protestants, Irish, attitudes towards 42-7; demography 37, 41, 53; migration of 10, 41-7, 59, 73, 92, 93, 94; Old World background 37-41; politicians 44; religion 50-53; self-identity 10, 36-7, 42, 47-50, 53-4, 108, *see also* Anglicans, migrants, Methodists, Presbyterians, Ulster
Protestant Political Association, 130, 132
Pukekohe 47, 53
Purcell, Peter 136
Pyke, Vincent 76

Queen of Nations 43-4, 46-7
Queen's Co. 58
Queensland, and Irish migration 78, 89, 90, 92, 102, 125
Queenstown (Cobh), Co. Cork 43, 46
Queenstown, Otago 136
Quillinan, James 99
Quinlan, John and Ann 9

Raphoe, Co. Donegal 50
Read, Gabriel 75, 76
Red Jacket 106
Redmond, John 119, 120, 121, 123, 140, 141, 143, 144, 146, 147, 148
Redmond, William 118, 140, 141, 145
Redwood, Archbishop Francis 150, 151
Reefton 92, 99, 136
Reid, Ellen 115
Reilly, Christopher 75, 76
Ribbonmen 118
Riversdale 122, 124, 125
Robinson, John 132, 133
Robinson, Mary 18
Roscommon, Co. 61
Rossa, O'Donovan 118
Royal New Zealand Fencibles 57-8

Russell, George 31
Ryan, Bert 127, 128, 129, 130, 132
Ryan, James 127
Ryan's Daughter 28

St Bathans 80
St Joseph's, Dunedin 9, 131
St Mark's, Remuera 51
St Mary's, Parnell 51
St Patrick's, Greymouth 90
St Patrick's Day 130, 132, 137, 139, 140, 142, 143, 150, 152
St Vincent de Paul Society 131
Sawyers Bay 124
Scotland 42, 55, 58, 62, 67, 68, 70, 71, 80, 82, 83, 88, 144
Scots, as immigrants 14, 49, 53, 55, 56-7, 58, 62-4, 65, 66, 77, 78-9, 80-84, 90
Scots-Irish 49-50
Scottish Interest Group (NZSG) 50
sectarianism 34, 41, 119, 121, 130, 150, *see also* anti-Catholicism, Hibernians, Irish diaspora studies, Orange Order
Shanahan, Martin 100
Shanahan, Mary 115
Shaw, George Bernard 32
Sheahan, M.J. 142, 143, 150, 151, 152
Sheedy, Daniel 90, 136
Silcock, R.H. 62
Silverstone, Mark 129
Sinn Féin, 11, 117, 120, 123, 125, 127, 129, 130, 132, 133, 144, 147-50, 152, *see also* Catholics, *Green Ray, New Zealand Tablet*, Orange Order
Skeffington, Francis Sheehy 121
Skibbereen, Co. Cork 87
socialists 117, 129, 132, 134
South Africa 28, 78, 143
South African Migration Project, Queen's University, Ontario 17
South Australia, and Irish migration 59, 89
South Canterbury 26, 28, 67, 126
Southland 26, 46
Spanish diaspora, the 19
Spillane, Thomas 122
Sprott, Rev. Thomas Henry 51
Stafford, Edward 43, 44, 49
Stead, J.B. 145
Stewart, George Vesey 42, 44, 46
Stone, Russell 47
Strabane, Co. Tyrone 48, 53, 58
Strong, Lizzie 115
Sullivan, Catherine 109, 111

Sullivan, John T. 122, 132
Sweetman, Rory 11
Sydney 17, 103, 125, 129, 132, 137, 144

Talty, Patrick 80
Tamaki 57
Tasmania 89
Tauranga 36, 105
Te Puke 105
Thackeray, William Makepeace 39
Thames 51
Timaru 27, 139, 144, 153
Timaru 90
Tipperary Co., 58, 59, 61, 64, 69, 70, 72, 73, 79, 81, 83, 84, 91, 93, 96, 97, 100, 103
Tohill, John 123, 126, 127, 128, 133
Tomacork, Co. Wicklow 89
Tonduff, Co. Antrim 112
Toronto 17
Tralee, Co. Kerry 69
Travers, William 44
Trinity College Dublin 38, 51
Troy, John 126
Tuam, Co. Galway 69
Tuapeka 75
Tyrone, Co. 45, 50, 58, 59, 61, 64, 68, 71, 72, 79, 90, 123

Ulster 33, 37-41, 42-7, 48, 58, 59, 60, 61, 62, 64, 67, 68-74, 79, 81, 83, 84, 85, 91, 92-94, 95, 101, 103, 108, 119, 145
Ulster New Zealand Trust, the 33
United Kingdom, *see* Great Britain
United States, and Irish migration 20, 23, 66-7, 78, 118, 123, 151
Uruguay 123

Vaney Neil, 26
Versailles Peace Treaty (1919) 150
Verdon, Bishop Michael 129, 149
Victoria, and Irish migration 57, 58, 62, 74, 75, 77-9, 80-86, 89, 90, 91, 92, 94, 98, 101, 103, 104, 135, 136, 150
Victoria, Queen 137, 143, 144
Vogel, Julius 44, 56

Waikato Immigration Scheme 45, 46
Waimate 28
Waimea 87, 101, 136
Wakamarina 76
Wakefield, Edward Gibbon 29

Wales 59, 80, 88, 120, 144
Walker, Elizabeth 114
Walshe, Rev. Thomas 100
Wanganui 26, 109, 114, 126, 151
Ward, Bernard 99
Ward, Crosbie 44
Ward, J.R. 40
Ward, Sir Joseph 143, 144
Waterford, Co. 64, 70, 111, 115
Watters, Rev. James 121
Weldon, Barbara 94
Wellington 17, 26, 107, 121, 122, 124, 126, 129, 140, 142, 144, 146, 150, 151
Welsh, as immigrants 56, 62, 77, 81, 82, 83, 84
West Coast 62, 74, 75, 76, 77, 79, 87, 89, 110; age of migrants 94, 95, 103; emigrant letters 102-3; geographical origins 91, 95, 103; Hibernians 135-8; marital status 94, 95; nomination files 96-8; numbers 90-91, 95; probates 98-102; religious affiliations 91-3, 95, 104; sex ratios 93-4, 95, 104; social networks 87-8, 96-103, 104; socio-economic background 94-5, 103
West Gragan, Co. Clare 86
West Indies 58
Western Australia, and Irish migration 89, 125
Westland 86, 87, 90, 91, 96, 98, 99, 101, 103, 136
Westport 87, 90, 93, 98, 100, 142
White Star 86
Whiteboys 118
Whyte, Bishop James 132
Wicklow, Co. 79
Williamson, John 44
Wilson, Helen M. 26
Windsor, Gerard 28
women, and children 112; attitudes to death 115-16; kinship ties 104, 112, 113-15, 116; impressions of colonial life 112-14, 116; marriage 109-10, 116; migration patterns 43, 61, 62-4, 65, 66, 73, 88, 106; on Otago goldfields 77-8, 79, 81, 82-4; the West Coast 90, 93, 94, 95, 99, 103, 104; voyage out 104, 108-9; work experiences 63-4, 66, 104, 109-11, 116; *see also* Irish diaspora studies, migrants
Wylde, James 97
Wyndham, George 144